# The psychophysiology of mental illness

**Social and Psychological Aspects
of Medical Practice**

Editor: Trevor Silverstone

# The psychophysiology of mental illness

Malcolm Lader BSc PhD MD DPM MRCPsych
*Member of External Scientific Staff, Medical Research*
*Council; Reader in Clinical Psychopharmacology, Institute*
*of Psychiatry, University of London; Honorary Consultant,*
*Bethlem Royal and Maudsley Hospital; Honorary Research*
*Fellow, Department of Pharmacology, University College,*
*London*

Routledge & Kegan Paul
London and Boston

First published in 1975
by Routledge & Kegan Paul Ltd
Broadway House, 68–74 Carter Lane,
London EC4V 5EL and
9 Park Street,
Boston, Mass. 02108, USA

Set in Monotype Imprint
and printed in Great Britain by
Richard Clay (The Chaucer Press), Ltd,
Bungay, Suffolk

ISBN 0 7100 8091 3

# Contents

# Figures

vii

# Preface

Psychiatric research has been unsuccessful in developing scientific methods of its own but has relied on a series of techniques borrowed from other disciplines. Too often the outside discipline has been chosen because of its current fashionable status rather than for its relevance, and the high hopes at the outset of such studies have lessened as concrete advances have failed to materialise. However, some disciplines have never seemed to foster unrealistically high hopes in their practitioners when using them in psychiatry.

For many years there have been groups of research workers in various parts of the world using physiological techniques to evaluate patients with psychiatric disorders. A steady accumulation of facts has occurred and, although the topic is still in its infancy, it is now a sturdy toddler rather than a helpless infant. There are huge gaps in our knowledge, inconsistencies and contradictions in our data, and probably naïveties and errors in our concepts. Nevertheless, sufficient information exists to influence our ideas about several mental illnesses, especially anxiety and schizophrenia. Often problems have arisen from the unscientific nature of much of psychiatry and the misapplication of techniques rather than from deficiencies in physiological theory and practice. Of course, the great practical and ethical problems of neurophysiological experiments in humans have limited the rate of advance into psychiatry of this particular subject, but endocrinology and other sub-specialities of physiology have been pressed into service as well.

For several years at the Institute of Psychiatry, University of London, and elsewhere, I have given lectures and conducted seminars on the topic of psychophysiology to postgraduate students taking further degrees in Psychiatry and Clinical Psychology. There has been no recent comprehensive published review of the whole topic and reference sources have been widely scattered, so that there appeared to be some need for a textbook on the subject. I

\*

have set out to give a general account of the use of physiological techniques in psychiatry with the emphasis on the empirical rather than the theoretical aspects of the topic. Because the boundaries of the subject are unclear I may have included some topics which others would regard as irrelevant and as no textbook can be encyclopaedic I must have inevitably omitted some equally important areas.

I hope at the very least the book will be of use to psychiatrists and psychologists in training to help them pass the sort of formal examinations which still exist. I would also hope that the subject-matter will be of genuine interest to them and also to medical practitioners, psychologists and members of all the professions concerned in the understanding and alleviation of mental illness. If this book stimulates some of these students to become actively engaged in research in this interesting field then I would feel that the effort which has gone into writing this book will have been amply repaid.

I am most grateful to Mrs A. Ginger for all her secretarial assistance with this book.

M.L

# Introduction

Darrow (1964a) defined psychophysiology as 'the science which concerns those physiological activities which underlie or relate to psychic functions'. This is undoubtedly a very wide definition as it could be construed to refer to an extremely comprehensive range of central nervous system functions. Others, e.g. Sternbach (1966), have been more concerned with the type of experimental approach which the psychophysiologist favours—the use of a polygraph, simultaneous recordings of several physiological functions, the concentration on autonomic measures, etc. There seems general agreement that psychophysiology concerns itself with experiments in humans, the equivalent studies in animals falling under the rubric of physiological psychology.

Nevertheless, despite varying opinions on what psychophysiology is, or even what psychophysiologists do, there are two fundamental principles which should not be lost sight of. Firstly, the functions which are recorded are physiological variables and must be measured with due regard to physiological considerations. For example, when recording finger pulse volume the physiologist does so with the digit supported at the level of the subject's heart because only in this position is the size of the pulse volume beat closely related to blood flow through the fingertip. Consequently, the psychophysiologist must also take recordings in this way, and if the behavioural requirements of the experiment make this impracticable, then either they must be modified or another recording technique or measure resorted to.

The second point is a less precise one but is basic to the distinction between physiology and psychophysiology. The measures used have to be shown to have some relevance to the behavioural events of interest. For example, in states of alertness the heart rate rises, sweating occurs and adrenaline is secreted. This prepares the body for further action should this prove necessary in the light of further events—Cannon's 'fight or flight'. However, the physiological preparedness is in excess of the *immediate* needs of the body and if further action is not required then the physiological functions will subside at a greater or lesser rate. What interests the psychophysiologist is the change in physiological functions in response to stimuli which produce psychological, behavioural changes. Such stimuli may be external (tones, flashes, disturbing films, etc.) or internal (ideation, affective changes, etc.). Of course, external stimuli will interact with central states to produce internal stimuli as well. The essential point is that the physiological changes are excess to immediate physiological requirements and are correlates of behavioural changes. Usually the subject will be in a state of physiological rest, sitting or lying, so that all the changes in response to stimuli are excess to physiological needs and can be directly quantified. It is illogical to alter the physiological needs, e.g. by exercising the subject, and then to regard the ensuing physiological changes, e.g. tachycardia, as reflecting in some way changes in psychological status.

Psychophysiology is thus a part of biological psychology (Lader and Venables, 1973), in which the biological correlates to behavioural events are studied. If a definition is regarded as necessary to the respectability of a fairly young branch of science then the following may suffice. Psychophysiology is the study of physiological variables which have a relevant correlation with behavioural events. The relevance has to be established in each experiment but usually the experienced psychophysiologist is able to design the parameters of the experiment so that the link between the behavioural and the physiological variables is as close as possible.

There is now a substantial body of data from experiments carried out in a psychophysiological context. In the past ten years the number of studies has multiplied several-fold and many departments of psychology in universities throughout the world have set up sections of psychophysiology. However, very few departments of physiology became interested in the subject so that the typical psychophysiologist today is a psychologist by training rather than a physiologist. An unfortunate consequence of this has been the tendency on the part of a few research workers to be ignorant of not only the finer points of physiological measurement but also its basic principles. However, a growing awareness of this problem has led to many psychologists equipping themselves for research by becoming properly trained in a well-established laboratory. Another result of the psychological bias has been the hypertrophy of statistical manipulations of data, the biological validity of which has remained in doubt. In addition, some of the physiological interpretations of the data, e.g. in terms of CNS structures, have been fanciful, being greeted more with puzzlement than derision by neurophysiologists. The neurophysiology favoured by some psychophysiologists lags about ten years behind that of neurophysiologists, and this tends to be more concentrated on certain structures. Thus, the 1960s were the decade of the reticular formation and the 1970s will probably elevate the limbic system to a pivotal role.

By far the greatest proportion of psychophysiological research has been carried out on normal subjects, typically students in North American psychology faculties. Although atypical of the general population it is probable that most of the empirical findings and the principles derived from them can be validly applied to the bulk of the population. This material was too vast to include in this book except in summary to form the background against which the findings in patients could be set. Furthermore, many of the studies and the theoretical aspects are of limited relevance to clinical problems. Very detailed accounts of normal psychophysiology are available in the *Handbook of Psychophysiology*, edited by Greenfield and Sternbach (1972), and in *Research in Psychophysiology*, edited by Venables and Christie (1975).

The affects (emotions, feelings) have been a favourite topic for psychophysiological research because of the marked, widespread physiological changes which occur. Anxiety, in particular, has been extensively studied for a variety of reasons. The relationship between the physiological changes and the perceived feelings has been a source of controversy but has acted as a spur to much fruitful research. Many psychiatric conditions are either primary disorders of affect, e.g. depression, mania and anxiety, or disturbances of affect are very obvious, e.g. in schizophrenia. It is therefore not surprising that psychophysiological techniques have been applied to these problems.

One approach has been to take groups of patients with a common diagnosis, e.g. anxiety state, and to compare them with a control group of some sort. This is the usual medical approach in which the assumption is made that there is an abnormality in the patient with respect to some function and that all patients with a common diagnosis will show that abnormality. Such an assumption says nothing about whether the abnormality is merely a concomitant of

3

the condition, whether it is involved in a symptom mechanism or whether it is causal in the sense of being an aetiological factor. For example, excess gastric acid in a patient with a peptic ulcer might reflect the fact that he has an ulcer, or it might produce pain by acting on the mucosal nerve endings, or it might have antedated the ulcer and been the 'cause' of it. It might also be coincidental, both the ulcer and the acidity being related to cigarette smoking. The use of psychophysiological measures is usually empirical. Firstly, it is established that the measure does relate directly to the illness or pathological mechanism of interest. Later the nature of that relationship, casual or causal, can be explored. In almost all instances in clinical psychophysiology, the physiological variable is acting as an indicator of some behavioural change in the patient, e.g. experiencing anxiety, and few examples of a more intimate relationship have yet been discovered.

This simple comparative approach raises two questions. Firstly, how homogeneous is the diagnostic category? In other words, are the patients in the group to be studied really alike with regard to their psychiatric features? The problems of diagnosis in psychiatry lie outside the scope of this book but the consequences of different psychiatric diagnostic styles are very relevant. One example must suffice. In the USA/UK diagnostic project (Cooper *et al.*, 1972), videotapes of patient interviews were presented to both American and British psychiatrists and their diagnoses analysed. The concept of schizophrenia used by the New York psychiatrists was much broader than that of their London counterparts, and included substantial parts of what British psychiatrists would consider to be depressive illness, neurotic illness or personality disorder and almost all of what they would call mania.

What are the implications for psychophysiology? If a general group of schizophrenics from the USA is the subject of study then that group will contain patients who by British (and probably Scandinavian and other West European) standards are manic, depressed or personality disordered. Conversely, a group of British patients diagnosed as depressives will have in its ranks patients who would be regarded by American (probably in most of North and South America) psychiatrists as schizophrenics. No problem arises when a European researcher evaluates data on American depressives or when an American examines the results from a psychophysiological study on European-diagnosed schizophrenics. When other groups are involved problems could arise.

However, many of the more experienced research workers in the USA are themselves dissatisfied with the wide criteria for schizophrenia and restrict their studies to 'core' or 'process' schizophrenics, or, better still, to those with unequivocal first-rank symptoms as recognised by Schneider (see below, p. 187). There seems little or no reciprocal recognition by European psychophysiologists that their depressive or manic categories might be too wide for North American tastes, but usually fairly severely ill patients are studied.

Other diagnostic categories may be even more equivocal. The problems of defining hysteria or psychopathy are enormous, especially if aetiological assumptions, particularly of a psychoanalytic nature, are allowed to govern the diagnosis. Simple definitions in behavioural terms are preferable at the moment until there is more consensus regarding the essential features of such syndromes.

No matter the diagnostic category of interest, the investigator should not assume that it is self-obvious what he is dealing with when he describes his groups as schizophrenic or depressed. A brief outline of the criteria or reference to a generally accepted schema (e.g. the Medical Research Council (1965) criteria for depressive illness) is essential for communication in this area.

What is particularly indefensible is to study broad groups of patients such as 'neurotic' and 'psychotic'. These words mean nothing in scientific terms and the data obtained from such a study are about as valuable.

The second problem in group-comparison research is to obtain a careful matching of normal controls and patients. Age, sex, social class, educational level and marital status are all important demographic variables. With respect to comparisons between in-patient groups, length of hospitalisation is undoubtedly a factor to take into account. The additional factors which should be considered in the psychophysiological context are probably many, but are largely unknown. Previous experience of laboratory situations is an important one and, paradoxically, patients may be more sophisticated in this respect than control subjects such as secretaries. Other variables which could conceivably be important are physical exercise, work habits, body build, sleep pattern, meal pattern, intake of patent medicines, smoking habits and probably many others. In general, age, sex and social class should be matched but recommendations regarding the other possible factors cannot be made because of lack of knowledge. Smoking may be a particularly important factor to be controlled in psychophysiological experiments because nicotine has so many autonomic effects, not only by a direct pharmacodynamic action but on withdrawal also.

With some psychiatric conditions, anxiety states being the best example, the abnormal emotion is deemed to differ from normal emotions in a quantitative but not a qualitative sense. Consequently, studying emotions in normal subjects would be expected to throw light on the mechanisms of morbid affects in patients. A large number of studies have been carried out in this framework but considerations of space have prevented me from any but a brief outline of such investigations.

In the next chapter, a fairly comprehensive account is given of the techniques used in psychophysiology. Detailed accounts of these techniques are available (Brown, 1967; Venables and Martin, 1967) but some are rather daunting for the novice to tackle. Sufficient detail is given in chapter 2 for the principles of measurement to be made clear and especial emphasis is laid on the biological aspects of measurement rather than on the electronic. The modifications required in many techniques for use in the psychophysiological context are described, and it is hoped that the newcomer to psychophysiology will be encouraged rather than dismayed by this aspect of the discipline. Recent developments such as the advent of digital computer techniques are included in order to emphasise the changes which such techniques have permitted in the more progressive and adequately funded psychophysiological laboratories. The polygraph is no longer the technical focus. As data from endocrinological studies are presented throughout the book, an account of techniques used in this area is given.

Chapter 3 comprises very brief accounts of some fundamental concepts in the psychophysiology of normal human subjects. Response specificity, orienting responses, the 'Law' of Initial Value and several other topics are outlined. The concept of arousal is first sketched and then some studies dealing with arousal, mainly in the form of anxiety, are presented in more detail. A full integration of all this material is postponed until the final chapter.

The next three chapters (4, 5 and 6) deal respectively with psychophysiological findings in anxiety, depression and schizophrenia. A comprehensive review is not attempted as the literature is large and scattered and many studies are not worth citing because of grave drawbacks. Of course, there are few if any investigations which have been reported which are totally satisfactory from the psychiatric, psychological and physiological viewpoints. Nevertheless, there are many in which as high a standard as possible has been maintained and these reports are given precedence. Other studies of lower standard but which illustrate some useful point are also outlined. Studies have not been included merely to criticise them for their shortcomings.

In chapter 7 a ragbag of conditions is included and psychophysiological findings discussed. Conversion hysteria and psychopathy are the main syndromes in this chapter but several others are dealt with briefly. The problem of the psychophysiology of psychosomatic conditions could form a book in itself, especially as practically every medical, surgical and gynaecological condition has been included in this broad and meaningless category at one time or another.

The final chapter attempts to draw together the various threads in the book. Some sort of coherent overview of the psychophysiology of mental illness is generally deemed to be necessary, but as psychiatry itself has not yet attained the formal status of a scientific discipline it is difficult to see how an empirical psychophysiological approach could be other than purely descriptive. Nevertheless, an attempt is made to describe more fundamental as well as more extensive approaches to this fascinating subject.

# 2                         Techniques

## Introduction

As we have seen in chapter 1, psychophysiology draws on the techniques of physiologists and uses them in a psychological context. A typical experiment consists in the measurement of one or more physiological variables while behavioural factors such as direction of attention, level of motivation or knowledge of results are manipulated. The essential point is that the physiological variable is being recorded and analysed for its psychological significance. However, the physiological system being monitored is primarily subserving a physiological function. For example, the heart pumps blood around the body and heart rate increases under conditions of psychological stress, such as being in a dangerous situation. But heart rate also increases during exercise so it is incorrect to conclude that exercise is a psychological stress because a tachycardia occurs. Consequently, in order to use physiological measures in the psychological context, the subject must be in conditions of physiological 'neutrality'; he must be sitting or lying quietly if cardiovascular or muscular activity is being studied.

A second consideration concerns the ethical aspects. For example, it is perfectly justifiable to introduce a catheter into an arm vein and on into the heart in a patient with cardiac abnormalities; this would not be justifiable in a normal subject or in a psychiatric patient because a small risk is involved and there is no direct benefit to the subject. Thus, there is a limit to the physiological techniques which can be legitimately used in psychophysiology. Many rely on surface electrodes rather than entering the tissues of the subject. Radioactive isotopes are seldom used in psychophysiology and then only in minimal doses.

Often, techniques are used or analysed in different ways in physiology and psychophysiology. For example, the neurophysiologist is interested in the form of electrical activity of muscle fibres and inserts a needle electrode into the muscle under investigation. The psychophysiologist is more concerned with the general level of activity of the muscle and to estimate this he applies surface disc electrodes to the skin overlying the muscle groups. The electrocardiogram furnishes another example. The cardiologist examines the waveform of the ECG in order to detect malfunctioning of the heart; the psychophysiologist is interested in the heart rate or, as a refinement, the inter-beat interval, and uses the ECG to trigger ratemeters or tachographs.

Some physiological measures are relatively neglected by physiologists yet intensively studied by psychophysiologists. The palmar skin conductance is the prime example, not meriting any mention in most standard physiology textbooks and yet being the most widely used psychophysiological measure.

An important difference between physiology and psychophysiology concerns the general experimental approach. Physiologists usually study fairly clear phenomena and look for obvious changes in these phenomena, e.g. changes in the firing rate of neurones. Psychophysiologists, applying their techniques in a psychological context, often deal with nuances of effect which may require statistical analysis to clarify. However, there are many areas of common concern, but still far fewer than in parallel animal research such as physiological psychology.

In this chapter the commoner psychophysiological techniques are outlined. For more detailed accounts see Brown (1967) and Venables and Martin (1967). An elementary account of the principles of instrumentation is given for those readers without any technical background. The physiology underlying the measures is briefly sketched in for psychologists whose physiology is rudimentary. The modifications to the measures when they are used in psychophysiology are dealt with in more detail as are the ways in which information is abstracted from the recordings.

## Basic technical aspects

Physiological measures can be roughly divided into those in which the bodily signal is already electrical and those in which it is not. Examples of the first category are the electrocardiogram (ECG) and the electroencephalogram (EEG). Types of non-electrical signal include volume and pressure changes, temperature and movement. With the latter type of signal it is convenient to convert the

9

non-electrical signal into an electrical signal, a voltage. It should be noted that transduction into electrical energy is a convenience, not a necessity. Thus pressure changes can be recorded using a distensible diaphragm upon which is mounted a stylus writing on a smoked drum; the pressure changes are thereby transduced into vertical movements of the stylus. However, this is cumbersome compared with the use of a pressure transducer, an amplifier and an ink-writing polygraph. The function of a 'transducer' is to change one form of energy into another, in this case to electrical energy, and a wide range of transducers is available. The non-electrical signal to be converted is the transduceable function; the principle by which the device works is the transducing method.

A commonplace example of the use of transducers is the record player. One transducer, the pick-up, converts the side-to-side movements of the stylus in the record grooves to electrical energy. This is amplified and then converted into sound waves by a second transducer, the loudspeaker cone.

Often there is a choice of transduceable function and transducing method. For example, respiration can be monitored by recording the temperature of air in the nostril or the movement of a tube around the chest, both transduceable functions. Temperature can be converted to a voltage signal by using a thermocouple or thermistor, both transducing methods. The requirements of a transducer are that it should not distort the signal appreciably, it should be sensitive to only the physiological event of interest, it should have a high efficiency and it should produce a good signal requiring only moderate amplification. The transducer should also be fairly standard and it is an advantage if it is small. Transducers have usually been developed in the physical sciences and some modification has often been needed in physiological applications.

## Types of transducer

*Strain-gauge* This device is usually a strip of material which changes its electrical resistance when stretched, as the length increases and the cross-sectional area decreases. A constant current is passed. By Ohm's Law, $V = IR$, where $V$ is the recorded voltage, $I$ the impressed current and $R$ the resistance of the strain-gauge. As $I$ is maintained constant, the voltage is proportional to the resistance and hence to the deformation of the strain-gauge. The changes are usually tiny and the signal change is consequently small but quite sufficient with present-day powerful amplifiers. Strain-gauges are often sensitive to temperature so that this must be compensated for.

Strain-gauges are widely used in psychophysiology to measure pressure changes and volume changes. A commonly used device consists of mercury filling a narrow-bore rubber tube. The resistance of the mercury column depends on the degree of stretch of the rubber, so that by wrapping the tube around a limb changes in the circumference of the limb can be detected. If the tube is placed around the chest wall an estimate of respiratory rate can be obtained.

*Piezo-electrical effect* Certain crystals and ceramic materials produce electrical energy when they are mechanically distorted. They are used in microphones and gramophone pick-ups. In physiological applications such devices are used as pulse detectors.

*Thermistor* This device alters its electrical resistance as its temperature changes. It is usually a wire made of metallic oxides, silicates and sulphides; typically a $1°C$ rise in temperature produces a 5 per cent drop in resistance. Thermistors are used to measure skin temperatures and in the nostril to monitor respiration. If a thermistor is heated slightly and placed in a stream of gas or liquid it is cooled, the degree of cooling depending on the flow rate.

*Thermocouple* If two dissimilar metal strips are joined at both ends and there is a temperature difference between the two ends, then an electrical current flows along the metal strips. If one junction is kept at a constant temperature, e.g. $0°C$, the current flow is proportional to the temperature at the other junction. Thermocouples can be used in the same applications as thermistors.

*Photo-electric transducer* There are several types of photo-electric transducers; in the most commonly used, light produces a voltage or a change in resistance in the transducer. In psychophysiology, the usual application is to record pulsatile flows by shining a light through a finger onto the photo-electric transducer. As the pulse beat reaches the finger it alters the transmissibility of light through the finger and this is registered as a change in voltage or resistance. In this use it is important that the light source does not heat the finger as this causes vasodilatation.

*Impedance techniques* If a high-frequency alternating current is passed through living tissues, the impedance to the current depends on many factors including both the dimensions and composition of the part studied. The impedance can be measured and if changes occur in the tissues, e.g. pulsatile blood flow, these will be reflected in alterations in impedance. The technique is versatile and can be used to measure blood flow in the head (rheoencephalography) (Lifshitz, 1963a, 1963b), in fingers and in limbs, and to monitor respiration. However, the technical problems are appreciable and there are difficulties in calibrating the impedance changes in terms of absolute volume changes.

## Electrical signals

So far we have dealt with strain-gauges which convert physiological signals into electrical energy and with impedance techniques in which the physiological signal alters an impressed electrical signal. There are many physiological signals which are, themselves, in an electrical form. The ones most commonly used in psychophysiology are the electroencephalogram (EEG), the electrocardiogram (ECG, in America EKG), the electromyogram (EMG) and the electrogastrogram (EGG). Eye movements also produce an electrical signal. All these signals have the following common requirements for their registration: they are picked up by electrodes attached to the body and the signals are amplified and then displayed in a convenient form.

### Electrode considerations

Electrode technology is a very complex subject which has received much attention from the more technical physiologists. Essentially, electrodes transfer bio-electrical phenomena from the body to the input of the amplifier without producing any appreciable distortion of the signal. The electrode presents both electrical and geometrical problems. The electrode must always be considered in relation to the contact medium which is placed between it and the body surface in order to produce a good contact.

The electrode and contact medium must be stable and not form a battery which would produce voltages of its own. A small current, however, inevitably flows through the electrodes for the following reason. An amplifier usually amplifies voltage, but to do so a minute current must inevitably flow through the inputs of the amplifier and hence through the electrodes. The magnitude of this current depends on the input impedance of the amplifier, the higher the impedance the less the current flow. This current flows through the electrodes and contact medium and through the body but is so small that it is undetectable by the subject. Nevertheless, there is a change in the electrode and contact medium composition because ions must flow to carry the current. Positively charged ions (cations), such as sodium, will flow to the negative electrode and negatively charged ions (anions), such as chloride, to the positive electrode. The build-up of these ions at the electrodes reduces the effective current by a process called 'polarisation'. This polarisation of the electrodes will eventually alter the recordings. It is, therefore, essential to use 'non-polarisable' electrodes whenever it is expected that the amplifier current will flow in one direction for an appreciable period. This occurs with direct current recordings when absolute voltage levels are required. In many psychophysiological applications only short-term changes in voltage are of interest, e.g. the ECG and EEG. For this purpose an alternating current system is sufficient and this means that the current through the amplifier will flow in both directions alternately. Consequently, the ion flow through the electrodes also repeatedly reverses its direction so that there is no build-up of polarisation. In practical terms it is much easier to obtain undistorted recordings when alternating current (AC) techniques are used than when direct current (DC) techniques are used. Consequently, unless there are pressing reasons to the contrary, AC recordings are preferable.

Other considerations of the electrodes are that they should be stable electrically and not produce intermittent voltages of their own. Good contact must be made between the electrodes and the biological surface, especially as the latter may be subject to movement, e.g. the skin overlying a contracting muscle. Wherever possible large electrodes are used, such as recording the ECG from the limbs. Where localisation is important (e.g. the EEG), small electrodes have to be used and the wide range of electrode types is witness to the lack of any completely satisfactory all-purpose electrode. The commonest type of electrode is a cupped disc with a central hole. It is glued to the skin with an acetone-soluble gum ('collodion') and the electrode is filled with electrode jelly by injecting it through a blunt needle into the electrode. Large electrodes (e.g. for the ECG) are merely strapped to the limb with a rubber band. More specialised electrodes include needle electrodes for particular EEG recordings and a wide range of similar devices and are dealt with under the sections on individual measures.

For bio-electrical signals like the ECG and EEG, hypertonic saline jellies or hypertonic zinc sulphate creams are most widely used. Sometimes abrasive powders are incorporated in the jelly to increase the contact. The skin site is usually prepared by dissolving surface oils and grease with alcohol or ether and then rubbing with an abrasive board or a blunt needle.

## Amplifiers

The design and construction of amplifiers suitable for bio-electric work is complex, but some knowledge of the more important characteristics of amplifiers is necessary for understanding psycho-physiological techniques. Commercially available amplifiers may still use valves but generally the latter have been superseded by transistors or integrated circuits.

The input circuit of the amplifier is that part into which the bio-electric signal is fed. In order that the amplifier should not distort the signal, the input circuit should have as high an impedance (i.e. a resistance to the flow of current) as possible. Input impedances of several million ohms are now easily attainable so that the bio-electric potential is hardly affected.

Practically all biological amplifiers are 'balanced' (or sometimes termed 'push–pull'). This means that the potential difference between two electrodes is measured by reference to 'earth' ('ground' in the USA), i.e. neutral potential. Consequently, the potential difference between each electrode and earth is amplified and the difference between the two electrodes is obtained as the algebraic difference. The great advantage of this arrangement is that extraneous voltage alterations, e.g. 50 Hz (cycles per second) interference, affect both electrodes simultaneously so that the algebraic difference, i.e. the real signal, is hardly affected. A good amplifier thus rejects unwanted external signals because it amplifies the real signals much more than the unwanted interference. The ratio of amplification of wanted signals to amplification of interference is termed the 'rejection' or 'discrimination ratio' and is typically above 10,000:1.

The amplification or gain of an amplifier can be expressed as the number of times a signal is amplified. For example, if an input signal of 10 microvolts produces 1 volt at the output then the gain is one hundred thousand times. Gain is sometimes expressed in decibels using the formula 20 $\log_{10}$ (output voltage/input voltage). In the above example, the gain would be

$$20 \log_{10} \left( \frac{1}{10 \times 10^{-6}} \right) = 20 \log_{10} 10^5 = 20 \times 5 = 100 \text{ db}$$

It is worth remembering that halving the gain is equivalent to a change of $-6$ db.

In any sensitive amplifier there is always some output even if the input leads are shorted. This is called 'noise' and is attributable to several causes, including random fluctuations in current flow and thermal agitation of electrons in components. Noise has components of all frequencies and therefore increases as the frequency range of the amplifier increases. Consequently, one should limit the frequency range of the amplifier to that appropriate to the signal. The smaller the signal to be amplified by an instrument then the lower must be the noise level.

Amplifiers are generally AC, i.e. they will not amplify constant voltages (DC) but only alternating changes in voltage. At either end of the frequency range there is a drop in sensitivity. Typically, for an EEG amplifier, the sensitivity is 30 per cent down at 0·5 Hz and 100 Hz ('turnover frequencies'). With these characteristics the loss is less than 1 per cent at 1·3 Hz and 80 Hz and the amplification should be as constant as possible for the frequencies between these values.

Some psychophysiological techniques require that steady voltages be measured and DC amplifiers, whose lower frequency response is thus 0 Hz, are necessary. These amplifiers are more complex and difficult to design than AC amplifiers. They are subject to a very gradual change in output level, termed 'drift', and changes in ambient temperature can alter their characteristics. One technique is to 'chop' the DC signal into short segments (say 2·5 ms in length) and to amplify these square wave segments as AC signals, finally reconstituting them in the output stage of the amplifier. Because of both electrode and amplifier problems, DC recordings are only resorted to when absolutely necessary.

## The recording instrument

In the past the 'end-product' of a psychophysiological experiment has almost invariably been a paper tracing obtained on a polygraph.

15

The principle is essentially the same as a galvanometer where the excursion of a needle is proportional to the current flowing through the coil. The needle is replaced by a pen, usually ink-writing, and a motor and chart-drive pulls a standard paper strip past the pen. The deflection of the pen from the mid-line is proportional to the voltage across the pen-oscillograph, the voltage being derived from the output stage of the amplifiers. The amplifier gain can be adjusted so that a standard signal produces a standard pen deflection, e.g. 10 $\mu$V cm$^{-1}$. The chart-drive is accurately controlled and there is usually a wide range of paper speeds, e.g. 0·15 mm s$^{-1}$ to 60 mm s$^{-1}$. If the paper is run fast enough, temporal relationships can be distinguished, e.g. the latency of a response.

Pen-writers have the disadvantage that their upper frequency response is limited due to the mechanical inertia of the pen and the friction of the pen on the paper. The response of the pen usually falls off fairly steeply above about 50 Hz. Various ingenious devices have been used to improve the frequency response, such as squirting the ink or using a beam of light projected onto photographic paper.

As the pen describes an arc as it deflects, both amplitude and timing errors may occur which increase the further the pen is from the mid-line. This error is relatively trivial except at the extreme of the pen's travel. Elaborate pen mountings and linkages have been designed to preserve the rectilinearity of response, but usually the frequency response then suffers.

Ink-writing polygraphs require careful maintenance as the pens tend to clog and block. However, the paper for them is cheap. Other types of pen are less temperamental but require more expensive special paper, e.g. heated pens writing on heat-sensitive paper.

The fundamental drawback of the polygraph is that its output is 'static' in the sense that manual intervention is needed to extract information from the tracing. In other words, the researcher has to take measurements from the tracing by hand in order to convert his recordings into data. No automatic processing is really feasible. Consequently, it usually takes much longer to analyse the recordings than it did to obtain them, especially if multi-channel recording is used. There has been a move in the more modern and sophisticated psychophysiological laboratories to relegate the polygraph to the status of a monitoring instrument and to record the physiological variables in a 'dynamic' form or even to process the variables 'on-line' into a computer.

## Analog tape recorders

A very convenient device for recording electrical signals in a usable form is the analog or instrumentation tape recorder. This resembles an ordinary audio tape recorder but is usually constructed to a much higher specification and is consequently more expensive. A basic difference in the electronics is that the analog recorder is capable of registering steady voltage levels, i.e. its frequency response goes down to zero. This is done by frequency modulation (FM) of a carrier wave signal. Analog recorders can also record audio signals, but separate amplifier circuits are necessary.

The upper frequency response depends on the precision of the engineering of the tape heads and the tape speed. A high-quality machine running at a tape speed of $1\frac{7}{8}$ inches per second will typically have a frequency response of 0–300 Hz.

Tape recorders have several speeds, e.g. $1\frac{7}{8}$, $3\frac{3}{4}$, $7\frac{1}{2}$, 15 and 30 inches per second. This facility can be used in two ways. Firstly, data can be processed at a faster tape speed than that at which they were recorded, thus saving analysis time. Secondly, events which occur very rapidly can be recorded at a fast tape speed and played back at a slow speed so that details can be discerned.

The tremendous advantage of the analog tape recorder over the polygraph is that the data are recorded in a 'dynamic' form, i.e. they can be transformed back into electrical signals. The output can be recorded onto a polygraph if a permanent record is required for visual analysis or it can be fed into a computer for automatic analysis. The data can be processed and re-processed as necessary. Some analog recorders can record six or seven channels on $\frac{1}{4}$ inch tape, and as tape of professional audio quality is adequate for most psychophysiological purposes the cost of tape is surprisingly low: seven channels of data up to 300 Hz in frequency can be recorded for two hours at a cost of £1 or so. Long-play tape is not recommended as being thin it tends to stretch too much.

## AUTONOMIC MEASURES

### Sweat gland activity, skin resistance and skin potential

Of all psychophysiological methods, the measurement of skin resistance is the most commonly used. As will be seen later, skin resistance is essentially an indirect way of assessing sweat gland activity. Direct methods of estimating sweating exist and will be briefly outlined first.

## Estimates of sweating

Over forty years ago, Darrow (1934) described a method for estimating sweating by passing a carefully controlled flow of dry gas over an area of skin and measuring the amount of moisture picked up. The moisture content can be analysed in a number of ways, thermal conductivity estimations being a fairly inexpensive and convenient method (Adams and Vaughan, 1965).

Another approach is to count the number of sweat glands in a measured area of skin secreting sweat at any particular instant. A commonly used method is the starch–iodide technique in which a dilute alcoholic solution of iodine is painted on the skin and starch-containing test papers applied. Each actively secreting sweat gland is represented by a blue-black spot. A similar method consists of painting the skin with tincture of ferric chloride and then applying a paper impregnated with tannic acid for 3 minutes (Ferreira and Winter, 1963). With both the starch–iodide and the ferric tannate method, the sweating can be quantified using a densitometer (optical opaqueness meter).

Direct counts can be made by illuminating the skin at an oblique angle (e.g. by a prism) and low-power microscopy, so that each active sweat gland appears as a glistening point. The skin can be photographed and counts made. A simple method consists of painting the skin with a coloured liquid plastic. Active glands prevent the plastic from setting and when the plastic 'skin' is peeled off they appear as holes which can easily be counted.

Although sweat gland counts are relatively simple techniques, they can only provide intermittent readings and detailed counts are tedious. They are not nearly as frequently used as the electrical methods.

## Electrical methods

These techniques are the most sensitive physiological indicator of psychological events yet available. They have been widely used but all too frequently misused. It has even been abused by certain non-scientific bodies. The measurement technique, although simple in principle, requires great care in design and in use and numerous sources of error can vitiate experimental findings. This complex topic is dealt with in detail in Venables and Martin (1967) and in Edelberg (1967). A particularly lucid, logical and brief account is provided by Montagu and Coles (1966).

## Resistance and potential

Broadly speaking, there are two main ways of estimating sweat gland activity electrically. In the first (the 'exosomatic' method), discovered by Féré in 1888, a small electric current is passed between two sites on the skin and the resistance between the two points measured. Responses to stimulation are always drops in skin resistance. Examples of skin resistance tracings from a subject first at rest and then when carrying out a mental arithmetic task are shown in Figure 2.1. (See also Figure 2.5 for examples of GSRs to auditory stimuli.) The second ('endosomatic') method consists of recording the naturally occurring potential difference between two skin sites (Tarchanoff, 1890). Responses in skin potential are usually biphasic, an initial negative component being followed by a positive one.

## Terminology

Unfortunately several terms exist for the various phenomena constituting the electrical properties of the skin. A distinction is usually made between the background skin resistance or skin potential level (often wrongly termed 'basal') and changes in those levels, abrupt or gradual, following stimuli. A further complication is that it is easier for technical reasons to measure the electrical resistance when using the exosomatic method, yet, as will be seen later, the reciprocal of resistance, conductance, is the more meaningful biological measure. It must be remembered that as sweat gland activity increases skin resistance decreases and skin conductance rises.

Abrupt responses to stimuli are variously known as psychogalvanic reflexes (PGRs), galvanic skin responses (GSRs) and electrodermal responses (EDRs). None of these terms is satisfactory but GSR seems to have the greatest usage. There is no clear distinction between GSRs of abrupt onset and rapid recovery and more gradual changes in level.

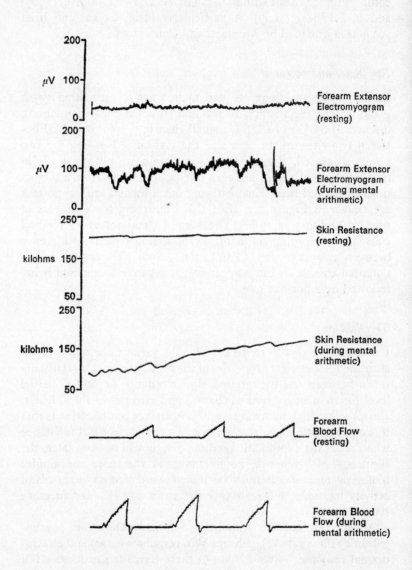

Figure 2.1 *Examples of* EMG, *skin resistance and forearm blood flow recordings from a subject at rest and carrying out a mental arithmetic task*

*Peripheral mechanisms*

For a long time the physiological basis of the skin resistance level and GSR was unclear, two possibilities being canvassed: (1) that changes in vascular tone underlay the GSR; (2) that sweat gland activity caused the GSR. Lader and Montagu (1962) carried out two series of studies in which skin resistance and finger pulse volume were recorded simultaneously from the same finger. In one series, atropine was introduced locally into the finger using an electric current (technique of iontophoresis) and resulted in the abolition of GSRs and the attainment of a high, steady skin resistance level without affecting vascular reactivity. In the other series, bretylium administered iontophoretically abolished vasomotor changes without affecting the GSR. As atropine blocks cholinergically innervated structures and as sweat glands are the only such structures in the fingertip (Dale and Feldberg, 1934), it was concluded that the GSR was entirely dependent on sweat gland activity.

Skin potential responses also appear to be dependent on sweat gland activity as they are largely abolished by atropinisation (Martin and Venables, 1966) although non-sudorific factors may also operate (Venables and Martin, 1967).

The GSR depends more on pre-secretory activity of sweat gland cell membranes than on the emergence of sweat. The probable mechanism is that the stimulus 'activates' the subject and produces a generalised sympathetic discharge which releases acetylcholine from the postganglionic neurones innervating the sweat glands. Depolarisation and momentary breakdown of the cell membranes then occurs, allowing the transient flow of ions and hence a drop in resistance.

*Conductance or resistance*

Ohm's Law states that $V = IR$, where $R$ is the resistance, $I$ the current through the resistor and $V$ the recorded voltage across the resistor. If $I$ is kept constant, the voltage recorded is directly and linearly related to the resistance. This forms the basis of the constant current method for measuring skin resistance. Ohm's Law can be re-formulated: $I = V/R$. Therefore, if a constant voltage is applied to a resistor, the current flowing through it is proportional $1/R$, which is the conductance. Thus, skin conductance can be measured using a constant voltage technique. Which is the preferable technique and unit of measurement?

Darrow (1934, 1964b) showed that the rate of secretion of sweat was linearly related to skin conductance. Similarly, Thomas and Korr (1957) demonstrated that conductance varies linearly with the number of active sweat glands. Since sweat glands form low-resistance pathways through the high-resistance stratum corneum of the skin they can be represented electrically as a number of switchable resistors in parallel with each other and with the high resistance of the stratum corneum (Figure 2.2). The resistance across the skin cannot be calculated directly but only in terms of conductances, since resistors in parallel are not additive like

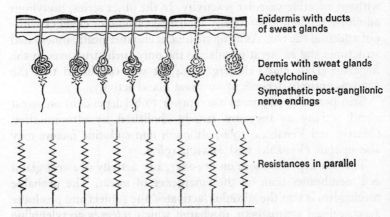

Epidermis with ducts
of sweat glands

Dermis with sweat glands
Acetylcholine
Sympathetic post-ganglionic
nerve endings

Resistances in parallel

Figure 2.2 *Diagrammatic representation of skin with sweat glands and equivalent electrical circuit*

resistors in series. Thus, the recorded conductance $G_1 = G_0 + ng$, where $G_0$ is the conductance of the stratum corneum, $n$ the number of active sweat glands and $g$ the mean conductance of an active sweat gland. As $G_0$ is negligible (about 1 $\mu$mho cm$^{-2}$ of skin), $G_1$ is proportional to $n$. If a stimulus is applied, $G_1$ increases to $G_2$ as $n_1$ increases to $n_2$. The number of additionally active sweat glands whose activity constitutes the GSR is given by $n_2 - n_1$ which is proportional to $G_2 - G_1$. Changes in resistance bear no relation to changes in sweat gland activity.

This model received direct support from an experiment of Lader's (1970) in which atropine was iontophoresed into the fingertip. Atropine takes some time for its effects to become maximal. During this time skin conductance drops steadily and GSR activity would be expected to fall away in a regular, monotonic fashion. GSRS were elicited from the atropinised finger and expressed as a proportion of the GSRS elicited simultaneously from a control finger treated with saline. When the GSRS were expressed as changes in conductance a regular, monotonic decrease in the relative size of the GSRS from the atropinised finger was found. Conversely, if GSRS were quantified as changes in resistance erratic changes in the relative size of the GSRS occurred before an abrupt drop to zero (Figure 2.3).

Thus, there seems little doubt that skin conductance bears a linear relationship to sweat gland activity whereas skin resistance

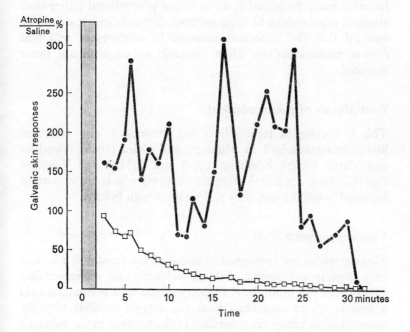

Figure 2.3  *Effects of atropine on the galvanic skin response*. The dotted area represents the time of iontophoresis of atropine into the middle finger and of saline into the ring finger of the left hand. The lower curve represents successive GSRS of the atropinised finger quantified as change in conductance and expressed as a percentage of the equivalent GSRS of the saline control finger, similarly quantified. The upper curve represents the same GSRS quantified as change in resistance and expressed as a percentage of the equivalent saline responses, also quantified as change in resistance.

is not a biologically valid unit at all. Nevertheless, sweat gland activity can still be estimated by recording skin resistance. GSRs are found by measuring the resistance at the start and at the trough of the response, converting each value to conductance and then subtracting them. Note that this is *not* the same as calculating the response as a change in resistance and then taking the reciprocal; this is not a valid measure.

Further transformations such as log or square root have been urged and may be advantageous in certain circumstances. Log transformations have the advantage that they take account of the fact that many biological systems follow proportional rather than absolute relationships to other systems. Nevertheless, it should be stressed that the important measure is conductance and that further transformations while desirable on occasion are never essential.

## Techniques of measurement

This is a complex topic which has spawned a large technical literature summarised in Montagu and Coles (1966), Venables and Martin (1967), Edelberg (1967) and Lykken and Venables (1971). There are certain technical aspects which are important for valid recording and they will be dealt with briefly.

### Constant current method

The electrodes are connected in series with a resistor $R$ which is very large in comparison with the subject's skin resistance (see Figure 2.4). For example, if a battery of 300 volts is connected via a resistor of 30 megohms, then the current remains virtually constant at 10 $\mu$amperes regardless of fluctuations in the subject's resistance. This current will be carried by the active sweat glands, the fewer the active sweat glands the greater the current through each one. It is thus impossible to state what is a 'safe' current density in the sense that the current will not interfere with sweat gland function. However, under usual conditions, current densities of about 10 $\mu$A cm$^{-2}$ of skin do not appear excessive.

There are several alternative methods of delivering constant currents, transistorised circuits being particularly convenient.

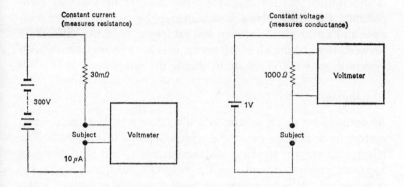

Figure 2.4 *Block diagrams for constant current method for measuring skin resistance and constant voltage method for measuring skin conductance*

## Constant voltage method

A low-voltage source (say 1 V) is connected across the subject and the current flowing is measured by placing a small resistor in the circuit and measuring the voltage drop across it. This drop is proportional to the current (Figure 2.4). The resistor should be of low value, say 1,000 ohms. As the voltage across the resistor will be of the order of millivolts fairly sensitive recorders are required, but these are well within the capabilities of modern instruments.

## Electrodes

The least complicated electrode system consists of one 'active' electrode on a fingertip or palmar surface and one 'inactive' electrode attached usually to the arm. The site of attachment of the latter electrode is abraded (with an emery board) so that its resistance becomes low and negligible in comparison with that of the active site. In this way changes at the active site only are recorded.

The alternative is to attach two 'active' electrodes to two sites such as adjacent fingertips. The changes are then a total of the changes at the two sites. If the constituent conductances are unequal at the two sites then the recorded conductance

$$G = \frac{G_1 \cdot G_2}{G_1 + G_2}$$

is determined predominantly by the smaller of the two components. Consequently, the relationship between total conductance and sweat gland activity will no longer hold. As differences between two palmar sites can occur, it is safer to use the unipolar system despite the necessity to abrade the skin.

*Polarisation*

As outlined on p. 13, whenever a direct current flows an electromotive force may be generated which opposes that current. The effect with respect to skin resistance measurement is to cause an apparent gradual increase in the subject's resistance above the true reading. Although there are several ways of obviating polarisation problems, the most common is to use non-polarisable electrodes. Silver–silver chloride and zinc–zinc sulphate systems can be used: the former suffers from the disadvantage that frequent re-chloriding is necessary as the current flow strips the chloride layer off the cathodic electrode; the latter system is suspect as zinc ions are non-physiological and may affect sweat gland activity.

The most suitable system is the double electrode developed by Lykken (1959), based on a commonly used device in the electronics industry. The current flows through one pair of electrodes and the voltage difference engendered is recorded from a second pair of electrodes. The two elements of each double electrode are in electrical contact via the contact medium. Polarisation products build up on one set of electrodes but do not affect the voltage across the recording electrodes. Unfortunately, this robust system cannot be used for recording skin conductance where the current itself is measured.

*Conductance or resistance?*

We have seen that conductance *units* are the appropriate biological measure but that either conductance or resistance can be recorded, a mathematical transformation then being applied in the latter case. The recording of skin resistance requires lower amplification and double-element electrodes are suitable. Skin conductance recording allows a constant current through each sweat gland and no arithmetical computations are required. If good laboratory facilities are available, skin conductance recordings are preferable because a true visual representation of levels and reactivity is obtained on the polygraph record. If field studies are to be undertaken, resistance measures have the advantage of a robust double-element electrode system. As computer analysis is now becoming commonplace, the reciprocal transformation no longer has to be done laboriously by hand.

Whichever technique is chosen, certain further precautions are essential for artifact-free recording.

*Electrode site*   The active electrode must be attached either to the palmar surface of the hands or the plantar surface of the feet, as these are the areas where sweat gland activity is relatively independent of ambient temperature and humidity. The volar surface of the distal phalanx of the thumb is a good area as it offers a flat extensive surface. The site should be inspected to make sure there are no small cuts which would reduce the skin resistance by acting as an electrical low-resistance pathway.

*Site preparation*   Swabbing the skin with alcoholic ether or carbon tetrachloride is not to be recommended as, although surface grease is removed, sweat gland activity may be decreased for a time by a direct local toxic action. Washing the hands with toilet soap and water is sufficient.

*Site masking*   As the sweat glands can be regarded as resistors in parallel, the larger the area recorded from the lower the resistance. Therefore it is essential to ensure that the recording is taken from a constant area of skin by using a masking device. Annular, self-adhesive, foam-plastic corn plasters are ideal for this purpose (Lykken, 1959).

*Constancy of site*   As the density of sweat glands may vary over the skin, it is necessary that the same site be recorded from in different subjects or in the same subject on different occasions. The central whorl of the finger- or thumb-print provides a useful reference point.

*Contact medium*   As the contact medium between the electrode and the skin will diffuse into the sweat gland ducts the contact medium should be as physiological as possible by approximating to the composition of normal sweat. A contact medium containing 0·05 M sodium chloride fulfils this condition for the main electrolyte constituent of sweat. Commercially available medical lubricating jellies are often suitable and very convenient.

*Calibration* This can be done quite simply by substituting a standard resistor of 100 kilohms for the subject.

## Skin potential

Because of the biphasic responses and because skin potential levels relate to general bodily factors such as potassium concentrations, one cannot recommend the routine use of skin potential in psychophysiological measures. Its use should be left to those with particular expertise and experience (Montagu, 1958).

The measurement of skin potential presents the same problems as the measurement of any other bio-electric potential. High-gain amplifiers with high-input impedance are essential as are non-polarisable electrodes and a physiologically appropriate contact medium.

## Interpretation of recordings

The background level of skin resistance (or conductance) varies continuously and trends can be estimated by taking readings at appropriate intervals and converting to conductance levels. For example, in Figure 2.1 (fourth tracing) a change in resistance can be seen, starting at 70 kilohms and rising to about 160 kilohms. The corresponding conductance values (conductance in micromhos = 1,000/resistance in kilohms (1 mho = 1/ohm)) are 14·3 and 6·3 micromhos and the change is 8·0 micromhos. The variability of the background level can be calculated.

The commonest aspect of the response which is analysed is the amplitude. Readings are taken at the onset of the response and at its peak and appropriate calculations carried out to derive the response in conductance terms. Other aspects of the response which can be analysed are the latency which requires a faster paper speed for accurate estimation and the rate of recovery of the skin resistance back to its prestimulus levels.

Spontaneous activity in the skin conductance can be estimated usually by counting the number of fluctuations above a certain criterion. For skin resistance recordings it is more appropriate to use a relative criterion, e.g. all fluctuations greater than 1 per cent of the background level, than an absolute criterion such as fluctuations above 1 kilohm in size.

## Salivation (Brown, 1970)

Saliva is produced by three pairs of salivary glands pouring their secretions into the mouth by means of ducts: (1) the parotid glands, situated in front of and below the ear; (2) the submaxillary glands, lying laterally in the floor of the mouth; and (3) the sub-mandibular glands which are further forward. The parotid secretes only about a quarter of the total saliva and the saliva secreted is serous (watery) (Schneyer and Levin, 1955). The sublingual secretes a mucous saliva and the submaxillary saliva of intermediate composition. The innervation of the salivary glands is complex with both sympathetic and parasympathetic fibres. Parasympathetic stimulation produces an increase in the flow of saliva which is also more concentrated; vasodilatation also occurs. Sympathetic stimulation results in vasoconstriction. Marked asymmetry is common between the glands on the two sides with respect to volume of secretion. Salivary secretion can be stimulated by chewing movements or by placing lemon juice in the mouth.

The earliest device for recording salivary flow consisted of a cup or disc attached over the opening of the parotid duct. A tube led to a drop-counter (Lashley, 1916). Various refinements have been introduced such as constant suction to attach the disc and electronic counting, but the device still has the drawback that it measures salivation rate in only one gland (usually the parotid). Six suction discs would be needed to measure total flow.

A very widely used alternative method employs dental cotton-wool rolls. Three dry cylindrical rolls are placed in an air-tight plastic container which is then accurately weighed. Using forceps, one roll is introduced in the floor of the mouth under the front of the tongue, the other two in the floor of the mouth laterally. The rolls are left in position with the mouth closed for 2 minutes and then rapidly removed and replaced in the plastic container. After 2 minutes, the procedure is repeated and again a third time. The containers are re-weighed and the mean of the three increases in weight is the salivary flow per 2 minutes. Care must be taken that the subject has not eaten, drunk or smoked for at least an hour and he should have been lying quietly with his mouth closed for at least 15 minutes. With these precautions, this simple unglamorous method is surprisingly accurate and sensitive.

## Heart rate

The heart rate is a widely used autonomic measure in psycho-physiology. The pulse rate is recorded from the periphery and is identical to the heart rate except in some pathological conditions such as atrial fibrillation. The heart rate is easy to measure because it consists of a series of discrete, identifiable events.

*Electrocardiography* The heart as it contracts gives rise to a complex potential change of the order of millivolts. These potentials are most easily recorded from the chest wall overlying the heart but they also spread down the arms and legs. Electrodes placed on each arm will usually record the electrocardiogram (ECG in Britain; EKG in America) quite satisfactorily. The electrodes are large metal plates which are fixed using rubber straps to abraded areas of the skin of the limbs. Hypertonic sodium chloride jelly is used as the contact medium. A medium-gain AC amplifier is sufficient to produce a signal of the order of a volt or two, which can be further processed. The limbs being recorded from should not be allowed to touch; the limbs should also be supported in some way as muscle activity can result in both movement and electrical artifacts.

*Other heart rate detectors* Other devices can be used to register heart rate and include a microphone to pick up heart sounds, pulse detectors over the apex thrust and radio-frequency imped-ance amplifiers to detect heart contractions. They are all less convenient than recording the ECG.

*Pulse rate detectors* Mechanical pulse detectors (strain-gauges) can be attached over an artery to record pulsations; they are prone to movement artifacts. Photo-electric devices can be fitted over a fingertip or onto an ear-lobe. Each pulse beat is accompanied by a change in the optical density of the part which is registered by the photometer. If blood flow is being measured in the fingertip or forearm, the plethysmograph will show fluctuations in volume corresponding to each pulse beat.

*Processing the signal* If a simple measure of rate per minute only is required, the ECG or pulse tracing can be recorded on paper on a polygraph and the beats counted. Often, however, more sensitive or shorter-term measures are required. This can be achieved in a clumsy and tedious way by running the paper at a fairly high speed, measuring the distance between beats, say the R-waves of the ECG, and converting this to inter-beat interval in milliseconds. Electronic means of processing the signal to provide the required information are available. In such devices, the first step is to detect the signal which then triggers an electronic pulse. The triggering is usually on an amplitude criterion such as towards the peak of the R-wave; a 'refractory' period is then introduced to prevent the device re-triggering on the subsequent T-wave. Thus, a series of electronic pulses is produced, each corresponding to a heart beat. These pulses can then be integrated so that a running average of the heart rate over the past, say 20 seconds, is written out by a pen. This type of recording is useful for heart rate changes with a time-course of minutes.

Another method, which preserves all the heart rate information, is the beat-to-beat cardiotachograph (Figure 2.5, bottom tracing). In this device, the interval between each two successive beats is displayed or recorded on a pen-recorder. For example, in one version, the pen moves down the paper at a constant rate. The pulse beat causes the pen to return to its baseline from whence it immediately starts its next traverse (see Figure 2.5). The slower the heart rate, the longer the inter-beat interval and the further the pen travels down the paper before being returned to its starting point. The inter-beat interval can be read off to the nearest 5 or 10 ms by reference to a standard pulse which is used to calibrate the system. This type of display allows the quantification of details of heart rate responses to discrete stimuli.

*Recording* The tracings obtained with a cardiotachograph usually show appreciable beat-to-beat variations. In young subjects sinus arrhythmia may be quite marked but can be easily distinguished because of its relation to respiration. Longer-term fluctuations also occur.

Heart rate responses to discrete stimuli, a loud tone or a shock, vary somewhat from subject to subject but generally take the form of an acceleration (tachycardia) maximal 4 to 5 beats after the stimulus and then a slowing (bradycardia) until 10 to 15 beats after the stimulus. In some subjects heart rate responses may consist almost entirely of cardiac slowing. Many investigators believe that the type of stimulation appears to influence the type of

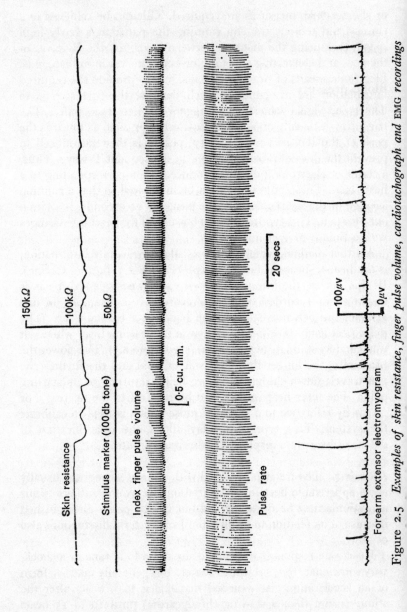

Figure 2.5 *Examples of skin resistance, finger pulse volume, cardiotachograph and* EMG *recordings*

response. However, the basic principles regarding the relationship between type of stimulus and the form of the response remain unknown.

## Blood pressure

The circulation of the blood is maintained by the heart which pumps blood into the arterial system to the tissues. The pulsatile output of the heart is cushioned by the elasticity of the arterial system: the arterial pressure in a major artery such as the brachial or femoral consists of a mean level upon which are superimposed the pulse changes. The highest pressure reached is termed the 'systolic pressure', the lowest the 'diastolic pressure'. The difference between the two is the pulse pressure. Mean blood pressure is the pressure recorded if the individual pulses are smoothed out, and it is dependent on the output of the heart and the peripheral resistance of the vascular tree.

The only accurate method for measuring blood pressure is to introduce a pressure transducer into an artery as is done in detailed cardiovascular assessments in cardiac patients. As it carries a slight risk of vascular thrombosis it is not suitable for use in normal subjects or psychiatric patients and indirect methods have to be resorted to.

The classic method is to wrap an inflatable cuff around the upper arm and to pump it up above systolic blood pressure (usually over 120 mm of mercury). The pressure is slowly lowered by opening a valve, and a stethoscope is placed over the brachial artery beyond the cuff. Characteristic sounds (Korotkoff sounds) are heard: systolic blood pressure is taken at the point where sounds can just be heard, diastolic pressure at the point where a sudden muffling of the sounds occurs. Practice is needed to take blood pressure in this way and, occasionally, uncharacteristic sounds occur, e.g. no muffling. Care should be taken that the arm is supported in such a way that the cuff is at the level of the heart. Typical readings are 120 mm of mercury systolic, 80 diastolic. (In scientific units, this is equivalent to 160 and 107 millibars or, better, 1,600 and 1,070 newtons per square metre.)

The blood pressure can be recorded 'blind' by having a moveable scale on the manometer. This is set arbitrarily and after the readings are taken they are corrected for the degree of offset of the scale by opening the manometer box and examining the true scale.

Many automatic devices have been invented to record blood pressure and, despite their ingenuity, the very number indicates that no one device is totally satisfactory. A typical method consists of an arm cuff which is automatically inflated and slowly deflated. A microphone over the brachial artery records the Korotkoff sounds which are amplified and then traced out on a polygraph over a tracing of the pressure changes. The systolic and diastolic pressures are then read off from the tracings at the pressure points corresponding to the onset and offset of the sounds. Refinements of this method consist of the automatic detection of the onset and offset of the sounds and the recording of the concomitant pressures. These techniques usually work satisfactorily in resting subjects but accurate recording of blood pressure in active subjects is still a problem. Comparison of cuff methods and intra-arterial methods suggests that the pressures are 10 mm of mercury lower using the cuff technique (Roberts, Smiley and Manning, 1953).

Simpler methods can be used to record systolic blood pressure alone. A small cuff is applied to the finger and inflated. Pulsations distal to the cuff are detected with a photo-electric or pneumatic plethysmograph or a crystal pressure transducer. As pulsations are detected the cuff is inflated until they disappear, whereupon the pressure is reduced again. The cuff pressure will thus 'hunt' about systolic pressure. In suitable resting subjects, the fluctuations about systolic pressure may be less than 5 mm of mercury. The technique is still prone to artifact in the active subject and the cuff has to be deflated periodically to restore the blood supply to the fingertip. However, a continuous record is obtained.

Because of the technical difficulties, blood pressure has been relatively unpopular as a psychophysiological measure. If both systolic and diastolic pressures are required, cumbersome arm cuff methods are necessary, giving intermittent readings only. Finger cuff methods are more convenient but in some subjects, especially if not at rest, it can be very difficult to obtain satisfactory recordings.

## Blood flow

Blood flow through an artery can be measured in animals by a variety of methods (electromagnetic, ultrasonic) but all necessitate wrapping the device around the artery. In humans catheterisation is required for measurement of flow in individual blood vessels and this cannot be used in psychophysiology. Instead, measurement of blood flow into the part of interest (arm, leg, hand, finger, head) is carried out by plethysmograph—the recording of volume changes.

Blood flow in the skin, as well as nourishing the skin tissues, regulates body temperature with vasodilatation occurring in conditions of heat. Muscle blood flow supplies oxygen and nutrient requirements to the muscle tissue and increases greatly during periods of muscular contraction. In conditions of heightened emotional arousal a redistribution of blood occurs with the skin and splanchnic areas being deprived of blood and the muscle blood flow increasing several-fold. Skin blood flow in the hand is solely controlled by sympathetic adrenergic vasoconstrictor fibres, vasodilatation being due entirely to release of constrictor tone. Muscle blood flow is more complex in its control (Barcroft, 1960). During exercise, metabolites accumulate and produce local vasodilatation. Adrenergic vasoconstrictor fibres maintain some tone. Cholinergic vasodilator fibres also play a role: although inactive at rest, during 'emotional stress' they produce marked vasodilatation (Blair et al., 1959; Wilkins and Eichna, 1941). Finally, circulating adrenaline, released from the adrenal medulla, also causes generalised muscle vasodilatation. Not only is the arterial side (arterioles) of the circulation under control but the venules are also influenced.

In summary, muscle blood flow, and to an even greater extent forearm or calf blood flow, is controlled in a complex manner; head or finger blood flow mainly reflects changes in skin blood flow which is under much simpler control. Nevertheless, both areas are capable of much interesting empirical data.

*Rationale* During the systolic phase of a pulse cycle, blood is ejected into the peripheral vascular tree. For a short while inflow into the limb or digit exceeds outflow and the member increases in volume. At the end of the ejection phase of the heart the rate of inflow drops, and during the diastolic phase outflow exceeds inflow and the limb or finger volume drops. The transient increase in finger volume is termed the pulse volume or blood volume pulse and is a Cartesian co-ordinate plot of the time-course of the net difference between inflow and outflow. As the rate of outflow is not known, the rate of inflow cannot be directly determined. However, it has been demonstrated that there is close correspondence between rate of blood inflow and size of pulse volume in normal

35

subjects when the limb or digit is at the level of the heart and variations in venous pressure are avoided. Under these conditions, the pulse volume may be regarded as an index of blood flow, although it cannot be converted into an absolute rate of flow.

Over a long period of time inflow must equal outflow or the member would be deprived of or engorged with blood. Over the short term differences can occur which are shown by changes in limb or digit volume. The main factor causing such 'blood volume' changes are alterations in the patency of venous plexus reservoirs. Changes in venous tone tend to parallel arteriolar changes and thus changes in blood volume often mirror alterations in blood flow. Nevertheless, no absolute measure of blood flow is obtained and this measure, while easy to record, needs cautious interpretation. Much less amplification is needed to record blood volume than pulse volume and the latter is seen as a small fluctuation in the blood volume tracing.

Absolute measures of blood flow can be obtained using venous occlusion. A cuff is wrapped around the limb and inflated to a pressure above that of the venous system but below diastolic arterial pressure (Barcroft and Swan, 1953). Arterial inflow continues while venous outflow is blocked so that the increase in volume of the limb is a direct measure of blood flow. Because engorgement soon occurs, occlusion is maintained for less than 10 seconds and readings can be taken not more frequently than two per minute.

Thus, there are three main ways in which estimates of blood flow can be obtained using plethysmography: measurement of pulse volume, of blood volume without venous occlusion and of blood volume with occlusion. All require measurements of volume and there are several ways of doing this.

*Fluid displacement* In these techniques the part under study which may be a finger or toe, or the hand or forearm, is enclosed in a rigid container. In the case of a digit, this consists of a thimble-like oncometer which fits loosely but is sealed to the finger with stop-cock grease. A polythene tube of low distensibility leads from the oncometer to a transducer. As the transducer is highly sensitive to volume changes air can be used as the fluid. Pulsations in the finger are transmitted to the transducer and converted to electrical signals (Figure 2.5, next to bottom tracing). As these signals are only of the order of a few microvolts, high-gain, stable amplification is necessary. If venous occlusion is required a small cuff is wrapped round the finger proximal to the oncometer.

For hand and forearm plethysmography, water-filled containers are used (Kelly, 1967). A loose rubber glove encloses the hand and fits the wrist sufficiently tightly to effect an air-tight seal but not so tightly as to interfere with venous drainage. In forearm plethysmography, the forearm is covered with a loose rubber sleeve fixed at either end round a suitable-shaped central hole in a rubber diaphragm. The diaphragms fit in either end of a tapered metal tube which encloses the forearm. The water in the plethysmograph must be maintained at body temperature, and it is filled to the height of a chimney at the top of the plethysmograph. Fluctuations in the height of the fluid can be recorded using a float carrying a stylus writing on smoked paper or by using a volumetric transducer (Figure 2.1). For occlusion of the hand, the cuff is wrapped around the wrist; for forearm plethysmography, the cuff is wrapped around the arm just below the elbow. In forearm plethysmography it is essential to exclude the hand from the circulation so a second cuff is wrapped around the wrist and maintained for periods of up to 20 minutes at pressures above systolic, i.e. about 150 mm of mercury (Greenfield, 1960). Venous occlusion plethysmography can be semi-automated by arranging the inflation and deflation of the cuffs by means of solenoid-operated valves.

*Girth plethysmography* A less cumbersome method relies on the relationship between the length, circumference and total volume of a cylinder. If length is unchanged, girth is a measure of volume and changes in girth of volume change. The usual transducer is a highly elastic rubber tube filled with mercury. The resistance of the mercury-in-rubber strain-gauge depends on its length, i.e. the girth of the limb. Such a device is much simpler to use than a fluid plethysmograph but presents problems of calibration. It is of most use for within-subject comparisons.

*Electrical impedance* As outlined earlier, volume changes in biological tissues are accompanied by changes in impedance to high-frequency alternating electrical currents (Geddes and Hoff, 1964). Thus, if the impedance is measured using such currents (100–200 kHz in frequency), changes corresponding to pulse beats are seen. This technique is very versatile as simple electrodes are used and can be attached to any part of the body. Calibration is

37

impossible and the part under study cannot be accurately determined as the exact current paths through the tissues lying between the two sets of electrodes cannot be accurately defined.

Rheoencephalography is the application of radio-frequency impedance plethysmography to the measurement of cerebral blood flow (Radvan-Ziemnowicz, 1967). However, despite much debate, controversy still exists concerning the validity of this method.

*Photoelectric methods* For the fingertip, photoplethysmography has been enthusiastically advocated (Weinman, 1967). Living tissue is transparent to red and infrared radiation (7,000–9,000 Angstrom units) while blood is relatively opaque. A beam of such radiation is used to illuminate the fingertip and the amount of light transmitted is measured using a sensitive photometer. The background level is a measure of blood volume upon which are superimposed fluctuations corresponding to the pulse volume beats. Again, absolute measures are not obtained.

*Analysis of recordings* For pulse volume recordings using a fluid plethysmograph the amplitude of the beats of interest can be measured and converted to volume changes using the calibration marks obtained by injecting a known quantity of fluid from a microsyringe. The volume of tissue from which the pulse fluctuations were obtained is estimated using a fluid displacement technique, and the pulse volume can then be expressed in terms of, say, mm$^3$ per 5 cm$^3$ of fingertip. Blood volume changes can similarly be quantified. With venous occlusion techniques, the slope of the volume line represents the rate of blood inflow. From the recording paper speed and the calibration constant of the recording system the rate of blood flow in millilitres per minute can be calculated and then corrected for the volume of forearm actually recorded from.

*Skin temperature* This technique has the virtues of precision and simplicity as temperature-sensitive devices such as thermistors are both accurate and small. However, the relationship between skin temperature and blood flow in the underlying tissues is complex and interpretation of results with this technique is not easy (Plutchik, 1956).

38

# Penile plethysmography

A specialised form of plethysmography comprises measurement of penile circumference. The most convenient transducer is a mercury-in-rubber strain-gauge which is slipped over the shaft of the penis (Bancroft, 1971). If erection occurs in response to a stimulus, e.g. projection of a slide of a nude, the strain-gauge is stretched. Such a technique has proved useful in helping to determine the sexual orientation of men with sexual problems and especially in following the progress of treatment.

# Pupillography

Techniques for the measurement of pupil size range from the most elementary to the extremely complex. The simplest technique employs a perspex strip out of one side of which are cut semi-circles of known dimensions. The strip is moved up and down in front of the subject's eye until a semi-circle matches the pupil. To keep light conditions constant a shaped metal tube about 30 cm long containing a small light is used. The observer presses his eyes to one end with the subject's face at the other and the perspex strip moves up and down in slots in front of the subject's face. Despite the primitive nature of this device, surprisingly accurate results can be obtained with even unco-operative subjects.

Another simple method consists of a black card containing a series of pairs of pin-holes at steadily increasing inter-pair distances (say from 1 to 10 mm). The subject holds the card up to one eye and looks through each pair of pin-holes in turn towards a light. He sees two circles of light which overlap at those pairs a small distance apart and are separate when looking through pin-hole pairs larger distances apart. One pair of pin-holes will give two circles which just touch and the distance between this pair of pin-holes equals the pupillary diameter. Co-operative, trained subjects are necessary.

A range of techniques depend on photography. The close-up camera is placed a standard distance from the eye and photographs of the eye are taken manually or automatically. As well as using film sensitive to light, ultraviolet and infrared systems have been used. The latter enables pupil sizes to be measured in the dark but because of the heat can be discomforting to the subject. Photographic techniques suffer from the grave drawback that only intermittent readings can be obtained.

The most sophisticated technique is the photo-electric one devised by Lowenstein and Lowenfeld (1958). A very narrow beam of infrared radiation is directed on to the eye and is electronically controlled so that it scans the eye like the spot on a television tube. The beam is either reflected by the iris or sclera or absorbed through the pupil. The reflected radiation from the subject's eye is picked up and amplified with a photomultiplier—a voltage appearing when the scan is over the iris, no voltage when the pupil is scanned. As the speed of the scan is known, the time during which no voltage is detected is proportional to the transverse diameter of the pupil. Both pupils can be scanned successively and, as only a narrow spot is used, no heating problems arise (Hakarem, 1967). This technique can also be used to measure pupillary responses (Goldwater, 1972). If the responses are small they tend to be lost in small spontaneous movements of the iris, but by using averaging techniques the signal can be retrieved from the background noise (see p. 54).

## Gastro-intestinal function

Gastric function in humans was first assessed by the subject swallowing a gastric tube. The contents of the stomach were aspirated and analysed. Alternatively, the tube had a balloon on the end which could be inflated after being swallowed and intragastric pressures recorded. However, such a bulky object could itself initiate contractions. More sophisticated pressure-sensitive transducers have been used but still necessitate the subject tolerating a gastric tube.

Techniques have been developed which involve the subject swallowing a small magnet, detected externally by a magnetometer (Wenger, Henderson and Dining, 1957) or a steel ball-bearing, monitored with a mine-detector (Davis, Garafolo and Gault, 1957). Radio-telemetry is a more elegant technique in which both pressure and pH can be transmitted (Staveney et al., 1966; Norman, 1969). The radiosonde pill can be allowed to pass through the gastro-intestinal tract or it can be tethered by a cord and its position determined radiographically. However, tension on the cord may cause great discomfort.

A different approach has been to attempt to record the electrical activity of the stomach using electrodes on the surface of the abdomen (Davis, Garafolo and Gault, 1957). Silver–silver chloride disc electrodes are used together with a sensitive DC amplifier. One electrode, the reference, is attached to the leg; the active electrode is attached to the abdomen, the upper left quadrant giving the best recordings. The electrogastrogram (EGG for short!) in the human consists of waves of about 0·5 mV in amplitude occurring about once every 20 seconds (Davis, 1959; Davis and Berry, 1963). This technique still has not been fully evaluated for use in psychophysiology (Russell and Stern, 1967).

Other viscera in which psychophysiological recordings of pressure and motility have been attempted include the bladder, rectum and oesophagus (Rubin *et al.*, 1962).

## SOMATIC MEASURES

### Respiration

The respiratory and cardiovascular systems are closely coordinated, the respiratory system serving to supply oxygen to the blood and to remove carbon dioxide from it, the exchange taking place in the alveoli of the lung. Respiratory function is regulated by the central nervous system, via centres in the pons and medulla which are influenced by higher centres to the extent of being under voluntary control. Emotional states alter respiration which is thus of interest to psychophysiologists (Dudley, Martin and Holmes, 1964). The most relevant variable for the psychophysiologist is usually minute volume which is rate of respiration per minute multiplied by the depth of respiration. Highly sophisticated techniques are used by the respiratory physiologist in the assessment of normal and diseased respiratory function, almost all neglected by the psychophysiologist who is generally content to measure respiratory rate only.

The quantitative measure of depth of respiration is the volume of each breath (tidal volume) which ranges in adults between about 400 and 650 ml. The classic way of monitoring tidal volume is to use a spirometer (Benedict–Roth), which is a closed system volume recorder. However, it is cumbersome and the subject requires training in its use as he tends to overbreathe at first. It is even stressful to anxious subjects. Another method is to assess changes in chest circumference using a band around the thorax and some type of strain-gauge, which yields a record of respiratory rate. Rate may not reflect minute volume as the tidal volume may alter independently or even inversely. Tidal volume is only assessed semi-quantitatively by using a single-girth strain-gauge, as the pattern of respiration may not be constant, i.e. change from predominantly thoracic to mainly abdominal. However, by using one strain-gauge around the chest and another round the abdomen quite good estimates of rate and depth of respiration have been obtained (Shapiro and Cohen, 1965). Probably the simplest method of assessing the rate of respiration is to fix a temperature-sensitive device to the upper lip. If a thermistor is used, changes in resistance occur, which correspond to the current of cold air on inspiration and warm air on expiration and which can be conveniently recorded using a slightly modified skin-resistance instrument.

Radio-frequency impedance methods have been assessed for the measurement of respiration (Geddes and Hoff, 1964), and this technique is an alternative to a strain-gauge round the chest.

Measurements of blood gases are routine in pulmonary physiology but for a variety of reasons, including the ethical inadvisability of arterial punctures, oximetry is generally used in psychophysiological studies. This consists of a photometer attached to an ear-lobe. Changes in the oxygen saturation of the blood in the ear-lobe are detected and recorded. The technique is less accurate than more direct methods.

Other techniques are available for measurement of airway resistance, lung compliance, etc., and are described in appropriate physiology books.

**Electromyogram**

Motor nerves to the muscles divide into many branches and ultimately innervate 100 to 200 muscle fibres (except in the extra-ocular muscles where the number is much smaller). When the nerve is activated, the impulse usually travels to all these fibres, which contract in unison thus forming what Sherrington termed the 'motor unit'. The nerve impulse is an electrical change which spreads over the muscle fibres and gives rise to a temporary depolarisation of the cell membrane followed by bio-chemical changes which result in the contraction of the fibres. The electrical changes can be detected and provide a more convenient measure of muscle activity than direct mechanical recording of muscle tension (Figure 2.6).

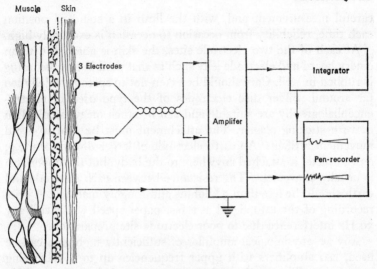

Figure 2.6  *Block diagram of* EMG *recording technique*

The amount of muscle tension depends on the number of motor units active and the rate of their repetitive firing. Although most movements involve change both in length and in tone of muscles, physiologists have concentrated on the study of the two extreme conditions, namely (1) *isometric contraction* and (2) *isotonic contraction* in which the tone remains constant but the muscle shortens. In the former condition the limb does not move; in the latter movement occurs. Under certain conditions (which are almost always met in careful psychophysiological experiments), there is a linear relationship between the amount of electrical activity (as a voltage–time integral) and the *isometric* voluntary tension in a muscle (Lippold, 1952). Therefore, the limb upon which the muscle mass of interest operates must not be allowed to move. For example, the arm must be resting comfortably in a designated position if forearm extensor activity is to be assessed. Foam-plastic cushions are useful for this purpose. One commonly used area where true isometric contraction may not be attained is the forehead, where frontalis activity results in scalp movements. In practice, though, useful estimates are still obtained.

*Technique*

For each muscle mass, standard electrode placements have been devised (Lippold, 1967). Very accurate location is possible by

43

careful measurement and, with the limb in a standard position each time, reliability from occasion to occasion is extremely high.

At each of the two electrode sites, the skin is abraded with an emery board and electrode jelly such as that used in ECG recording is rubbed in well. Care should be taken not to spread the jelly too far around. Silver disc electrodes of the type used in electro-encephalography are suitable and can be stuck on with collodion or with sticking-plaster. The attachment must be firm to avoid movement artifacts. An earth electrode of larger dimensions, e.g. an ECG plate, is attached anywhere to the body, but the upper arm is usually convenient. The resistance between each electrode and earth should be less than 5 kilohms and roughly matched. A brief recording of the EMG signal at a fast paper speed will reveal any 50 Hz interference due to poor electrode site preparation.

Any AC physiological amplifier of sufficiently high gain can be used, EEG amplifiers with upper frequencies up to 1 kHz being appropriate. The EMG has a frequency spectrum from about 16 Hz to over 1 kHz. Polygraph pens fall off in performance above 50–60 Hz so the paper-tracing is not a complete record of the signal. A cathode-ray oscilloscope is necessary to see all the detail.

However, in psychophysiological applications, frequency information is not required and it is convenient to integrate the signal. This can be done in several ways (Shaw, 1967), an example of the output from a commercially available EMG pre-amplifier and integrator being shown in Figures 2.1 and 2.5. The electromyograph is converted from a series of spikes oscillating either side of the baseline into a much smoother 'envelope' which represents the rectified and summed signals over a short preceding period of time (typically a time-constant of 200 ms). Therefore, the elevation of the tracing above the baseline is a measure of the EMG activity (Figure 2.7).

The system is calibrated by substituting an AC signal of known peak-to-peak amplitude for the EMG recording. A 50 Hz sine wave is usually used although it is rather a poor substitute for the wide-frequency and spikey EMG signal. However, as long as the system amplifies equally over the entire range ('level response'), the error is negligible.

The commonest method of analysis is to take readings in milli-metres from zero baseline at appropriate time intervals and to convert these to microvolts by reference to the calibration marks. Mean values, trends and variability over a period of time can then

μV

'Raw'

μV

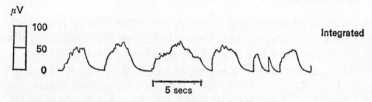

Integrated

5 secs

Figure 2.7   *Comparison of 'raw' and integrated* EMG

be calculated. EMG responses to discrete stimuli such as tones are
not easy to quantify and may be obscured by movement artifacts
if a startle response occurred. Fluctuations in EMG levels take the
form of brief bursts of activity often accompanied by visible
twitches and can be counted.

The distinction between 'relevant' and 'irrelevant' muscle
activity is an important one (Benson and Gedye, 1961). Relevant
activity refers to EMG potentials in muscles fulfilling a direct
function, e.g. maintaining posture, or performing a task, such as
the activity in the ipsilateral forearm muscles during a reaction
time task. Irrelevant activity occurs in muscles not directly involved, such as the contralateral forearm muscles in the above
example. This activity could be zero without interfering with the
maintenance of posture or the carrying out of a task, and the
amount of such irrelevant activity is a reflection of emotional
arousal.

*Gross movements*

The movement of a limb can be monitored by attaching an accelerometer to it. As its name implies, the accelerometer transduces
acceleratory forces into resistance changes. A voltage is obtained as

45

the output which varies according to the movement of the limb and which can be amplified and recorded (Sainsbury, 1964).

For whole body movements an ingenious device has been developed using ultrasonics. An ultrasonic beam is directed into the room in which the subject is sitting or standing and any movements are registered as alterations in the signals bounced off the subject and picked up in the receiver. The technique is quite safe and very convenient (Sainsbury and Costain, 1971).

## Finger tremor

Superimposed on normal voluntary muscular activity is a repetitive rhythm of about 9 Hz. The most tenable explanation for this relates to the servo-loop controlling muscle length which is believed to have oscillations in it of about 7 to 10 Hz. Whatever the mechanism, if the fingers are held in a steady, unsupported position, a tremor occurs which increases in states of heightened emotion.

Finger tremor can be measured by attaching an accelerometer. The varying voltage obtained as the output signal is amplified and recorded. By using computer techniques such as frequency analysis, the characteristics of the waveform can be analysed.

## Eye movements

Several types of eye movement have been categorised (Shackel, 1967). Saccades are the standard everyday movements which take the eyes from one fixation point to the next. Typically, a fixation pause lasts from 0·25 to 1 second and the eyes then move to their next position with a saccade of from 50 to 100 ms duration. Another eye movement which has been studied is smooth tracking, when the eyes closely follow a moving point. Blinking is also of interest and occurs at intervals of about 2–10 seconds, each blink lasting 200–400 ms. During blinking, the eyes rotate upwards.

There are several methods of measuring eye movements (Peters, 1971). A contact lens with a small mirror on it can be inserted, upon which is focused a light beam. Or the light beam can be reflected tangentially off the cornea itself, although this technique is limited to small movements only.

An electrical technique relies on the presence of a standing voltage between the front and back of the eye, the corneo-retinal potential. If the eye moves in any direction the potential field also moves, and changes in it can be detected by suitably placed electrodes around the orbits. For studies in which only the frequency, number or rough direction of eye movements are required, AC amplifiers with a bandwidth of 1–40 Hz are suitable. The sensitivity has to be high, signals of 5–500 μV being measured. DC recording is essential for accurate quantitative purposes so that non-polarisable electrodes must be used. Silver–silver chloride electrodes of the type used in skin potential recording are suitable.

To record up and down movements of the eyes electrodes are attached above and below the orbit. To record side-to-side movements of both eyes electrodes can be placed on the outer extremities of the orbits. To record side-to-side movements of each eye separately, e.g. to study convergent movements, electrodes must also be attached to the inner canthi of the eyes, on the side of the bridge of the nose.

Blink rate has been utilised on occasion in a psychophysiological context (Martin, 1958).

## Electroencephalography

### Introduction

In the latter part of the nineteenth century it became possible to record both standing potentials (DC) and potential variations (AC) from the cerebral tissue of animals. In 1929, Hans Berger published the first report of minute voltage fluctuations on the human scalp which he attributed to brain activity and termed the electroencephalogram (EEG). In the succeeding years the clinical relevance of the EEG was established with respect to paroxysmal conditions such as epilepsy and space-occupying lesions such as tumours. For these purposes multiple-channel recordings are essential and visual analysis is efficient in detecting abnormal waveforms. However, for psychophysiological research purposes such techniques proved inadequate and laborious. The advent of computers, especially small laboratory machines, has revived interest in the EEG as a psychophysiological variable because mathematical analyses of varying degrees of complexity are now feasible. The following account will confine itself entirely to the techniques of research electroencephalography.

TECHNIQUES

*Electrodes*

Most EEG work entails AC recordings, as the investigator is only interested in transient variations in potential difference between two sites on the scalp and not in steady DC potential differences. Non-polarisable electrodes, e.g. silver–silver chloride, are not essential unless the surface area is small as, for example, with fine-needle electrodes. With modern amplifiers of high input impedance, no significant distortion will occur with electrodes of surface area greater than 5 mm².

For DC recording, carefully prepared, selected and tested electrodes are essential, silver–silver chloride being commonly used.

There are several different types of scalp electrode. One type consists of a small, slight-domed, silver button, 1 cm in diameter, with a hole in the centre and a tag with the lead on it at the side. The electrode is stuck onto the scalp with collodion and electrode jelly is squirted through the hole into the dome of the electrode using a small syringe and a blunted needle. The electrode can be accurately applied and usually stays on for as long as necessary, but is awkward to remove as the collodion tends to harden.

An alternative consists of a short length of silver tubing, threaded on the outside and ending in a flared extension. A lead is soldered in the threaded end and the electrode screwed into an insulated mounting. The flared end is covered with lint and cotton-wool, secured with a rubber band and soaked in saline. The electrodes can be held in place with a rubber cap. If only a few electrodes are to be applied each can be mounted in a tripod spring system which lightly grips the hair. This electrode is useful if a succession of brief recordings are to be taken at frequent intervals, e.g. in following the time-course of a drug's effects on the EEG.

*Application of electrodes* The electrode site is swabbed with an antiseptic grease solvent such as 2 per cent hibitane in 70 per cent alcohol. The scalp is rubbed with an emery board or slightly scratched with a blunt needle, and electrode jelly, usually containing hypertonic saline, is rubbed in. Care must be taken to confine the electrode jelly to the electrode site.

*Electrode placements and linkage* There is still some argument regarding electrode configurations, partly because the theoretical considerations are complex and partly because the clinical electro-

48

encephalographer is particularly concerned with localisation of EEG phenomena. The simpler system is the bipolar system in which it is assumed that electrical changes occur under both electrodes and that the EEG consists of the difference between the electrical activity at the two electrodes. The 'monopolar' system attempts to localise the activity to one electrode only, either by selecting an inactive site for the second electrode or by using a set of electrodes over the scalp and joining them together ('common reference derivation'). The former ploy depends on the choice of an electrically silent second electrode site which is very difficult in practice, even extra-cerebral areas having a variety of electrical activity such as the ECG. The common reference system has some theoretical disadvantages. For psychophysiological purposes, bipolar derivations are preferable as localisation is seldom important.

There are standard 'montages' such as the ten–twenty system in which over twenty electrodes are attached to the scalp and sixteen or more channels recorded from simultaneously (Jasper, 1958). In psychophysiology, one is more interested in the detailed analysis of one or two channels. In general, alpha activity is more evident from the occipital regions and eye-blink artifacts are less here. However, as the requirements for each study differ greatly no specific recommendations can be made except that the muscular areas of the scalp and the neck regions should be avoided, especially in tense individuals. We have found one electrode on the vertex and one in the left tempero-parietal region satisfactory for most of our studies in patients.

*Amplifiers*

This is again a very complex topic with great ingenuity being shown by technically sophisticated electroencephalographers. The requirements for AC recordings are fairly standard: high input impedance of at least 1 megohm and preferably 10 megohm; freedom from 50 Hz interference; high sensitivity with an amplification of at least 100,000 times; good frequency response, say from 0·5 Hz to 1,000 Hz; a low 'noise' level; and linearity of response. These are all easily available in modern amplifiers. For DC recordings, stability, i.e. freedom from drift, is essential.

*Recording of* EEG

The standard way of recording the EEG is to use a pen-writing oscillograph which provides a paper tracing (Figure 2.8). The

Figure 2.8 *Frequency analysis of two channels of* EEG. The vertical deflection of the lowest pen represents the voltage in each wave-band for each channel successively. (By courtesy of Dr M. Driver, EEG Dept, The Maudsley Hospital)

disadvantages of such an output for research purposes are detailed on p. 16.

*Artifacts* An artifact in electroencephalography is any recorded waveform which does not stem from cerebral activity. The equipment itself may develop faults due to faulty contacts; the characteristics of components such as resistors, capacitors and transistors may alter with ageing or eventually break down. Electrical interference is a very common source of artifact and is easily recognisable as it is usually due to the 50 Hz (60 Hz in the USA) alternating mains current. Insufficient electrode preparation is almost always the cause but occasionally it may be some major source of interference such as faulty X-ray equipment. Movement artifacts are prone to occur with pad electrodes and with poorly applied stick-on electrodes. In clinical work artifacts from the patient may be very troublesome and in some cases ineradicable. For example, electromyographic potentials may obscure the EEG in tense patients and attempts to 'relax' such patients are usually unsuccessful. Eye movements such as blinks produce large potential shifts but can be minimised by recording from electrodes situated coronally across the head equidistant from the eyes; this obviates the effect of vertical movements of the eye (which occur during a blink) but not those of side-to-side movements. Other sources of artifact in the patient include arterial pulsations, the ECG, sweating and swallowing. An experienced electroencephalographer can detect artifacts, determine their cause and take steps to remove them.

## Analysis of the EEG

*Visual* The EEG is a complex waveform, continually changing, and as it differs somewhat taken from different areas of scalp it defies complete description and analysis. As a first step the EEG frequencies can be divided on clinical grounds into four wavebands: less than 4 Hz is termed 'delta'; from 4 to less than 8 Hz, 'theta'; 8 to 13 Hz inclusive, 'alpha'; and faster than 13 Hz, 'beta'. Alpha frequencies should be distinguished from 'alpha rhythm' which besides being 8–13 Hz in frequency is most prominent towards the occipital area of the head, with the subject's eyes closed. Various frequencies can be present simultaneously, e.g. 25 Hz activity being superimposed on slow-wave activity.

51

However, in visual analysis it is the frequency most obvious to the naked eye which is described.

In psychophysiology, the commonest method of visual analysis is to estimate alpha activity as this lessens or disappears when the subject becomes alert. The per cent alpha time (alpha index) is the percentage of time in which the electroencephalograph shows alpha waves above a certain amplitude criterion, say 10 μV. Responses to stimuli can be quantified as the time following each stimulus during which alpha activity disappears and is replaced by beta activity.

*Automated* Visual analysis of the EEG has established its usefulness in the clinical context but for psychophysiological research automated methods have been developed. One group of methods is designed to automate visual analysis. For example, electronic filters can be built which will pass alpha frequencies above a pre-set amplitude. By deflecting a pen when alpha frequencies are detected, a square wave representation can be derived and the device used to estimate the alpha index or the alpha blocking time (Milstein and Stevens, 1967).

Simple integration of the EEG has been used and this measure gives a rough index of the average amplitude of the EEG. A more sophisticated variation of this technique is to filter the EEG signal into a series of wavebands (Kaiser *et al.*, 1964). A typical set of wavebands is 2·4–4 Hz, 4–7·5 Hz, 7·5–13·5 Hz and 13·5–26 Hz (Figure 2.9). Fairly simple and cheap electronic filters are available and the outputs of these filters can then be rectified and integrated over any required period of time. Although these wavebands

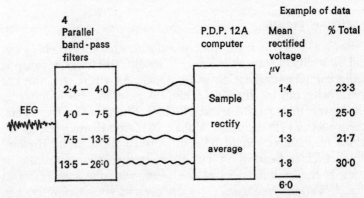

| | 4 Parallel band-pass filters | P.D.P. 12A computer | Example of data | |
|---|---|---|---|---|
| | | | Mean rectified voltage μv | % Total |
| EEG | 2·4 — 4·0 | Sample rectify average | 1·4 | 23·3 |
| | 4·0 — 7·5 | | 1·5 | 25·0 |
| | 7·5 — 13·5 | | 1·3 | 21·7 |
| | 13·5 — 26·0 | | 1·8 | 30·0 |
| | | | 6·0 | |

Figure 2.9 *Diagrammatic representation of broad wave-band analysis*

correspond to delta, theta, alpha and beta frequencies, the outputs of the filters convey different information from the electroencephalograph. For example, even when no alpha rhythm is evident on the paper record, there will still be some output from the 7·5 to 13·5 Hz filter. However, this reflects the tendency of visual analysis merely to pick out the dominant frequency pattern. We have found broad-waveband frequency analysis to be simple in practice and to yield empirical results of a useful nature, e.g. in detecting drug effects.

Another group of methods is based on the assumption that the EEG is a continuous and stable function of time which can be analysed mathematically. Some of these methods use very complex 'time series' analyses and sometimes it appears that the biological significance of the EEG is being lost in a welter of higher mathematics. Many of these techniques assume that the EEG can be usefully described in terms of a range of constituent sine waves. In a fairly widely used technique, one or two channels of EEG are fed into a group of narrow-band filters which are tuned to pass frequencies of, say, 7·0–8·0 Hz, 8·0–9·0 Hz, etc. The output from each filter is integrated over 10 seconds and then displayed as a pen deflection (Figure 2.8). Of course, if the outputs of several appropriate filters are coalesced, the same data as broad-waveband filters are obtained. Although it is usually necessary to carry out the frequency analysis using specially built electronic equipment, if computer facilities are available direct mathematical analyses of the EEG can be carried out. The determination of the amplitudes of the constituent sine waves presumed to comprise a complex waveform is called Fourier analysis. The computations involved in Fourier analysis are complex and several 'short-cuts' exist such as the 'Fast Fourier Transform' and auto-correlation function analysis.

Another method of computer analysis is to analyse the period of each unfiltered EEG wave and to plot out the numbers of waves of each period. As the period is determined by measuring the time (in milliseconds) between successive crossings of the zero voltage point, this method of analysis is often termed 'zero-cross' analysis. Not only the number of waves in each period but their mean amplitude can be determined by the computer.

It can be seen that the automatic analysis of the EEG can entail both higher mathematics, complex electronics and computer technology. It is with such methods that any hope of progress lies because the analyses are objective and large amounts of EEG data can be processed. Nevertheless, the EEG remains an empirical measure in the sense that its physiological basis is obscure and automated analyses make both biological and mathematical assumptions which are impossible to verify.

## Evoked responses

Recording and analysis of the EEG provides information about relatively slow-term changes. In the past decade techniques have become available for detecting short-term responses in the EEG to stimuli such as flashes of light and clicks (Shagass, 1972). As these responses are superimposed on ongoing activity the problem is to extract the signals, i.e. the responses, from the noise, i.e. the background EEG. The methods used are based on the assumption that the elements of the response have a constant relationship to the stimulus, whereas the background activity is random with respect to the stimulus. Thus, the stimulus is presented repeatedly and the epochs of EEG following the stimuli are summed and averaged. For example, sixty-four clicks can be presented at intervals of about 7 seconds and EEG epochs of 0·5 seconds following the clicks are analysed. A characteristic waveform becomes apparent.

The usual procedure nowadays is to use a computer to sample, store, add and average the EEG epochs. The EEG is fed into an analog-to-digital converter (A/D converter) input of the computer (see p. 59). Characteristically, five hundred samples are taken every 1 ms in each epoch.

The computer may be specially devised for averaging procedures (so-called 'computer of average transients' or CAT) or be a small general-purpose laboratory computer which is specially programmed for averaging experiments.

It might be thought that the more the epochs averaged, the clearer would be the averaged evoked response, as the signal-to-noise ratio should increase. This is true in general but the signal-to-noise ratio is actually a function of the square root of the number of epochs. Therefore, in order to double the signal-to-noise ratio, four times as many stimuli must be presented.

The technique also assumes that the signal is maintained constant. If the signal varies in some regular way, then the average response may not be very meaningful. For example, if sixty-four stimuli are presented and the latency of a sharp wave component steadily lengthens, then the average will be a smooth hump which does not represent the true response. Some idea of the variability of the response can be obtained by calculating the variance as well as the mean of the response. In general, the fewer the number of stimulus presentations, the more likely is the average response extracted from the epochs to be meaningful.

The stimulation can be auditory, such as a click, a tone or a burst of white noise (Geisler, 1960). Visual stimuli may be a flash of light or a black and white pattern, such as a chequer board, which is displaced momentarily so that the position of the white elements is transiently occupied by black elements and vice versa. Tactile stimuli include tapping the fingernail and the powerful but un-physiological electrical shock to the skin overlying the ulnar or other superficial sensory nerve.

The response can be roughly divided into specific responses of short latency (up to about 40 ms) and non-specific responses of longer latency. The characteristic short-latency tactile (somato-sensory) response is that recorded from the scalp overlying the cortical sensory receiving areas contralateral to the stimulated nerve. It is very small or absent on the ipsilateral scalp side. The potentials are believed to reflect depolarisation processes in the primary cortical areas. Short-latency responses in the auditory evoked response may also reflect such depolarisation but the primary visual receiving areas lie too deeply in the calcarine fissure for their depolarisation to be convincingly demonstrated.

Of more interest to the psychophysiologist are the later responses, as these appear to be related to psychological variables such as attention and alertness. A characteristic auditory response is shown in Figure 2.10. The non-specific responses to auditory stimuli are elicited best at the vertex of the head and somato-sensory and even visual evoked responses are easily seen in this region of the head. Consequently, in many studies the EEG is recorded from two electrodes, one situated on the vertex, the other typically on the mastoid area (behind the ear) or on the occipital or posterior temporal regions. The choice of electrode position is governed by many factors, but, in general, the further apart they are the larger the response. In other details the EEG recording is the same for the background EEG, but the upper frequency re-sponse should be at least 300 Hz and it must be remembered that any electrical activity, intra- or extra-cerebral, time-locked to the

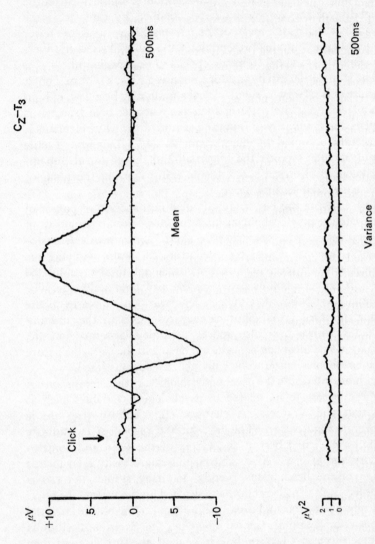

Figure 2.10 Mean and variance of 200 EEG responses evoked by clicks

stimulus will be apparent in the averaged response (Bickford, Canter and Bickford, 1966). Eye blinks are a common source of artifact but can usually be recognised because they are massive, occur later than about 250 ms following the stimulus, and greatly increase the variance of the evoked response. In doubtful cases, recording and averaging from electrodes above and below the eyes will determine whether a blink artifact is being introduced into the evoked response (Wasman et al., 1970).

A related phenomenon is the 'contingent negative variation' (CNV) or 'expectancy wave' (Tecce, 1971, 1972). For this, a conditioning paradigm is used in which a warning stimulus is given followed by an 'imperative' stimulus to which the subject must make a response. After pairing of the stimuli a few times a characteristic change is seen in the EEG between the stimuli, particularly over the frontal regions of the scalp. This takes the form of a steady negative-going deflection (relative to the frontal regions) which returns to the baseline when the second stimulus is received. Because this deflection is small (a few microvolts) and is superimposed on continuing EEG activity, averaging techniques are required to quantify it accurately. Because the shift in potential is a steady one, either DC recording or recording with a long time-constant (at least 8 seconds) is necessary. DC recording of the EEG is technically difficult so long time-constant amplifiers are used and the interval between the warning and the imperative stimuli must be kept relatively short (say 3 seconds).

## Sleep studies

Despite the fact that we spend a third of our lives asleep, the study of sleep did not achieve much momentum until comparatively recently. Behavioural observations and self-reports were complemented by all-night electroencephalographic recordings. Earlier views held that sleep was a unitary phenomenon, merely showing a continuum in depth. Aserinsky and Kleitman (1953, 1955) laid the foundations of modern sleep studies when they observed periods during sleep when rapid, conjugate eye movements occurred, accompanied by low-voltage, high-frequency EEG patterns (see also p. 90).

For all-night sleep recordings of EEG, stick-on electrodes are used, several channels being recorded simultaneously. Eye movements are monitored by recording from electrodes on the outer

57

canthi of the orbits. As a qualitative recording is usually adequate, i.e. the detection of rapid eye movements (REM), AC electrode-amplifier systems are commonly employed. The electromyogram, e.g. from the chin region, is often also recorded, as muscle activity becomes very low in the REM stage of sleep.

The analysis of the records can be done manually or by using automated computer techniques to categorise the tracings into the five stages of sleep. A diagram can then be constructed of the time spent by the subject in the various stages of sleep throughout the night.

## SPECIAL CONSIDERATIONS

### Telemetry

The majority of psychophysiological experiments can be satis-factorily performed using wires attached to the patient and leading to the amplifying equipment. In some cases, however, there are definite advantages in transmitting the recorded variables from the patient to the recording equipment using radio waves. Occasion-ally, useful data can only be obtained in this way. Mentally disturbed children often will not tolerate lying on a bed or sitting in a chair but will quite happily play in a room despite the attach-ment of electrodes and the transmitter. The monitoring of patients in real-life agoraphobic or socially phobic situations furnishes another example. The most dramatic instance of telemetry of physiological variables is that of astronauts in space flights.

The technical problems are large but not insuperable, especially if single-channel recordings are sufficient. The commonest tech-nique uses frequency modulation (FM) in which the amplitude of the physiological signal modulates (i.e. alters) the frequency of the carrier wave. The basic advantage of this technique is that the physiological signal, when demodulated at the receiver, is not affected by changes in the amplitude of the carrier wave; conse-quently, the patient does not have to maintain a constant position with respect to the receiver. If a carrier wave of about 100 MHz is used (1 megahertz = 1 million cycles per second), a commercial FM radio receiver can be used to detect, demodulate and amplify the signal. In the UK a frequency in this region has been reserved for purposes of medical research. The range of transmission is usually less than 50 metres.

Some light-weight, reliable and relatively cheap telemetry systems are now becoming available commercially and should broaden the scope of psychophysiological research.

An alternative to telemetry is to record the physiological variable onto a miniaturised tape recorder carried in the subject's pocket. This technique has been applied to the long-term recording of blood pressure in order to characterise the normal patterns throughout the day. The technique is particularly useful in monitoring phobic patients without the need to trundle after them with a telemetry receiver.

## Computer techniques

A wide range of computer techniques are now available to ease the work of the psychophysiologist, and some laboratories have their own computer. In this complex field, it is easy to make mistakes in the choice of equipment or in the use of available equipment for the purposes of psychophysiological research. While every psychophysiologist's approach and requirements must inevitably differ, there is still a common pattern in the type of research carried out and, consequently, in the applications for computer facilities.

For data to be analysed by a digital computer they must be in digital, i.e. numerical, form. This of course applies to most forms of analysis; in the conventional analysis of polygraphic recordings, the psychophysiologist measures off points against the scales on the chart paper. With computer facilities an appropriate voltage output of the polygraph amplifier is led into an analog-to-digital (A/D) converter of the computer. Sampling of the input voltage and A/D conversion takes place under command from the computer program, the voltage at the time of the execution of the command being converted to a number and made available to the rest of the computer system. Since it is the voltage analog which is actually measured, an appropriate conversion factor must be supplied separately to the program, relating the measured voltage to the psychophysiological variable being analysed.

Each time a sample is taken and digitised an item of data is produced. As the computer repeats the process, data accumulate in the computer forming a 'data file'. The primary form of data storage comprises a network of tiny electromagnetic rings termed the 'magnetic core'. Any part of the core can be used at any time and can be 'accessed' very rapidly. In small and even medium-sized computers, the data produced in the average psycho-physiological experiment would soon exceed the storage capacity of the magnetic core. Therefore, the data have to be transferred in batches to secondary storage, usually in the form of a magnetic disc or magnetic tape. Very large amounts of data can be stored in this way, but access to the data is slower. Another form of data storage is onto paper tape punched electromechanically. This is relatively slow (say, one hundred numbers per second) but is usually adequate for the psychophysiological measures on a slower time-scale, e.g. skin conductance and heart rate.

Data output can take many forms depending on the require-ments of the research worker. A very useful system for monitoring and for manipulating data consists of displaying them on a cathode-ray oscilloscope with provision in the program for further pro-cessing. Probably the neatest way of dealing with the data is to process them in the laboratory computer, storing the final data on disc or tape. Statistical programs can then be written which can finally analyse the data.

Usually a computer works at its own rate; for example, if it has to square and sum 1,000 numbers it will do this as fast as it can. However, in 'real-time' working, data are fed into the computer as the events governing that data occur. Thus, if an event recurs every 10 ms, then data will go into the computer once every 10 ms. The upper rate of data input is limited by the speed of the input devices such as a paper-tape reader or an A/D converter. In 'real-time' working, a computer may spend a very high proportion of its time idling in between bursts of data input. 'On-line' working means that the user has direct access to the computer from his terminal in contrast to 'off-line' working where data accumulates away from the computer and is fed in in batches. 'Real-time' working is always 'on-line' but not vice versa.

*Methods of using computer facilities*

(1) The commonest method of harnessing computer facilities in psychophysiological research consists of *scoring* the paper record from a polygraph and using a computer to analyse the data. The data from the polygraphic recording are transferred by being punched on cards or paper tape. This technique is, of course, applicable to all forms of research, the computer merely being used as a large and speedy calculating machine.

(2) The simplest digital method for data acquisition and manipulation is the *data logger*. This relatively inexpensive device consists of an A/D converter which samples one or more psychophysiological channels at pre-set intervals. The digital values are punched onto paper tape or, in the more sophisticated models, stored on digital magnetic tape. The paper or magnetic tape is subsequently fed into a computer and data manipulation, calculations, etc., carried out. The disadvantage of the data-logging system is the necessity for an intermediate, tangible form of the data as magnetic or paper tape. The second disadvantage, the relatively slow sampling rate, is only a limiting factor in psychophysiological experiments using rapidly changing variables such as the EEG. Even then, many loggers can digitise quickly enough onto magnetic tape.

(3) An *instrumentation coupler* consists of a device which samples and digitises variables on command, but instead of outputting the data in tangible form they are transmitted to a central computer, which thus controls the data input. The instrumentation coupler is an interesting new development as it utilises the power of large computers without the need for intermediate, tangible forms of data.

(4) *Special-purpose computers* have been used for the past ten years or so to average electroencephalographic-evoked responses. The essential difference between these computers (e.g. 'computers of average transients', CAT) and general computers is that the program is wired in the special-purpose computer and therefore its execution is very rapid as the computer does not have to interpret coded instructions as in the general computer. Consequently, a special-purpose computer is capable of sampling 125 data points in a millisecond, although this facility is only of importance where very transient signals are being analysed, e.g. in bio-physical applications. Special-purpose computers have a limited number of programs, e.g. averaging, interval and dwell histograms and correlograms, and a limited choice of parameters such as sampling speed. Also, the output of data is often cumbersome, paper tape being usual. However, the special-purpose computer is appreciably cheaper than the smallest general-purpose laboratory computer.

(5) *General-purpose laboratory computers* have become widely available in the past few years and are ideal for psychophysiological experiments. There are two approaches to this type of instrument. A basic small digital computer can be bought to which are added A/D converters, relay controls, etc., as required. Alternatively, the

manufacturer's 'package' can be bought already containing all these features.

Such computers are usually small in terms of core but digital magnetic tapes or discs provide an effective and quite large 'back-up' storage. Typically, one tape can store a quarter of a million numbers, which usually suffices for all but the most overenthusiastic psychophysiologist.

Several channels can be input via the A/D converters and usually all can be sampled within a millisecond.

### Types of experiment particularly suitable for on-line computers

The small general-purpose on-line laboratory computer is in many ways very suited to psychophysiological research. The relatively slow rate of data acquisition allows manipulations to be carried out between sampling and also the total of data accumulated is not sufficient to overload the tape or disc storage. It is, however, in the running of psychophysiological experiments that the on-line computer provides the greatest flexibility. Very complex stimulus parameters can be easily programmed. For example, in one of our studies, the computer presents twenty trains of stimuli, each train consisting of ten auditory clicks to which the subject responds by pressing a key. The inter-click interval in any train is either 8–12 seconds or 2·5–3·5 seconds, and the inter-train interval is 16–24 seconds. Furthermore, 4–8 seconds before the first click in each train a warning light flashes on. After each click the reaction time is computed and then displayed on a counter to give immediate feedback to the subject and to maintain his motivation. The electroencephalographic evoked response to the clicks is measured as is the EEG in between the clicks and skin conductance level at the time of the click. Such complex experiments would be very difficult to perform without an on-line computer. Furthermore, although the original program took a few days to write and have running perfectly, modification of stimulus parameters can now be carried out very easily.

Experiments involving feedback or instrumental conditioning are also very easy to perform. In the feedback type of study the subject's physiological background levels or responses are measured and then displayed to the subject in some way. A meter needle or brightness of a light, pitch or loudness of a sound can all be used. With the instrumental-conditioning type of experiment the subject is 'rewarded' for making the 'correct' response. For example, if his heart rate drops, he earns a small sum of money. The computer can calculate the responses very rapidly and immediately reward the subject if the criterion has been reached, thus ensuring close contiguity of reward.

## Choice of equipment

The choice of equipment and technical strategy for someone embarking on psychophysiological research is so dependent on a large number of factors such as funds available, type of research envisaged, previous experience, local expertise, etc., that it is impossible to lay down hard and fast rules. Some advice is fairly obvious. Thus, the available computer facilities should be very carefully explored as the opportunity to use automatic methods of analysis should never be missed. The laboratory should be scoured for unused or even obsolete pieces of equipment; very often a derelict EEG machine or pen-recorder will be unearthed which after overhaul will be quite serviceable as a monitoring instrument, enabling higher priority to be given to the purchase of an analog tape recorder. Whenever possible, equipment should be borrowed from a colleague or the manufacturer and tested out thoroughly to make sure it is suitable for the proposed purpose. In this way costly mistakes can be avoided.

Local electronic expertise should be recruited both to advise and to build instruments. For example, a skin-resistance instrument can be built surprisingly cheaply.

The adequacy of servicing arrangements should be confirmed as it is most frustrating to have an experimental programme held up while a spare part is temporarily unavailable. Modular apparatus is very convenient in this respect as a module can be exchanged, leaving the equipment functioning while the defective module is repaired.

Versatility is an important consideration. The requirements of an experimental psychophysiological laboratory may alter rapidly, especially if there is the usual turnover of staff. In this respect the small laboratory computer has enormous advantages as, being programmable, it is supremely versatile.

The ideal arrangement is to have a computer serving one or more laboratories either on a time-sharing basis or with each laboratory using the computer in turn. The experiments are carried out in

*

real-time directly on-line into the computer so that there is no tedious manual analysis to be performed after the experiment.

Experiments are monitored on a polygraph, if necessary, but the record of the experiment is kept in dynamic form on analog tape.

The type of experimental system in use in the author's laboratory is shown in Figure 2.11.

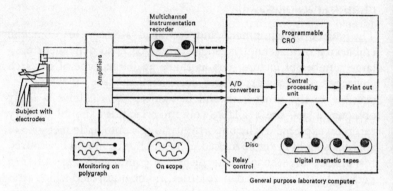

Figure 2.11 *Diagrammatic representation of a typical recording system in a psychophysiological laboratory*

## ENDOCRINOLOGICAL MEASURES

### The adrenal cortex and adrenal medulla

The adrenals each consist in effect of two separate glands, one surrounding the other. The outer gland, the adrenal cortex, secretes glucocorticoids which have widespread effects on the metabolism of carbohydrates, fats and proteins, a mineralocorticoid which controls sodium and fluid balance, and some sex hormones. The adrenal medulla is essentially a sympathetic ganglion in which the post-ganglionic cells have lost their axons and become secretory in function.

### Adrenal cortex (Ganong, 1963; Jenkins, 1968)

The adrenal cortex consists of interlacing cords of granule-containing cells interspersed with venous sinuses. The cortex is divided into fairly distinct zones, the zona glomerulosa on the outside with the zona fasciculata and zona reticularis on the inside.

The two inner zones secrete glucocorticoids while the mineralo-corticoid is secreted by the outer zone only (Stachenko and Giroud, 1962; Symington, 1962).

Biologically active extracts of the adrenal cortex were prepared in the late 1920s but it was not until the late 1930s that the isolation and analysis of adrenal steroids was carried out by workers in Switzerland and in the USA. Using large amounts of bovine adrenal glands to produce small amounts of crystal-like material, cortisone, corticosteroid and cortisol were identified. The adrenal residue after the removal of crystalline substances also proved to be active, containing a substance found to be an important regulator of electrolyte concentrations and now known as aldosterone. Although about fifty steroids have been separated from the extracts of the adrenal cortex, some are present in minute amounts, some are intermediate compounds in the chain of synthesis and some may be artifacts of the extraction process.

There is much species variation in the type of adrenal cortical secretion. In man, cortisol (hydrocortisone) and aldosterone are the most important, as evidenced by the clinical observation that patients with adrenal insufficiency can be maintained in health by giving these two hormones or their equivalents. The human adrenal also secretes some corticosterone, which is the predominant steroid in some animals, e.g. rodents. The normal total daily secretion of cortisol is about 20 mg, of corticosterone 2 mg and of aldosterone 0·1 mg. The concentrations of these compounds in plasma are approximately 10 $\mu$g, 1 $\mu$g and 0·01 $\mu$g respectively per 100 ml of plasma. Cortisone, which was the first of these compounds to be used in the treatment of inflammatory diseases such as rheumatoid arthritis, is present in only minute amounts in adrenal blood and is probably a metabolite of cortisol.

In addition to these compounds, the adrenal also produces androgenic steroids. These are not important under normal conditions.

Cortisol in the blood is largely bound to plasma proteins; one protein is an alpha globulin known as corticosteroid-binding globulin or transcortin, the other protein is plasma albumin. Cortisol is normally 94 per cent bound to protein and it is only the remaining 6 per cent which is actually immediately available for biological activity.

The adrenocortical hormones are steroids, a complex class of compound (Klyne, 1963). They contain three fused cyclohexane

rings and a cyclopentane ring, and stereochemical isomers exist
(Figure 2.12). It is usual to refer to the adrenal steroids by their
common names, such as cortisol, which is certainly much more
convenient than the systematic name. For example, the systematic
name for cortisol is $11\alpha,17\beta,21$-trihydroxypregn-4-ene,3,20-dione.
Reference should be made to biochemical textbooks for a full
exposition of this complex topic.

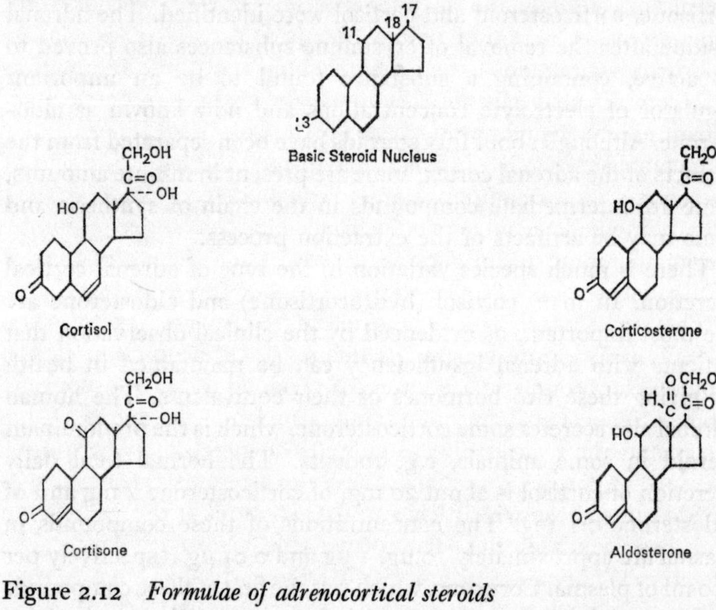

Basic Steroid Nucleus

Cortisol

Corticosterone

Cortisone

Aldosterone

Figure 2.12 *Formulae of adrenocortical steroids*

Cortisol is synthesised in the adrenal cortex from cholesterol,
progesterone being an intermediate compound. A series of hydroxylation processes takes place. Aldosterone also follows a similar
pathway and corticosterone is also a precursor of this compound.

The breakdown pathways of the adrenocortical hormones are
also very complex, with whole ranges of metabolic products
(Dorfman and Ungar, 1965). The chief metabolites of cortisol are
11-oxo-derivatives which are excreted in the urine as the glucuron-
ides. Aldosterone is metabolised by reduction and then conjugated. The rate of metabolism of adrenocortical hormones is
fairly rapid; the normal half-life of cortisol is 80 minutes, that of
aldosterone 33 minutes (Tait *et al.*, 1962). Thyroid gland activity
also alters metabolism of the adrenal cortical hormones. During

pregnancy the metabolism of cortisol is affected by a change of protein-binding which is increased so that less of the cortisol is available for breakdown.

## Estimation of adrenal steroids in urine

Many laboratories have concentrated on the estimation of urinary steroids because the techniques are somewhat simpler than those for plasma steroids and an integrated measure of adrenocortical function over a period of time is obtained. A major disadvantage of urinary estimations is that the metabolism of these compounds is so complex that it is not easy to ascribe changes in one urinary constituent to changes in its plasma precursor. Also, abnormalities of metabolism or renal function may profoundly alter patterns of excretion, both quantitatively and qualitatively. Most routine urinary methods estimate whole groups of steroids. Separation by chromatographic techniques is necessary for the estimation of individual steroids.

The 17-oxosteroids (17-ketosteroids) all have a keto group $(C=O)$ at C-17 and generally contain a total of nineteen carbon atoms. They comprise a mixture of metabolites derived not only from adrenocortical hormones but also from secretions of the testes and the ovaries. These steroids do not provide a specific measure of cortisol secretion. The 17-oxosteroids can be further divided into those which have an oxygen atom at the 11-position and those which do not. The former (the 11-oxy-17-oxosteroids) are entirely adrenal in origin, partly from cortisol and partly from adrenal androgens. The 11-deoxy-17-oxosteroids form a larger proportion of the 17-oxosteroids and contain metabolites of both adrenal and testicular origin. The 17-oxosteroids are found in the urine conjugated either with glucuronic acid or with sulphate. The technique usually used in the UK yields a deep purple colour with the Zimmerman reagent; the intensity of the colour is estimated with a spectrophotometer (Medical Research Council Committee, 1963). In young (aged 20–40) males, the normal range of values is 10–25 mg in 24 hours; in females it is 5–17 mg in 24 hours.

The 17-oxogenic steroids (17-ketogenic steroids) are of more importance as they more directly reflect cortisol levels. The pre-existing 17-oxosteroids are first removed and then the total 17-oxogenic steroids are converted to 17-oxosteroids and estimated using the Zimmerman reaction (Norymberski, 1961). Metabolites of cortisone such as tetrahydrocortisol, tetrahydrocortisone, the cortols and cortolones constitute the bulk of the 17-oxogenic steroids. Normal values in males range from 5 to 21 mg in 24 hours, in females from 4 to 16 mg in 24 hours.

An alternative technique which has been widely used in the USA is the Porter–Silber reaction in which 17-hydroxycortico-steroids react with phenylhydrazine to yield a yellow colour (Glenn and Nelson, 1953). Fewer cortisol metabolites take part in this reaction than the Zimmerman reaction so the values are lower— 4·1–14 mg in 24 hours in males, 2·8–12 mg in 24 hours in females. The technique is generally referred to as the estimation of urinary 17-hydroxycorticosteroids.

## Estimation of adrenal steroids in blood (Dixon et al., 1967)

Cortisone and corticosterone can be estimated using a fluorimetric method (Mattingly, 1962). As both compounds contribute to the fluorescence, the technique really measures 11-hydroxycortico-steroids. However, the method has the disadvantage that non-steroid constituents of the blood may also fluoresce. The Porter–Silber reaction mentioned above can be adapted for plasma estimations and yields values for a morning sample (9–10 a.m.) of 6 to 25 μg of cortisol per 100 ml of plasma.

The rate of secretion of cortisol can be estimated by administering a small quantity of cortisol radioactively labelled with carbon-14 or tritium. This isotope is diluted by the endogenous secretion of cortisol and the rate of dilution can be estimated by taking serial blood samples or a 24-hour urine sample. The urine method relies on the separation by paper chromatography of a metabolic product such as tetrahydrocortisol which is derived in toto from cortisol. The normal range of cortisol secretion in the adult is 6·3–28·6 mg in 24 hours, with a mean value of 16·2 (Cope and Pearson, 1965).

Cortisol levels in the blood are not constant throughout the day but show a pronounced and regular diurnal variation (Perkoff et al., 1959). The level is highest about 8 a.m. falling rapidly during the morning and then less sharply during the afternoon and evening to reach its nadir around midnight. Lymphocytes in the blood show the opposite pattern, being lowest in the morning (Elmadjian and Pincus, 1946). Reversal of the sleep period as in night workers is accompanied after a few days by a reversal of the cortisol pattern.

Similarly, time changes as in transcontinental travellers are also accompanied by equivalent shifts in the cortisol pattern.

Recent work has shown that the normal pattern of cortisol secretion consists of about seven to nine major episodes throughout the day, with sharp rises and falls in plasma cortisol concentration, and with cessation of cortisol secretion between episodes. The secretory programme seems to fall into four unequal phases: (1) minimal secretory activity lasting about 4 hours late at night around bed-time; (2) a small pre-secretory nocturnal phase over the ensuing 2 hours; (3) the main secretory phase lasting the rest of the night; and (4) a period of intermittent waking secretory activity for most of the day and evening (Weitzman *et al.*, 1971).

Body build is another important factor influencing the excretion of both 17-oxosteroids and 17-oxogenic steroids. The level of 17-oxosteroid excretion is related to the muscle mass of the body. The excretion of 17-oxogenic steroids is, by contrast, related to height and weight but, as there is little relationship to either muscle or fat, it must be assumed that the clearest relationship is with the length and width of bones. It is speculated that muscles may need oxosteroids for their maintenance, the contents of the limb medullary cavities may need corticosteroids for theirs (Tanner *et al.*, 1959).

Assessments of psychological state and estimates of body size both correlated significantly with 17-hydroxycorticosteroid excretion in twenty-seven USA army recruits. Combining the variables resulted in a better prediction of steroid excretion than either variable alone (Rose, Poe and Mason, 1968). This was replicated in a further 46 basic trainees (Poe, Rose and Mason, 1970).

*The assessment of pituitary-adrenal function*

The polypeptide hormone, adrenocorticotrophin (ACTH), is secreted by the anterior lobe of the pituitary and stimulates the production and release of cortisol secretion. Plasma ACTH levels can be estimated using radioimmunoassay techniques which are very specialised.

ACTH is itself released by a neurohormone which is secreted in the median eminence at the base of the hypothalamus and which passes down pituitary portal vessels to the anterior pituitary. The release of corticotrophin-releasing factor (CRF) appears itself to be suppressed by high levels of cortisol, the system thus forming a negative feedback loop (Kendall, 1971).

69

ACTH may be injected as a test of adrenal cortical function. In normal subjects, an injection of 40 units of ACTH–zinc results in increases 5 hours later ranging from 10 to 50 μg of cortisol per 100 ml of plasma (Jenkins, 1968).

A test of the integrity of the feedback control of ACTH release is provided by the administration of the drug metyrapone ('Metopirone'). This inhibits the synthesis of cortisol, cortisol levels drop, ACTH production is stimulated and large amounts of the cortisol precursor 11-deoxycortisol are secreted and can be estimated in the urine as a 17-oxogenic steroid.

Another method of testing this feedback loop is to give large doses of a glucocorticoid such as dexamethasone. This suppresses ACTH secretion and cortisol levels in the blood fall markedly.

Indirect estimates of adrenocortical function (such as increases in circulating neutrophils and decreases in lymphocytes (Hoagland *et al.*, 1946) and eosinophils) have been used in the past (Cleghorn and Graham, 1950), but such measures are no longer accepted as specific indices.

*Estimation of aldosterone*

This is difficult to measure because of the small amounts present in body fluids. Isotopic or radioimmunoassay techniques have been developed but are time-consuming to carry out.

Sachar (1967a) has enumerated them ethodological pitfalls in research using adrenocortical indices. The range of corticosteroid excretion in normal subjects is wider than first appreciated and partly depends on sex, age and body weight. As with the majority of psychophysiological studies it is thus important to control for these factors. A variety of drug treatments may interfere with corticosteroid estimations in at least three different ways. Firstly, a direct chemical interference may occur, e.g. phenothiazines produce artificially low values for plasma and urinary 17-hydroxy-corticosteroid estimations. Secondly, drugs may interfere with the release of ACTH from the hypothalamus. Thirdly, the metabolism of cortisol may be altered by the induction effects in the liver of barbiturates and phenothiazines accelerating its hydroxylation. Even if medication is held constant, induction of liver enzymes may occur and progress, thus causing changes in cortisol metabolism over time. It is important that 'drug-free' patients be studied.

## Adrenal medulla (von Euler, 1956)

Noradrenaline and adrenaline (norepinephrine and epinephrine respectively in the USA) are both secreted by the chromaffin tissue in the adrenal medulla whereas the adrenergic nerve endings of the sympathetic nervous system release predominantly noradrenaline. In man 80 per cent of the catecholamine output in the adrenal vein is adrenaline. The adrenal medulla is not essential for life.

Noradrenaline is formed by the hydroxylation and decarboxylation of tyrosine, dopa and dopamine being precursors along the way (Figure 2.13). Adrenaline is formed by methylation of nor-

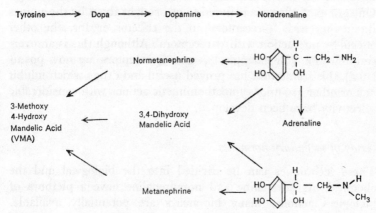

Figure 2.13 *Synthesis and breakdown of catecholamines*

adrenaline. Phenylethanolamine-*N*-methyltransferase (PNMT), the enzyme which catalyses this last step, is found in appreciable quantities only in the medulla. The usual level of noradrenaline in the blood is about 0·8 ng ml$^{-1}$(0·8 $\times$ 10$^{-9}$ gm ml$^{-1}$), of adrenaline 0·1 ng ml$^{-1}$.

The catecholamines, adrenaline and noradrenaline, are rapidly removed from the circulation by absorption into tissues and by enzymatic breakdown. Very small amounts appear unchanged in the urine. The major breakdown pathways involve either conjugation (with glucuronide or sulphate) or methylation and oxidation to 3-methoxy-4-hydroxymandelic acid (vanillylmandelic acid, VMA). In normal subjects 30 μg of noradrenaline, 6 μg of adrenaline and 700 μg of VMA are excreted in 24 hours.

The release of medullary catecholamines is part of the diffuse, generalised adrenergic discharge provoked by emergency situations.

Cannon called this the 'emergency function of the adrenal medulla'. In the medulla, the catecholamines are stored in the form of granules and their secretion into the circulation is triggered by acetylcholine released from the terminals of pre-ganglionic neurones which innervate the medulla.

Adrenaline and noradrenaline have a very wide range of effects in the body (see Table 1, p. 73). Some of these effects mimic those of the sympathetic nervous system but others are direct metabolic effects. On the basis of the differential effects of noradrenaline, adrenaline and the closely related compound, isoprenaline, the effects of the catecholamines have been divided into two groups. One group of effects is believed to be brought about by the amines interacting with 'α-receptors' in the effector organs, the other effects by interaction with 'β-receptors'. Although this is an over-simplification (for example, $\beta_1$- and $\beta_2$-receptors are now postulated), this framework has proved useful and drugs which inhibit one or other group of sympathomimetic actions with considerable selectivity have been developed.

*Assay of medullary hormones*

These techniques can be divided into the biological and the chemical. As adrenaline and noradrenaline have a plethora of biological actions, many bio-assays are potentially available. Among the classical bioassays for adrenaline is the measurement of blood pressure rise in a spinal cat. Alternating doses of unknown and standard preparations are injected intravenously, utilising dosages which give submaximal responses. The method is accurate to within 10 per cent. Rats can also be used and are cheaper. Another classical assay system is a strip of rabbit ileum suspended in an oxygenated bath. Inhibition of naturally occurring contractions can be induced with one part of adrenaline to 230 million of bathing fluid. More recently a technique using observed changes in the calibre of the blood vessels of the denervated rabbit ear has been found sensitive.

Chemical methods are usually simpler and less time-consuming but may result in the estimation of related compounds as well as adrenaline and noradrenaline. One method using ethylenediamine compounds and fluorimetry yields values consistently higher than with the bio-assay methods.

Adrenaline and noradrenaline can be estimated in the plasma

**Table 1**

*Some effects of noradrenaline and adrenaline*

|  | Noradrenaline | Adrenaline | Main receptor type involved |
|---|---|---|---|
| *Blood vessels* | | | |
| Coronary | dilate | dilate | β |
| Skin and mucosa | constrict | constrict | α |
| Viscera | constrict | constrict | α |
| Skeletal muscle | slight constriction | dilate | β |
| Brain | slight constriction | slight dilatation | α |
| Kidney | slight constriction | moderate constriction | α |
| *Peripheral resistance* | rise | drop | |
| *Heart* | | | |
| Myocardial excitability | increase | increase | β |
| Force and rate of contraction of *isolated* heart | increase | increase | β |
| *Blood pressure* | | | |
| Systolic | rise | rise | |
| Diastolic | rise | drop | |
| *Pulse rate* | drop (reflex bradycardia) | rise | |
| *Bronchial muscle* | relaxation | marked relaxation | β |
| *Gastro-intestinal tract and urinary bladder* | | | |
| Motility | decrease | decrease | β |
| Sphincters | contract | contract | α |
| *Metabolic effects* | | | |
| Oxygen consumption | slight increase | increase | — |
| Blood sugar | slight increase | increase | — |
| Blood lactic acid | slight increase | increase | — |
| *Subjective sensations* | feelings of slight stimulation | feeling of stimulation | — |

73

and cerebrospinal fluid and in the urine. Because of their rapid turnover, spot estimations of catecholamine levels in plasma may not be very representative, especially if long-term powerful stimulation procedures are used. The half-life of catecholamines in plasma has been estimated to be about 100 seconds. The time required for complete replenishment of circulating catecholamines is only 30 seconds. Therefore, with very short-term changes, plasma samples may again not be fully representative of the hormonal changes occurring. The problems arising in the estimation of plasma catecholamines have been well documented by Carruthers *et al.* (1970).

Urinary samples give, in effect, a time-integral of catecholamine excretion. However, for urinary estimations to be valid, it must be assumed that the small proportion of catecholamines excreted unchanged remains constant throughout the experimental conditions employed (Elmadjian, Hope and Lamson, 1958). There is no evidence for or against this assumption. Another possible source of artifact is that the stimulation procedure has some effect on renal blood flow, glomerular filtration and tubular secretion and re-absorption, which might itself alter the clearance into the urine of the catecholamines. Advocates of urinary catecholamine estimations as indicators of bodily response to stimulation conclude that 'while it may be true that the free catecholamines in urine do not provide a *quantitative* measure of catecholamine release, they do at least probably indicate whether or not the release has been augmented or reduced' (Levi, 1972). In other words, catecholamine excretion is a non-linear but progressive function of catecholamine production. For reflecting changes in adrenal medullary and sympathetic function over a time-scale of 1–3 hours, urinary estimations are preferable to plasma estimations, even if the latter be repeated several times.

## Thyroid hormones

The hormones elaborated by the thyroid gland regulate growth, differentiation of tissues and oxidative metabolism. They are unique in containing the element iodine, which allows the application of special methods to their study. A complex array of iodine-containing compounds is found in the body arising from the ingestion and absorption of iodine-containing foods, from

74

thyroid gland activity and from the peripheral breakdown of the secreted substance.

## Physiology

The thyroid gland is a bilobed structure located on the sides of the trachea just below the larynx. Thyroid tissue has a rich blood supply and consists of follicles containing a colloid substance, thyroglobulin. The thyroid hormones are thyroxine ($3,5,3',5'$-tetraiodothyronine, $T_4$) and $3,5,3'$-triiodothyronine ($T_3$), which are both secreted by the thyroid gland, the former in much larger quantities than the latter (Figure 2.14). There is some evidence

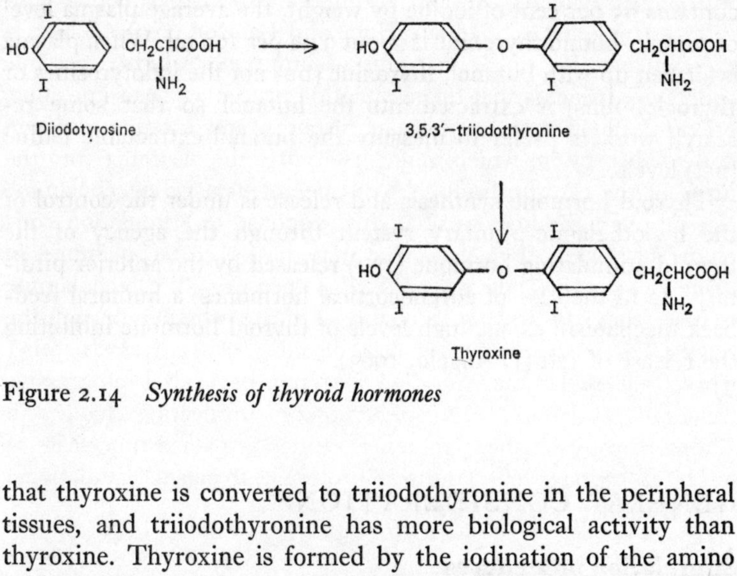

Figure 2.14  *Synthesis of thyroid hormones*

that thyroxine is converted to triiodothyronine in the peripheral tissues, and triiodothyronine has more biological activity than thyroxine. Thyroxine is formed by the iodination of the amino acid tyrosine and then by combination of two molecules of diiodotyrosine to form one of thyroxine.

The thyroid gland must be capable of concentrating normal dietary iodide which is a trace element nutritionally. An active transport mechanism is involved so that the gland takes up iodide from the blood. Thus, the radio-iodine uptake test provides a very sensitive and direct means of evaluating glandular activity. A minute dose of radioactive iodine is given by mouth and the accumulation of radioactivity in the gland at various times

75

thereafter is measured by counting the gamma rays emitted with a collimated (i.e. directional) scintillation counter. The [131]I isotope has a physical half-life of eight days and is generally used. The [132]I isotope has the much shorter half-life of 2·4 hours and can be used where repeated estimations at short intervals are required. The normal thyroid gland takes up about 25 per cent of the administered dose in 24 hours. The overactive thyrotoxic gland takes up a higher percentage, as much as 75 per cent, whereas the underactive hypothyroid gland takes up much less, below 10 per cent.

The thyroxine released by the thyroid gland (about 80 μg per day) is bound to plasma protein in the blood stream. This protein-bound iodine (PBI) in the plasma normally ranges between 3·5 and 8·0 μg per 100 ml. As 95 per cent of the PBI is in thyroxine which contains 65 per cent of iodine by weight, the average plasma level of protein-bound thyroxine is about 9 μg per 100 ml. When plasma is shaken up with butanol, thyroxine (but not the iodotyrosines or thyroglobulins) is extracted into the butanol so that some research workers prefer to measure the butanol-extractable iodine (BEI) levels.

Thyroid hormone synthesis and release is under the control of the hypothalamic-pituitary system through the agency of the thyroid-stimulating hormone (TSH) released by the anterior pituitary. As in the case of adrenocortical hormones, a humoral feedback mechanism exists, high levels of thyroid hormone inhibiting the release of TSH (D'Angelo, 1963).

## GENERAL CONSIDERATIONS

### Stimulation procedures

There is a welter of stimulation procedures which have been used in psychophysiology. There are no stimulation manoeuvres specific to psychophysiological research, and physiology and psychology among other disciplines have contributed stimulation procedures. The choice of stimulation procedure or whether to use one at all devolves on the particular theoretical and practical approach of the experimenter.

Firstly, the decision must be taken as to whether any form of stimulation will be resorted to or whether so-called 'baseline' or 'background' activity levels will suffice. Although these are also euphemistically referred to as 'resting' levels, the experimental situation itself—coming into a laboratory, having electrodes attached or venepunctures carried out—is a very powerful stimulation procedure (Sabshin *et al.*, 1957). It has been shown many times using a variety of variables that the initial levels are always raised, often to a marked extent. This does not invalidate the use of laboratory procedures but emphasises that, on the first occasion at least, no really 'resting' readings are possible. On subsequent occasions, readings approximating more to basal values can be obtained in normals. However, in psychiatric patients, adaptation to laboratory situations may be slow or even absent. This lack of adaptation can be exploited as differences between normal subjects and psychiatric patients, agitated depressives, for example, will become more and more evident on repeated testing occasions (Clemens and Selesnick, 1967).

An alternative approach to using a stimulation procedure is to attempt to relax the individuals. This can be done by simple means such as reassurance and verbal instructions or by using drugs to induce drowsiness or sleep. The best example of this technique is the 'sedation threshold technique'. In this technique, a barbiturate, usually thiopentone sodium or amylobarbitone sodium, is injected intravenously at a constant rate until an 'end-point' is reached (Shagass, 1954). The 'end-point' can be electroencephalographic, such as the appearance of fast-wave low-voltage activity (Ackner and Pampiglione, 1959); autonomic, such as the disappearance of skin conductance fluctuations (Perez-Reyes, Shands and Johnson, 1962); neurological, such as the onset of slurred speech (Thorpe and Barker, 1957) or nystagmus (Fink, 1958); or behavioural, such as the inability to do simple mental arithmetic. The amount of drug injected in mg kg$^{-1}$ body weight is then calculated and forms the variable of interest.

Stimulation procedures can be classified according to their temporal characteristics and according to type of stimulation. Short-term stimuli can be flashes of light or auditory tones, longer-term stimuli mental arithmetic tasks or viewing upsetting movie films. The short-term stimuli may be repeated at discrete intervals to form an habituation procedure or different types of stimuli paired as in classical respondent conditioning techniques. Long-term stimuli include 'real-life' situations such as parachute

77

training or combat in war. Naturally occurring situations such as earthquakes can be utilised but there are practical problems in mounting such a study and difficulties in systematically gathering data.

Most stimuli used in psychophysiological experiments can be roughly divided into physical, physiological, pharmacological, psychological and psychiatric. Of course, a stimulus may have elements of another type so these headings are not mutually exclusive. For example, viewing a horror film is psychologically disturbing but there is also the visual input which can be quantified in physical terms. Conversely, apparently innocuous physical stimuli may have some unexpected psychological connotations, e.g. one of my patients was upset by a click stimulus because it reminded him of a habit his loathed employer had of snapping his fingers at him.

Physical stimuli in psychophysiology are essentially those which consist primarily of sensory input. The stimuli are in the usual sensory modalities—auditory, visual, tactile and, occasionally, gustatory and olfactory. The advantage of this type of stimulation is that the sensory input can be quantified in absolute physical terms.

Physiological stimuli utilise known bodily responses. For example, if a hand is immersed in ice-cold water, generalised vaso-constriction occurs with a rise in blood pressure—the 'cold-pressor test'. Similarly, adrenocortical stimulating hormone (corticotrophin, ACTH) can be injected and the adrenal response estimated.

If the substance administered is a drug, then a pharmacologically induced response may result. An example is the injection of methacholine (mecholyl), a cholinergic substance which has marked cardiovascular effects including a drop in blood pressure (Gellhorn and Miller, 1961).

The stimulation procedure may be designed to elicit behavioural responses. There are a wide range of such stimuli including mental arithmetic, psychomotor tasks, memory tests, etc. Any psychological testing procedure can be used in a psychophysiological context. Psychiatric stimuli are less commonly employed than behavioural stimuli and are really a sub-section of such stimuli. An example is the recording of psychophysiological variables during an interview procedure.

## Experimental conditions

Many of the experimental conditions of an experiment are dictated by the physiological measures being used. For example, if finger blood flow is being estimated, the ambient temperature must be kept within the narrow range of 24 to 27°C. Humidity may also need to be controlled if climatic extremes are experienced (Wenger, 1962).

The most usual laboratory configuration is for the patient to be in a small room with the leads from the attached electrodes passing through into an adjacent room which houses the recording equipment. The advantage of this system is that the patient does not see a daunting array of electronic equipment.

It is advisable for the recording room in which the patient is situated to be sound-proofed or sound-protected. It must be remembered that the aim of this is to lessen the passage of extraneous sounds into the room, not to prevent sounds coming out of the room. Too often the purpose of the sound-proofing is mistaken and an anechoic chamber with sound-absorbent walls results. The key areas to sound-protect are the doors and windows. Often it is more useful to lay rubber flooring or carpet in the corridor outside the room than to try to sound-proof the intervening wall.

An intercom system by which the patient can speak to the experimenter is very useful, especially with anxious patients who may need reassurance. A one-way glass panel through which the patient can be observed is an important item, or closed-circuit television can be used.

## Experimental strategies

This is a very important topic especially with regard to the future development of psychophysiology. In chapter 1, some of the problems in clinical psychophysiology were outlined and experimental strategies to attack these problems given.

In general, the main strategy concerns the adequate provision of controls (Pollin, 1962). In one approach, the classical medical approach, a group of patients characterised by one particular feature such as delusions or agitation is compared with a group of controls, matched for a series of factors of greater or lesser importance such as age and sex. The control subjects may be 'normals', i.e. individuals who have not shown concern about themselves with respect to the feature of interest (e.g. depression) sufficient to present themselves to a doctor or who have not shown deviant behaviour (e.g. manic restlessness) sufficient for people around them to become concerned. Control subjects may be taken from hospital patients such as those recovering from acute appendicitis in an attempt to control for admission to hospital. Thirdly, psychiatric patients who have not shown the feature of interest may be used as the control group.

An alternative is to use patients as their own control, e.g. before and after recovery. However, the treatment given may alter the psychophysiological measure so that it is confounded with the effects accompanying recovery.

Normal subjects can be used in certain ways in strategies to elucidate psychophysiological changes in emotions. Anxiety can be engendered by using stimulation procedures such as calling out the names of the colours of strips of paper passing rapidly behind an aperture while the subject's voice is relayed back to him with a delay of 0·2 second (Wing, 1964). This technique has the weakness that no control is exercised over the type of emotion produced, which need not necessarily be anxiety but may be embarrassment, anger, frustration, resentment or even indifference.

## Conclusions

In this chapter, we have ranged over a variety of techniques from the simple, such as skin temperature, to the complex, e.g. the computer-averaged evoked response. The methods often border on the limits available, such as the meticulous chemistry needed in plasma steroid estimations. All these techniques have one thing in common: to a greater or lesser extent the variables estimated reflect psychological states in the subject.

# Some psychophysiological concepts 3

---

## Introduction

Although much of psychophysiology as applied to the study of mental illness proceeds on an empirical level, some knowledge of the concepts developed in the subject is essential to place the findings in perspective. The most extensively used concept in clinical psychophysiology is that of arousal: this concept is dealt with briefly in this chapter and again in the final chapter. Other concepts such as autonomic balance, stress and response specificity are also outlined. For a full exposition of these topics, reference should be made to the large volumes edited by Greenfield and Sternbach (1972) and by Venables and Christie (1975). One topic which I have dealt with in a little more detail is that of sleep, in view of the greatly increased interest in this topic in recent years.

The main purpose of this short chapter is to act as an introduction to the succeeding clinical chapters, to provide a framework within which these studies can be evaluated and to furnish the reader with some appreciation of how controversial some of these concepts are.

## Autonomic balance

This concept arose out of the formulations of Eppinger and Hess (1910) who regarded involuntary muscle activity and glandular function as being under the dual but antagonist control of the sympathetic and parasympathetic divisions of the autonomic nervous system. They postulated that any change in the balance between these two controlling systems might be expected to produce widespread disturbances in bodily function. Individuals were regarded as varying in the point of balance. Those with increased tone or activity of the sympathetic nervous system were in a condition of 'sympatheticotonia'; those with parasympathetic over-activity were in a state of 'parasympatheticotonia'. Symptoms associated with the former condition were dilated pupils, moist palms and tachycardia; parasympatheticotonia was accompanied by a slow pulse, dry skin and constricted pupils.

Darrow (1943) has reviewed studies designed to evaluate individual differences in autonomic balance and functioning. Very little support for the concept was forthcoming and the concepts of Eppinger and Hess fell into desuetude, especially in the UK and USA, as more modern concepts regarding the functioning of the autonomic nervous system became current. Nevertheless, the original concepts were resuscitated by Wenger (1941) who reformulated them somewhat so that autonomic balance referred to the relative activities in the adrenergic and cholinergic branches of the autonomic nervous system (see also Wenger, 1947).

Wenger and his associates have worked since the 1940s undertaking a large series of studies evaluating autonomic nervous system activity in groups of children and adults, normal and diseased (summarised in Wenger and Cullen, 1972). Measures included salivary output, salivary pH, dermatographia latency, dermatographia persistence, palmar conductance, volar forearm conductance, systolic blood pressure, diastolic blood pressure, pulse pressure, heart period, sublingual temperature, finger temperature, respiration period and pupillary diameter. With some of these measures it is difficult to understand how the autonomic nervous system could be involved anyway and with others the techniques as described appear crude.

The earlier results demonstrated that individuals did indeed differ in autonomic functioning, that these differences were normally distributed, that an individual's functioning tended to remain constant from year to year and that anxiety patterns in the personality or as symptoms affected the autonomic balance. These results are unexceptionable and predictable. Later studies, far less convincing, purported to uncover patterns of autonomic functioning which appeared to have some association with physical conditions such as hypertension, arthritis and asthma and with anxiety or fear (Wenger, 1966).

There have been few investigators who have used this particular approach and therefore there has been little or no replication of Wenger's work. While the data viewed empirically are most useful in establishing norms for various groups of subjects, it is doubtful if the concept of autonomic balance is of much value in the light of modern views of autonomic functioning.

## Orientation reaction and orienting responses

Pavlov's later work was mainly concerned with the condition reflex, but he recognised the importance of what he termed the 'investigatory' or 'what-is-it' reflex. In a frequently quoted paragraph, he stated (1927):

> It is this reflex which brings about the immediate response in man and animals to the slightest changes in the world around them, so that they immediately orientate their appropriate receptor organ in accordance with the perceptible quality in the agent bringing about the change, making full investigation of it. The biological significance of this reflex is obvious. If the animal were not provided with such a reflex its life would hang at every moment by a thread. In man this reflex has been greatly developed with far-reaching results, being represented in its highest form by inquisitiveness—the parent of that scientific method through which we hope one day to come to a true orientation in knowledge of the world around us.

This reflex is generally termed the 'orientation reaction' and it comprises many components, the 'orienting responses' (Sokolov, 1963). The main changes are:

(1) Changes in sense organs: pupillary dilatation, lowering of retinal threshold to light.

(2) Changes in skeletal muscles governing sense organs: widening of palpebral fissure, retraction of nictitating membrane in animals, eyes turn towards the source of visual stimulation; head turns towards the source of sound, ears 'prick' up in animals, sniffing occurs in animals.

(3) Changes in general skeletal musculature: ongoing actions are temporarily arrested, rise in general muscle tone.

(4) Changes in EEG: alpha waves disappear if present, slower waves indicating somnolence disappear.

(5) Autonomic changes: re-distribution of blood from skin and splanchnic areas to muscles, sweat gland activity in palms of hands and soles of feet increases, tachycardia followed by bradycardia but sometimes bradycardia alone (Graham and Clifton, 1966; Uno and Grings, 1965).

If the novel stimulus is very powerful, e.g. a rifle shot, the response takes the form of a 'startle reflex' (Landis and Hunt, 1939). A very rapid and transient flexion of the entire body occurs, the eye blink being the most stable element of the reflex and also the fastest with a latency of 40 milliseconds. There is no real qualitative difference between the startle reflex and the orientation reaction. The startle reaction is strong and fast, the orientation reaction weaker and more prolonged. Orientation reactions have also been divided into phasic and tonic forms, the former being more rapid and shorter-lasting than the latter.

## Stress

This much-used word has an unfortunate ambiguity of meaning. In physics it refers to external forces on an object and the deformations in that body are termed strain. Selye (1936, 1950), on the basis of morphological changes in the adrenocortical system in response to a variety of influences including fasting, cold, acute infections and trauma, concluded that the pituitary-adrenal cortex axis responds generally to a wide range of stimuli. He termed this the General Adaptation Syndrome and unfortunately described the changes in the organism as 'stress' (rather than 'strain'). Attempts have been made to salvage the semantic confusion by using terms like 'stressor' for the external stimuli (Levi, 1967).

Mason (1972) has cogently criticised the concept, or at least the application of it: 'Somehow the categorical concept of stressful conditions seems to have circumvented work concerning systematic consideration of discrete stimuli, body receptors, and the underlying mediating mechanisms'. It has become fashionable to describe stimuli as 'stressful' merely because they are powerful and then to presume that a Selye-type response must ensue. Indeed, very often the term 'stress' is used in such a loose way both for external stimuli and for the bodily responses. Without denigrating Selye's empirical work, one can now express the opinion that the concept of stress is so diffuse as to be not merely meaningless but even misleading.

## The 'law' of initial value

This states that the true response of a variable to a stimulus decreases as the true pre-stimulus level increases. In other words, as the level rises the response diminishes. Although elevated to the status of a 'law' of science by Wilder (e.g. 1957) it is not nearly as clear-cut or as well established as its name would imply. It has of course been known for many years in the physical sciences that the estimation of a change was more or less dependent on the level upon which that change was superimposed. However, in psychophysiology, the belated realisation of this relationship has led to a series of mathematical manipulations of the data, the ingenuity of those manipulations being matched only by their entire divorce from basic biological principles. Some investigators have attempted general solutions of the problem (e.g. Benjamin, 1963; Oken and Heath, 1963) but the topic has become more and more complex. In general, biological phenomena follow logarithmic laws, as Gaddum (1945) pointed out, so that if the original data appear unsatisfactory in statistical terms a logarithmic transformation should be resorted to. If the data are still unworkable then the experiment was probably poorly planned or hastily executed.

## Response specificity (Engel, 1972)

Response specificity can be roughly divided into two categories, namely stimulus specificity and individual specificity. The former refers to the tendency which a particular stimulus has to evoke particular characteristic response patterns in the subject. For example, showing pictures of nude women to male subjects is very likely to produce penile erection. Individual specificity is the tendency which any subject has to produce a characteristic pattern of responses. Thus, one individual may show a great deal of heart rate response to a stimulus yet little sweat gland response, whereas another subject may have the reverse pattern (Lacey, 1959; Steinschneider and Lipton, 1965).

The first form of individual response specificity is 'intra-stressor stereotypy'. In response to a particular stimulus, an individual will display the same pattern of response on successive testing occasions (Lacey, 1950; Lacey and Van Lehn, 1952). An extension of this work led to the concept of 'inter-stressor stereotypy', in which the pattern of response tends to remain idiosyncratic to the individual across varying types of stimulus. Thus, mental arithmetic and the cold-pressor test would result in a similar response pattern in a subject. Two studies (Lacey, Bateman and Van Lehn, 1953; Lacey and Lacey, 1958) designed to evaluate this hypothesis

85

were performed and indicated that some subjects did indeed tend to give similar response patterns to different stimuli; other subjects were far more variable. Schnore (1959) and Dykman *et al.* (1959, 1963) confirmed these findings but Wenger *et al.* (1961) opined that the similarities between many of the stimuli and the temporal proximity of the stimuli could account for the reproducible response patterns in the subjects.

Furthermore, in Lacey's experiments, the stimuli such as a word fluency test and mental arithmetic were presented when the subject was at the same skin resistance level each time. Thus, after one stimulus, the experimenter waited until the subject's skin resistance had returned to pre-stimulus levels. The response pattern may well be dependent on the pattern of 'resting' level of activity in the various measures at the time of stimulus onset. If so, it is possible that the resting levels rather than the response pattern is characteristic of any particular individual.

Stimulus specificity was studied by R. C. Davis and his colleagues, who showed response patterns depended at least as much on the type of stimulus as on the individuals (Davis, Buchwald and Frankmann, 1955). In these studies (Davis, 1957), the subjects were stimulated by warmth, cold, affectively toned stimuli, etc., and the response patterns obtained were more closely dependent on the stimulus than on the individual. Thus, 'situational stereotypy' appeared more important than 'individual stereotypy'.

It would seem that both individual and stimulus factors are important in determining the pattern of a response in accord with the conclusions of Engel (1960) and Engel and Bickford (1961).

### Habituation, adaptation and acclimatisation

The central nervous system possesses the undoubted property of modifying its responses in the light of previous events. This is seen at its simplest in the phenomenon of habituation, which may be defined as that biological phenomenon which is manifested by the progressive diminution in the size of responses evoked by successive identical stimuli applied at discrete intervals (Lader, 1971). It is a widespread phenomenon throughout the entire biological kingdom (Harris, 1943). Some biologists have regarded habituation as the simplest form of learning—of learning not to respond to irrelevant stimuli (Humphrey, 1933). One of the criteria for an habituatory process is the return of the response if the parameters of stimulation are altered or if an extraneous stimulus intervenes (Thompson and Spencer, 1966). This property distinguishes habituation from sensory accommodation on the one hand and effector system fatigue on the other.

Orienting responses are prone to habituate (Sharpless and Jasper, 1956). These responses cause widespread disruption in the organism and needless repetition would be biologically disadvantageous. The Pavlov school studied habituation under the term 'extinction of the orienting reaction', and Pavlov (1927) extended his Theory of Internal Inhibition to explain the extinction. He postulated an internal inhibitory state being set up in response to the stimulus which tended to dissipate over time. Massing of the stimuli would cause a build-up of inhibition and extinction of the response. The disinhibiting effect of an extraneous stimulus was a crucial difficulty for Pavlov's theory and he had to resort to the idea of 'irradiation' from the cortical 'centre' of the extraneous stimulus.

Adaptation is another term frequently used to describe changes in response to an altering stimulus situation. Although the term is sometimes used synonymously with habituation, it is best reserved for long-term changes, e.g. return of a background measure such as heart rate to pre-stimulus levels.

Acclimatisation refers to the changes in measures back towards resting levels after a subject has been placed in a novel laboratory situation.

## Bio-feedback

This is an area of psychophysiology which has excited a great deal of interest in the past few years. Many papers have been published on this topic (e.g. see Barber *et al.*, 1971). The techniques evolved are dependent on up-to-date electronic technology such as on-line computers and graphic displays.

Feedback training is like any other training with repeated trials, knowledge of results, etc., with the difference that the performance to be enhanced is an internal physiological change instead of an external behavioural one. The technique has three requirements:

(1) The physiological variable whose level, responsivity, etc., it is wished to control must be monitored continuously and with

sufficiently sensitive techniques to detect small moment-to-moment changes.

(2) Information regarding changes in the physiological variable of interest must be relayed accurately and rapidly to the subject. This information can be continuous (e.g. a needle on a dial registering pulse rate, the frequency of a tone reflecting skin conductance level) or discontinuous (e.g. a light coming on when the blood pressure drops 5 points following a tone signal). In animals the latter type of information can be combined with reward, e.g. food or water, or electrical stimulation of the 'pleasure' areas of the brain. In general, in humans continuous feedback is more effective than dichotomous information as fewer or shorter sessions are apparently needed in the feedback training.

(3) The subject must be motivated to learn. Although curiosity, anxiousness to please and competitiveness may suffice for some subjects, monetary reward may have to be resorted to.

A typical experiment consists in monitoring the heart rate via ECG electrodes and using a ratemeter to derive the mean ongoing heart rate. This is 'fed back' to the subject by display on a meter and he is instructed to lower the mean heart rate as much as possible. Another group of subjects will be instructed to raise heart rate. Other variables which have been used in this context include the EEG (Lynch and Paskewitz, 1971), the EMG, skin conductance, blood pressure, skin blood flow, salivation and gastric motility.

There are probably several mechanisms by which control is obtained over the physiological function. Respiration, voluntary muscle contractions or even ideation could act as an intervening mechanism. Because of this attempts have been made to differentially condition the two sides of the body with respect to GSR or vasomotor responses. This is a more rigorous test that fundamental physiological processes are involved.

The implications for mental illness are several-fold. Firstly, elucidation of the mechanisms underlying feedback control might throw light on what goes wrong when normal control is disturbed. Hypochondriasis might be related to some disturbance of this sort. Control of abnormal physiological functions, such as hyperacidity in the stomach and epileptic discharges in the EEG, has been attempted and opens up a wide range of therapeutic possibilities. Thirdly, the techniques are ideally designed for helping tense patients to relax, e.g. by EMG feedback.

## Activation and arousal

Cannon (1915) described the mechanisms whereby the body prepares for emergency action during fear and rage and he emphasised the 'energy mobilisation' aspects of the changes. Elizabeth Duffy, in a series of papers and books (1941, 1951, 1957, 1962, 1972), developed the idea that all behaviour has a common dimension of energy release, both overt and covert. The extent of the energy release is determined by the degree of effort required by the situation as interpreted by the individual. She suggested that the other dimension of behaviour is 'direction' of energy release. Because of its biochemical implications 'energy release' is not a good term.

Lindsley (1951) propounded a theory of 'activation' which holds that the cortex is activated by the upward discharge of lower centres—the thalamus, hypothalamus and diencephalic reticular formation. When the discharge level is low, the subject is asleep or drowsy, i.e. his level of activation is low. The other end of the continuum represents extreme emotions, such as terror and rage, with a high level of activation. Implicit in these theories is the idea that a stimulus increases activation in order that the organism be more capable of reacting appropriately (Berlyne, 1960). However, as Schlosberg (1954) has pointed out, the level of activation carried to excess becomes disorganising.

The term 'arousal' has also been extensively used in psychophysiology. Originally in the Middle Ages it was a term used in hawking. Physiologists often use it in a qualitative sense—an animal is either 'aroused' or 'non-aroused'. Psychophysiologists use it as an alternative term to 'activation' to describe the behavioural continuum which can be defined in operational terms as ranging from sleep, drowsiness, an inalert state and normal waking through heightened emotional awareness and uneasiness to states of emotion culminating in extreme emotions such as rage, panic and revulsion.

The concepts of arousal and activation are crucial to much of psychophysiology, especially that of psychiatric patients, and further development of these concepts is set out in the final chapter.

## Sexual arousal

Mainly from the work of Masters and Johnson (1966), a great deal is known of the physiological changes accompanying sexual arousal. However, this topic lies mainly outside the scope of this book as the physiological changes are not indicators of psychological status except in a very general sense, i.e. it is not strictly psychophysiology. Excellent reviews of this topic have been provided by Zuckerman (1971).

## Sleep studies

Interest in the phenomena of sleep has increased greatly in the past twenty years following the demonstration of associations between certain physiological characteristics of sleep and the recall of dreams (Aserinsky and Kleitman, 1953, 1955). Consequently, the literature on this topic has grown enormously and has been well reviewed by Snyder and Scott (1972). Many psychiatric conditions are accompanied by disturbances of sleep so that some knowledge of the main characteristics of sleep is helpful in evaluating studies on the psychopathology of sleep (Kales and Berger, 1970).

Sleep was originally regarded as a unitary state with various depths of sleep along a continuum. This simple concept was upset by Aserinsky and Kleitman (1953, 1955) who discovered that bursts of conjugate, rapid eye movements (REMs) occurred periodically throughout the night. These clusters of REMs were associated with low-voltage, high-frequency EEG waves. Dream recall was present about 80 per cent of occasions when the subject was roused from REM sleep but in less than 10 per cent of times when awakened from non-REM sleep (Dement and Kleitman, 1957a).

Dement and Kleitman (1957b) re-classified the EEG changes in sleep into the following four stages: (1) low-voltage, fast waves but no sleep spindles apparent; (2) spindle activity of 14–16 Hz superimposed on a low-voltage background; (3) delta activity—high-voltage 1–2 Hz activity occupying less than half the record; (4) delta activity present for more than half the time. REM sleep usually occurs when Stage 1 sleep follows another stage and is associated with low-amplitude, fast-frequency waves and a marked decrease in the tone of head and neck muscles. Other names for REM sleep include paradoxical sleep, dreaming sleep and rhombencephalic sleep. In young adults, there are four to six REM sleep periods in a night's sleep, occurring cyclically at intervals of 70 to 110 minutes. The REM periods become progressively longer during the night. About 20 to 25 per cent of the total sleep time is spent in REM sleep, 5 to 10 per cent in Stage 1, 50 per cent in Stage 2 and 20 per cent in Stages 3 and 4.

At birth, 40 to 50 per cent of total sleep time is spent in REM sleep, the percentage dropping during the first months of life. In children, there is a high proportion of Stages 3 and 4 which drops during adolescence to yield the adult pattern. In the elderly, the proportion of REM sleep is about the same as in young adults but as the total sleep time is less, the absolute amount of REM time is also less. The most obvious change is a marked decrease or even absence of Stage 4 sleep.

Dreaming can occur during non-REM sleep but the reports of subjects when awakened from this stage are somewhat atypical of dream reports. With wakening from REM sleep, the reports closely resembled spontaneous dream reports and the dream recall deteriorated as the time from the end of a REM period to awakening was prolonged. By eight minutes there was very little recall. Dreams from REM periods later in the night were more easily recalled. External stimuli, such as flashing a light or spraying water on the subject's skin during non-REM sleep, did not initiate REM periods but were incorporated into dream material recalled on awakening one minute later.

As mentioned earlier, certain muscles in the head and neck such as the external laryngeal muscles lose tone during REM periods. Heart rate and respiration become more irregular and skin conductance fluctuations increase. A high proportion of REM periods are accompanied by penile erections. Adrenal cortical and medullary hormones appear to increase during REM sleep.

The significance of REM periods is still unclear although REM stage sleep deprivation studies have shown that there is a specific need for REM sleep which has to be made up at a later time. However, the psychological disturbances such as hallucinations and delusions which follow REM sleep deprivation may be a function of total sleep deprivation.

An immediate result of the re-orientation of our concepts regarding sleep has been the elucidation of certain phenomena occurring during sleep: somnambulism, enuresis and narcolepsy and catalepsy. Thus, somnambulism in children occurs in non-REM sleep, usually Stages 3 and 4, and the sleep-walking is heralded by a burst of high-voltage slow-wave activity in the EEG. Such EEGs are typical of younger children so that there may be a delay in maturation of the EEG of sleep-walkers. Enuresis has also been studied during all-night sleep recordings. Typically the 'enuretic episode' begins in Stage 4 sleep and is ushered in either by a K-complex or a paroxysm of delta waves associated with bodily restlessness. Sleep patterns then change to Stage 2 or non-REM Stage 1 and micturition occurs (Gastaut and Broughton, 1965). Patients with narcolepsy and catalepsy have their sleep and their day-time attacks characterised by a REM period with lack of muscle tone during the onset. This contrasts with normal sleep in which at least an hour of non-REM sleep elapses before a REM period. It has been suggested that the conjunction of narcolepsy and catalepsy constitutes a distinct syndrome and that patients with sleep attacks without the other features should be considered separately (Dement, Rechtschaffer and Gulevich, 1966).

Many other interesting aspects of sleep have been explored, one of the most fascinating being the biochemistry of sleep (Williams, 1971). Nevertheless, many questions remain, an intriguing one being the suggestion that REM stages represent a periodic alteration in brain function which occurs throughout the 24 hours but is only easily detectible during sleep.

# Anxiety

4

## Introduction

Anxiety is the affect which has received most attention, especially from those engaged in using autonomic and somatic measures as indicators of 'arousal'. The reasons for this concentration are several-fold. First, anxiety is an emotion which we have all felt and do experience frequently. Consequently, the study of anxiety is of direct and important relevance to normal psychology in a way that schizophrenia is not. Second, anxiety-proneness varies from individual to individual and many theories of personality afford great prominence to the influence of trait anxiety on behaviour. Neither depression nor schizophrenia are nearly as important in this respect. Third, pathological or morbid anxiety, i.e. anxiety which is more severe, more persistent or more pervasive than the individual is accustomed to and can bear, appears to be quantitatively but not qualitatively different from 'normal' anxiety, i.e. that affect which we all experience at some time or another. Consequently, study of anxiety states should throw light on normal anxiety and vice versa. Fourth, anxiety is easy to induce in normal individuals and is then quick to subside so that a convenient research paradigm is available. And, fifth, anxiety has been heuristically viewed as an over-arousal state which provides a strong theoretical framework in which to relate experimental data.

Krause (1961) has listed six types of evidence for the detection of anxiety, especially of a transitory nature. The introspective report is perhaps the most important and there are grounds for giving it criterion status. It is the best indicator we have although it is subject to bias and it is ultimately unanalysable. Unconscious anxiety is a much more controversial concept which needs biological validation. The second indicator is as a response to stress, i.e. it is dependent on the properties of the stimulus which should

93

induce a perception of impending harm or evil. This cognitive appraisal of the stimulus varies from individual to individual (Lader, 1972), i.e. each subject has his own stressors. For this reason, this indicator is not a good one. Third, anxiety is characterised by a set of physical signs and symptoms: a sense of constriction in the chest, tightness in the throat, difficulty in breathing, epigastric discomfort or pain, palpitations, dizziness and weakness in the legs, dryness of the mouth, sweating, vomiting, tremor, screaming, running in panic and sudden micturition or defaecation. The detailed measurement and evaluation of the accompanying physiological changes is the particular interest of the psychophysiologist (Krause, Galinsky and Weiner, 1961). Of course, other emotions such as rage and ecstasy also produce physiological changes so these indicators of anxiety need continuous concurrent validation by reference to other indicators of anxiety, such as subjective reports.

The fourth type of evidence in Krause's list is clinical intuition, an inferential covert process. One can experience one's own anxiety but only perceive indications of another's anxiety. Nevertheless, the rating of overt anxiety is a highly practical and common procedure. Molar behaviours, e.g. facial expression and gesture, form the fifth type of evidence, the sixth being change in task performance.

Several types of laboratory situation have been used, both to induce anxiety in normally calm subjects and to standardise the recording procedure for anxious patients. Malmo et al. (1948) listed the main requirements of a useful 'stress' situation as: (1) the external stimulation should be uniform and controlled; (2) it should be relatively mild; (3) though mild, it should produce objective changes; (4) definite differences in test reaction should be detectible when individuals whose reactions differ clinically are exposed to the situation. These workers used a thermal pain stimulator. Motion picture films of distasteful, anxiety-provoking scenes such as circumcisions in Australian aboriginals or gory industrial accidents have been extensively used (e.g. Lazarus et al., 1962). Grinker et al. (1957) utilised an anxiety-producing interview but acknowledged that there were very complex stressor–patient relationships.

More complex situations have been used. For example, Weybrew (1959) studied eight male applicants for posts as prison officers. They were made to supervise two 'prisoners' (in reality, psychologists) while they erected a tent. The prisoners subjected each candidate to taunts and abuse.

## Normal anxiety

The assessment of the physiological changes accompanying the anticipation of a painful stimulus such as an electric shock has been used as a 'model' of anxiety-induced changes. During the anticipatory period before the shock, skin conductance rises and the number of spontaneous fluctuations increases (Miller and Shmavonian, 1965). Katkin (1966) told half of his subjects to expect a shock and the other half just to rest. No shock was given to either group but the expectation group had much higher rates of spontaneous fluctuations. The subjects were also categorised as high in affect or low in affect depending on their scores on the Affect Adjective Check List. The high-affect subjects in the expectation group were slower to recover to resting levels after the stress period.

Heart rate acceleration occurs in the half-minute period preceding an expected shock except for the last few seconds when deceleration occurs. Subjects who have not experienced the shock previously show more tachycardia than subjects who have been shocked before (Deane, 1961, 1964). The greater tachycardia in the naive subjects occurs whether the shock is to be mild (0·2 mA) or strong (4·0 mA) (Elliot, 1966).

Palmar sweating, measured colorimetrically, increased in 4-year-old children when read a mildly anxiety-provoking story (Lore, 1966). However, there was no control for the 'mental effort' of listening to the story and this objection can be raised against some similar studies. Paradoxically, sweat gland activity *dropped* in patients prior to a surgical operation (Harrison, MacKinnon and Monk-Jones, 1962).

Examinations provide convenient real-life situations for assessment of the induction of anxiety. In an early study of this type, twenty-three students were tested before and after an examination, various cardiovascular variables being measured (Hickam, Cargill and Golden, 1948). Blood pressure was slightly elevated, heart rate markedly raised (by a mean of 19 beats per minute) and peripheral resistance diminished prior to the examination. However, in this type of study, some sort of control for the effects of repeated testing is necessary.

*

A similar study involved the radio-telemetric monitoring of pulse rates of physicians in a midday staff conference and of medical students presenting cases (Ira, Whalen and Bogdonoff, 1963). Again marked rises were found during the stress.

A very extensive evaluation of anxiety in a fear-provoking situation has been carried out by Fenz and Epstein (1967). Sport parachutists were studied, with records of skin conductance levels and heart rate throughout the day prior to the jump, in the aircraft before the jump and on landing. Ten novices were compared with ten experienced parachutists. On all measures the curves of novices and veterans were similar to begin with, e.g. when arriving at the airport, during take-off, etc. Then the curves diverged, the novices showing a marked rise with peaking at the time of the jump. Thus the novices' heart rate rose sharply to a mean of 145 beats per minute just before the jump, while the experienced parachutists showed a drop at this point. This was interpreted as indicating the development of inhibition of anxiety as training proceeded (Fenz and Jones, 1972).

Several studies have explored the relationship between anxiety-proneness (trait anxiety) and psychophysiological measures. One early study was negative, no relationship being found between scores on the Taylor Manifest Anxiety Scale and palmar sweating (Lotsof and Downing, 1956). In other studies, high scorers on the Taylor Scale have been found to have higher EMG levels (Rossi, 1959), more eye blinks (Lovaas, 1960), and slower habituation of the orienting response (Katkin and McCubbin, 1969; Koepke and Pribram, 1967) than low scorers. Similarly, high scorers on a Test Anxiety Questionnaire had higher skin conductance levels than low scorers (Kissel and Littig, 1962) and subjects with high neuroticism scores on the Eysenck Personality Inventory were more reactive with respect to the GSR than low neuroticism subjects (Coles, Gale and Kline, 1971).

A more psychoanalytic approach was favoured by Bogdonoff, Bogdonoff and Wolf (1961). They interviewed twenty-four normal subjects attending a dentist's surgery routinely and divided them into 'aggressive' and 'defensive' individuals. A Lashley disc was placed over a parotid opening and the salivary flow rate estimated before, during and after tooth-drilling. There was no difference in salivation between the groups at rest but the aggressive group showed a marked increase in secretion during stress whereas the defensive group produced a marked fall.

## Anxiety states

Anxiety in the clinic is 'an indescribable foreboding or dread of personal doom' (Grinker, 1961). As such it is common in many psychiatric conditions, both organic and functional. One approach has been to attempt to correlate affects like anxiety, arising in any context, with psychophysiological measures. Even if the usual classificatory scheme of psychiatry is used, many studies, especially early ones, used very broad categories such as 'psychoneurotic' and 'psychotic'. Such groupings have long been severely criticised (e.g. Bowman and Rose, 1951), and Darrow (1933), in a lucid exposition of the pitfalls awaiting the investigator in the area of the physiology of psychiatric patients, stresses the importance of using patients homogeneous with respect to some prominent clinical feature.

In the sections that follow, the results of psychophysiological investigations into psychiatric patients will be outlined, measure by measure.

## Autonomic measures

### Sweat gland activity

The earliest studies, reviewed by Golla (1921) and Prideaux (1920), concentrated on methodological considerations of the nature of the GSR. Anxiety neurotics were described as having low skin resistance (increased sweating) and small responses (Solomon and Fentress, 1934). Ödegaard (1932), in a very thorough and systematic evaluation of the skin potential in psychiatric patients, remarks that patients with anxiety give unstable, active records. The GSR was even suggested as a test for neuroticism but the data supporting this assertion are unconvincing (Herr and Kobler, 1953, 1957).

Palmar sweating was measured chemically (Silverman and Powell, 1944a) and found to be increased in psychoneurotic patients awaiting discharge from an army general hospital, as compared with normal subjects (Silverman and Powell, 1944b). Most of the patients were suffering from anxiety states.

A mixed group of thirty-six psychiatric patients was ranked for anxiety and divided into the eighteen high-anxiety and eighteen low-anxiety subjects (Piercy et al., 1955). The GSRs to shocks, lights and to a deep breath were measured but no differences were found between the groups with respect to level or reactivity. Nor was S. B. G. Eysenck (1956) able to differentiate between broad groups of 'neurotics' and 'normals'.

A heterogeneous group of anxious and depressed patients was rated for anxiety, depression and hostility on the basis of an interview (Zuckerman, Persky and Curtis, 1968). The presence of anxiety correlated with the frequency of spontaneous skin conductance fluctuations but this variable did not distinguish between the patients and a group of normal control subjects. Similarly, anxious patients had higher skin conductance levels than depressed patients (Gilberstadt and Maley, 1965).

Wing (1964) asked her subjects to call out the colours of strips of gummed paper mounted on a drum as the strips rotated and were exposed to view for a short time through a window. The colours were difficult to name, being non-primary, and to increase the difficulty of the task the subject's voice was relayed back through earphones with a delay of 0·2 second. The patients had higher skin conductance levels throughout the procedure but the mean number of fluctuations was equal in the two groups.

Lader and Wing (1964, 1966) carried out a detailed evaluation of the GSR in anxious patients. In a preliminary study in sixty-four student subjects, an habituation paradigm was developed consisting of a ten-minute rest period followed by the administration of twenty identical auditory stimuli of 100 decibels intensity and 1 second duration, the inter-stimulus interval varying randomly between 45 and 80 seconds. The background skin conductance, the GSRs to the stimuli and the spontaneous fluctuations were analysed. A method of calculating the rate of habituation was developed based on the exponential course of the habituation process.

In the second experiment, the physiological measures were compared during the habituation procedure in a group of twenty patients with anxiety states and twenty matched normal control subjects. In the normal group, the conductance levels dropped over the course of the recording session whereas it rose in the patients. Habituation of the GSRs was much less rapid in the patients who also had a greater number of spontaneous skin conductance fluctuations. In the patients, significant correlations were obtained between ratings of overt anxiety on the one hand and habituation rate and number of fluctuations on the other: the

98

more anxious the patient appeared, the less rapid was habituation and the more the number of fluctuations.

The twenty patients with anxiety states were given one week's treatment with placebo and one with amylobarbitone sodium 200 mg per day in a balanced cross-over trial with double-blind procedure. The recording of physiological variables was carried out at the end of each week. Skin conductance levels over the course of the test rose on the placebo occasion but dropped after the week of drug treatment. Habituation of the responses was accelerated by the barbiturate which also lowered the frequency of fluctuations, as compared with placebo. Clinically, only physical symptoms were helped by the drug.

Next, a comparison of the physiological and clinical effects of amylobarbitone and chlorodiazepoxide was carried out. After a pilot study to establish roughly the equieffective dose levels of the two drugs, a formal two-plus-two-plus-one bio-assay was carried out. The treatments were amylobarbitone sodium 150 and 300 mg per day, chlordiazepoxide 22·5 and 45 mg per day, and placebo; each of thirty patients received three of the five treatments in a fully balanced incomplete block design, each drug being given for one week with full double-blind precautions. Skin conductance level, responses and fluctuations yielded highly significant treatment effects, enabling the computation of dose–effect curves, equivalent dosages and fiducial (confidence) limits.

This series of experiments demonstrated the sensitivity of skin conductance measures to sedative drug effects. The physiological measures showed much more consistent drug effects than did clinical ratings and allowed a much more precise estimate of the relative effectiveness of the two drugs.

In a further study, Lader (1967) carried out the habituation procedure on the following groups of subjects: (1) anxiety with depression; (2) anxiety states; (3) agoraphobics; (4) social phobics; (5) specific phobics; and (6) a large number of normal subjects (see Figure 4.1). Habituation rates were slowest in the first group, becoming progressively faster through the groups to the normal subjects and specific phobics. Fluctuation rate followed a similar rank order being highest in Group 1 and lowest in Group 6. The specific monosymptomatic phobics had physiological measures in the normal range whereas all the other groups differed significantly from normal. For a sub-sample of the patients in this study, slow habituation rate and high spontaneous fluctuation rate were

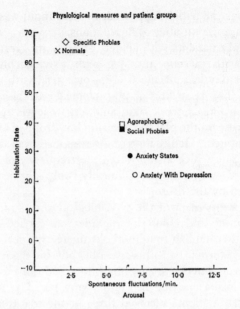

Figure 4.1 *Relationships between habituation rate and arousal in various groups of psychiatric patients*

associated with a poor response to systematic desensitisation (Lader, Gelder and Marks, 1967).

A further examination of sweat gland activity was recently carried out by Bond, James and Lader (1974). Thirty patients with anxiety states were compared to thirty age- and sex-matched normal controls. Skin conductance recordings were made while the subjects sat passively listening to a series of auditory clicks (P condition) and then while the subjects performed a reaction-time task in response to the clicks (A condition). In the normal subjects the skin conductance level was higher during the active task and in the patients the level remained the same: the mean level in the patients was nearly twice that of the controls. Skin conductance variability dropped during the active task and was higher in the controls, especially at rest. Fluctuation rate rose in both groups during the active task and was lower in the controls during the passive task (Figure 4.2).

Habituation of the GSR was examined by Stewart *et al.* (1959) in a group of ten anxiety neurotics, a group of eighteen schizophrenics and a group of twenty-seven manic-depressives. The anxious patients took significantly more trials to reach zero response than the other two groups, but as no control group was included, it could not be stated whether the rate of habituation of these patients was abnormally low. The data of Dureman and Saaren-Sepp'a'l'a' (1964) can be interpreted as indicating delayed habituation in anxious patients. However, another study of anxious patients failed to reveal any differences from normal in the rate of GSR habituation (Tan, 1964).

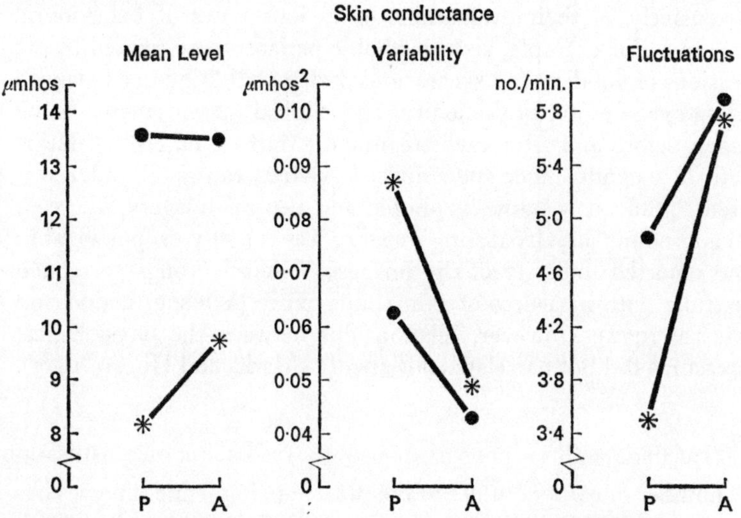

Figure 4.2 *Difference between patients* (●——●) *and normals* (*——*) *with respect to some skin conductance variables recorded under passive* (P) *and active* (A) *conditions*

Howe (1958) evaluated habituation and conditioning in anxiety states and normal subjects. Extinction of the conditioned response was impaired in the anxious subjects.

Psychophysiological measures have proved particularly useful in evaluating fear responses in phobic subjects and the response of these patients to behavioural treatments (Paul, 1969). Geer (1966) delineated two groups of female students, those with a high rating for fear of spiders and low for fear of snakes, and those with low ratings for both animals. All the subjects were shown slides which were at first neutral in content but were then of snakes in one half of the subjects, spiders in the other half. The high-fear spider group showed the largest GSRs to the spider slides followed by the low-fear group shown spiders. Both groups shown snake slides gave small responses. Some adaptation to repeated presentation of the spider slides was apparent.

Students with phobias of speaking in public have been treated with desensitisation procedures and their progress monitored by recording heart rate, respiration and skin conductance (Van Egeren, Feather and Hein, 1971). Similarly, Agras (1965) has followed the progress of patients during desensitisation over several sessions.

Marks and his co-workers have used physiological measures very extensively in their evaluations of various types of behavioural therapy. For example, sixteen phobic patients were treated by six sessions of flooding and six sessions of desensitisation in a balanced cross-over design, physiological and clinical measurements being taken before and after each treatment (Marks et al., 1971). Heart rate, skin conductance and subjective anxiety ratings all differentiated significantly between phobic and neutral imagery. Increase in autonomic activity during imagery was roughly proportional to the reported intensity of the imagery. Clinical ratings correlated usefully with measures of skin conductance (Watson, Gaind and Marks, 1972). However, relationships between the physiological measures did not correlate consistently (Marks and Huson, 1973).

## Pulse rate

A number of earlier studies of the pulse rate in mental illnesses has been reviewed by Altschule (1953). In general, the pulse rate is either normal or raised in patients with 'neurosis' or 'neurocirculatory asthenia', an old term for anxiety states with predominantly cardiovascular symptoms. White and Gildea (1937) reported that the resting heart rate was higher in patients with anxiety states than normal controls. During a cold-pressor test, the heart rate remained higher in the patients and was more variable. Similar increased variability was noted in another study (Whitehorn and Richter, 1937). Glickstein et al. (1957) discerned two sub-groups among a group of nineteen anxious patients undergoing tests on four successive days: one group had very high anxiety levels and a high initial heart rate which declined gradually; the second group was less anxious and had lower heart rates which showed distinct responses to each of the stress procedures.

Ackner (1956b) found similar resting pulse rates in anxious patients and normal subjects although the mean pulse rate of the former group tended to drop a little more with the onset of sleep than that of the latter group. Nor did Jurko, Jost and Hill (1952) note any difference in pulse rate between a mixed group of psychoneurotics and a normal group.

Lader and Wing (1966) found a definite tachycardia in anxious patients (a mean of 92 beats per minute) as compared with normal controls (76 beats per minute). Both groups declined at about the same rate during the recording session. A similar finding was noted by Bond, James and Lader (1974), a group of anxious patients having a mean pulse rate of 81·2 beats per minute as compared with normal values of 74·5 beats per minute ($p < 0.05$). Kelly (1966) also reported the pulse rate of anxious patients to be raised.

## Blood pressure

Hall (1927) recorded the blood pressure of seventy-one psychoneurotic patients. In the 'neurasthenics' and 'psychasthenics', the blood pressure was generally lower than normal; in the anxiety neuroses, the blood pressure was raised and labile.

A detailed evaluation of blood pressure in psychoneurotic patients during a series of psychological tasks and cold-pressor tests showed that the patients' blood pressure rose before the tests, rose further during the tasks and then dropped a little. The controls' blood pressure rose little during the tasks but dropped much more after. Throughout the session the controls' blood pressure gradually dropped and became less reactive whereas the patients' levels and reactivity were maintained. The authors concluded that the adaptation of psychoneurotics to repeated stress is impaired (Malmo, Shagass and Heslam, 1951). In a further study, the most consistent difference between psychoneurotics and normals was the continuation of blood pressure rises in the patients during the later phase of stress when the controls' blood pressure was beginning to drop (Malmo and Shagass, 1952). Similarly, in normals the post-interview levels were lower than those before the interview, whereas with anxious patients the reverse obtained (Innes, Millar and Valentine, 1959). A small elevation in blood pressure in anxious patients was reported by Kelly (1966).

## Blood flow

The earlier work on the peripheral vasomotor system and emotions, normal and abnormal, was comprehensively reviewed by Ackner

(1956a). Psychoneurotics had diminished blood flow in the hands as compared with normal subjects (Abramson, Schkloven and Katzenstein, 1941). Anxious patients were reported to show a 'shift to the sympathetic', i.e. to be vasoconstricted (Van der Merwe, 1948).

Ackner (1956b) compared the pulse volume amplitudes of a group of 10 calm mental patients, 13 anxious patients (mostly anxiety states and agitated depressives) and 12 normal subjects known to be of a calm disposition. The pulse volumes of a finger were recorded twice under resting conditions and once in quinal-barbitone-induced sleep. The normal subjects had the largest pulse volume at rest with no change during sleep; the calm patients had smaller pulse volumes with some vasodilatation ensuing during sleep; in the anxious patients, the pulse volumes were the smallest and sleep was accompanied by a marked vasodilatation. There was no overlap between the anxious patients and the other subjects with respect to the size of the sleep-induced vasodilatation.

Forearm blood flow levels in anxious patients were studied by Kelly (1966) both at rest and with the patients attempting to do mental arithmetic under harassment. The data were compared with those from normal controls. The mean resting level of the controls was 2·2 ml per 100 ml arm volume per minute and for the anxiety states 4·8 ($p < 0.001$). Under stress conditions the blood flow of the controls rose to 8·8 and of the patients to 8·2, i.e. the difference at rest was lost.

In a larger-scale study, Kelly and Walter (1969) recorded the blood flow rates of several groups of patients. Chronic anxiety states had the highest resting levels of forearm blood flow of all the groups of patients. One negative study was that of Harper *et al.* (1965) who found no difference, either at rest or during stress, between control subjects and a group of 10 phobic women. Calf plethysmography was used to record muscle blood flow in 30 patients selected for psychotherapy (Vanderhoof and Clancy, 1964). After treatment, correlations were calculated between the percentage change in symptom check lists with treatment and the blood flow readings. Significant positive correlations around the 0·6 level were found. However, such correlations were also found for patients who received control treatments consisting merely of rest periods.

ANXIETY

*Pupil size*

Using flash photography, L. S. Rubin (1964) compared 11 neurotic patients—mainly anxiety states and obsessionals—with 11 normal controls, with respect to pupil size at rest, during and after a cold-pressor test. In the former two conditions no differences were apparent between the groups; however, following the stress the normals' pupils rapidly constricted to their pre-stress values whereas the patients' pupils remained dilated for 7 minutes before recovering.

## Somatic measures

*Respiration*

In an early study using a spirometer, Finesinger (1944) reported that anxious and depressed patients had increased sighing-type respirations and many irregularities in the respiratory pattern. Such irregularities in anxious patients were found in another study but were even more marked in schizophrenic patients (Jurko, Jost and Hill, 1952).

Anxious patients have a lower respiratory efficiency—expressed as the ratio of total ventilation to total oxygen extraction—than normal control subjects (Coppen and Mezey, 1960a). Furthermore, their energy expenditure is higher. Both these abnormalities were lowered on administration of 200 mg of amylobarbitone sodium.

Respiratory rate is generally increased in anxious patients as compared with control subjects (e.g. Goldstein, 1964).

*Electromyogram*

The EMG has been used in many psychophysiological studies of anxious patients. In one, the EMG was recorded from forearm extensor, masseter and sternomastoid sites in 10 anxiety states and 10 control subjects, at rest and during the repeated application of white noise stimuli (Davis, Malmo and Shagass, 1954). There were no differences between the groups with respect to resting EMG levels. Patients tended to respond at all 3 sites whereas the controls showed greater responses in the head and neck than in the forearm. Consequently, for the forearm site only, responses were greater in the patients than in the controls. This was so both for immediate responses to the auditory stimuli and for later secondary rises in EMG level. These differences were only present for responses to stimuli 1–4.

The frontalis EMG was found to be a better discriminator between patients and controls than neck or forearm muscles (Malmo and Smith, 1955). Irene Martin (1956) divided her neurotic patients into 'dysthymics' (anxious, depressed and obsessional) and 'hysterics' and recorded frontalis and forearm extensor EMGs during several relaxation periods and several task situations. The resting levels were generally higher in the dysthymics than both the hysterics and a group of control subjects, especially towards the end of the recording session. The stress procedures did not generally differentiate the groups except for an interview situation which produced much higher levels in the neurotics. In another study, EMG levels were elevated in psychoneurotic patients as compared with normals, especially in those patients with low alpha activity in the EEG (Bartoshuk, 1959).

An extensive survey of EMG activity in anxious women was carried out by Goldstein (1964) who recorded from 7 sites. At rest the patients had significantly higher levels than normals for masseter and forearm extensor EMG and a white noise stimulus induced greater responses in patients as compared to normals with respect to the sternomastoid, frontalis, forearm extensor and gastrocnemius muscle sites. It appeared, therefore, that anxious subjects can be differentiated more easily from calm subjects during stimulation procedures than at rest.

Another approach has been to select patients for objective signs of muscular tension such as rigidity of posture and stiffness of movements (Davidowitz et al., 1955). Tense patients showed greater residual EMG activity after they had stopped pushing a button than did control subjects. On re-trial, the EMG levels dropped significantly in the controls but remained the same in the patients. The patients also produced more anticipatory movements. Impairment of motor control was reported in anxious patients in another study (Malmo et al., 1951).

Electromyographic techniques have also been used in investigations of symptom mechanisms in patients. Cameron (1944) asserted that patients with tension and anxiety states fell into 3 categories: those in whom the skeletal musculature was mainly involved, those in whom the smooth musculature was mainly involved and those in whom both types of musculature were involved.

Patients with complaints of headache and neck tension were compared with patients without such localising symptoms and with normal controls during pain stimulation (Malmo, Wallerstein and Shagass, 1953). With pain stimulation to the forearm there was increased EMG activity in the symptomatic patients' forearm muscles as compared with the other patients. With stimulation to the forehead, however, the frontalis muscle potentials were higher in the patients with symptoms in the head and neck than in the other patients. It was concluded that this raised EMG is due to a central conflict over whether to withdraw the arm or head respectively from the painful stimulation and hence headache is also due to some central conflict. This explanation was preferred to the alternative theory that headache is due to a response of neck muscles to stress because these muscles are intrinsically more sensitive in these patients.

An interesting electromyographic study of symptom mechanisms was carried out by Sainsbury and Gibson (1954) who made out an inventory for 30 anxious and tense patients, recording their symptoms, feelings and bodily complaints attributable to muscular overactivity (head sensations, backache, etc.). EMGs were recorded from the frontalis and forearm extensor muscles. The patients were divided into two groups depending on whether their symptom scores were above or below the median on the inventory. The former group had higher EMGs at both sites than the less anxious and tense patients. There were 7 patients who complained of headache or head sensations at the time of recording; they had higher frontalis EMG levels than the remainder of the patients but forearm levels were not different. Conversely, 14 patients complaining of stiffness, 'rheumatics' (without joint pains) and aching in the arms had higher forearm muscle potentials than the remainder.

The relationship of psychodynamic themes to localised muscle tension during psychotherapy has been explored (Shagass and Malmo, 1954). Forearm tension rose with 'hostility' themes and leg tension with 'sex' themes.

Conditioned eye blink responses were acquired more rapidly by agoraphobic than by social and specific phobic patients, but there were no differences between the groups with respect to extinction of these responses (Martin, Marks and Gelder, 1969).

*Finger tremor*

The amplitude of tremor has been reported to be increased in anxious patients for all frequencies (Redfearn, 1957). With eye closure tremor amplitude drops in normal subjects but not in anxious patients (Carrie, 1965).

## Electroencephalogram (Hill, 1963; Ellingson, 1954)

The EEG findings in anxiety states have been fairly consistent and quite predictable. In an early study comparing 100 psychoneurotics with 100 normals, alpha activity was found to be less abundant in the patients, especially those suffering from chronic anxiety states (Strauss, 1945). This was confirmed by Brockway et al. (1954) in an extensive study of a heterogeneous group of patients with the common symptom of anxiety. In normal subjects, the dominant alpha frequency followed a normal distribution with a mean of 10 Hz; in psychoneurotics, the distribution was bimodal with peaks at 9 and 10·5 Hz. In anxiety states the distribution was normal with the dominant frequency at 11·2 Hz. The proportion of beta activity was higher in the patients (Brazier, Finesinger and Cobb, 1945). Automatic quantification using a wave analyser has confirmed the association of anxiety and fast activity (Kennard, Rabinovitch and Fister, 1955).

Thus, the EEGs of anxious patients consistently show less alpha and more beta than normal (Lindsley, 1950). Ellingson (1954) dismisses this as insignificant, attributing it to the patients' inability to relax. However, this is in itself a distinguishing characteristic of anxious patients, of which the EEG provides objective evidence.

One study has been outlined in which no differences were found between anxious patients and control subjects (Wells and Wolff, 1960), but this is an exception.

### Evoked responses

Photic stimulation produces harmonic driving in the EEG. The amount of such induced harmonic activity has been reported to vary with the anxiety level of the patient, increasing with heightened anxiety (Ulett et al., 1953). Shagass (1955) used photic stimulation at 10 and 15 Hz in 29 normals, 31 anxiety states, 30 psychoneurotic depressive patients and 37 psychotic depressives. The ratio of responses at 15 Hz to those at 10 Hz was significantly higher in the anxiety states than the control subjects who in turn had a higher ratio than both the depressive groups. The differences were mainly attributable to better driving at the higher frequency for the anxiety group. Such results do accord with the increased beta activity in the resting EEG of anxious patients.

Alpha-blocking has been examined in two groups of female college students scoring at the extremes of the Cattell-Scheier Anxiety Battery. The highly anxious subjects had fewer responses than the calm subjects (Sayer and Torres, 1966). This might possibly be due to inattention to the external stimuli on the part of the anxious subjects.

*Contingent negative variation* (Walter, 1966; Tecce, 1972)

Various aspects of the continent negative variation (CNV, expectancy wave) have been described as abnormal in anxious patients. Forty neurotic patients with high anxiety levels, average age 39, were compared with 40 normals, mean age 33. Eye movement potentials, a source of artifact in CNV work, were balanced out. The warning stimulus was a click which was followed a second later by a series of flashes to which the subject responded by pressing a button. Two sets of 12 acquisition trials were followed by 2 sets of 12 trials during which a distracting tone was sounded. The mean CNV during acquisition was 16 microvolts in the patients which was significantly less than the mean normal value (20 μV). During distraction the CNV initially decreased markedly but was steadily restored in the normals to give an overall mean value of 14 μV. In the patients, the CNV remained attenuated at a mean level of only 4 μV (McCallum and Walter, 1968). As the authors are at pains to point out, the patients were receiving drugs (mainly anxiolytic agents) at the time of testing but the continuing distractibility presumed to be the cause of the diminution of the CNV is striking. Anxious patients also show slower habituation of the CNV as the stimuli are repeated (Walter, 1964). This suggests that the anxious patient continues to be expectant after the first stimulus at a time when the normal subject has completely habituated and finds no novelty value in the stimulus.

Confirmation that the CNV is attenuated in anxious patients has been forthcoming (Dongier and Bostem, 1967; Bostem *et al.*, 1967). It would appear worthwhile to include CNV recordings in the assessment of evoked response function in anxious subjects and patients. The interpretation of the findings would not be simple because the psychophysiological significance of the CNV remains unclear. Both arousal and attention influence the CNV, not to mention other kinds of electrophysiological activity such as autonomic functions and potentials associated with motor movements (Tecce, 1972). All this assumes that the CNV has been satisfactorily recorded and that eye movement potentials have been eliminated.

## Endocrine measures

### Adrenocortical function in normals

A great many studies have been carried out evaluating adrenocortical function in normal subjects under a variety of conditions. A selection of these studies is outlined here in order to underline the sensitivity of adrenal cortical indices to changes in stimulation conditions with accompanying affective alterations.

Venepuncture itself, or at least the anticipation of it, appears to raise plasma cortisol levels. For example, in 15 volunteer subjects, the mean plasma cortisol level was 24 µg per 100 ml on the first occasion, but only 11 and 15 µg per 100 ml on two subsequent occasions (Davis et al., 1962).

Opportunity has been taken of college examinations as real-life stressful situations of a high magnitude (Dreyfuss and Feldman, 1952; Schwartz and Shields, 1956). For example, 17-hydroxycorticosteroid levels in the urine rose quite markedly in 10 students during examinations (Melick, 1960). A very detailed analysis of this situation was carried out by Connell, Cooper and Redfearn (1958) who tested volunteer subjects, soldiers and students, before and during an important examination and also over both short and long periods of physical activity. The emotional stress of the examination caused a definite increase in the urinary excretion of 17-oxogenic steroids but only a slight increase in 17-oxosteroids. Short periods of physical exercise produced no alteration in the 17-oxogenic steroid excretion and a modest increase in 17-oxosteroid excretion. During prolonged physical stress extending over several days, there was a progressive decrease in 17-oxosteroid output but no alteration in 17-oxogenic steroid excretion. The authors adduce evidence for increased peripheral utilisation of cortisol during exercise and suggest that increased cortisol production following emotional stress is a preparatory manoeuvre for physical exercise. Plasma corticotrophin levels also appear to be raised during examinations (Hodges, Jones and Stockham, 1962).

The relationship between plasma cortisol levels and Taylor Manifest Anxiety Scores was found to reach significant levels in 78 students taking an oral examination in medicine (Bloch and Brackenridge, 1972).

Stressful situations have included soldiers in combat or in parachute training (Persky, 1953), the latter offering a graded series of stressful tasks from training on the ground, down chutes, off towers and finally from airplanes (Basowitz et al., 1955). Soldiers in training were exposed to five simulated situations by Berkun and his colleagues (1962): (1) an aircraft emergency during flight; (2) the disruption of a military exercise by misdirected incoming shells; (3) a forest fire; (4) apparently radioactive fallout; and (5) the soldier was made to feel responsible for a situation in which a comrade seemed seriously injured. Ratings of affect and urinary corticosteroids were measured. Situations (3) and (4) had relatively little effect on the physiological index. Situations (1) and (2) produced definite increases in steroid output. Situation (5) had the greatest effect in this respect.

An extremely complex and dangerous manoeuvre in military aviation is landing an airplane on an aircraft carrier. Anxiety ratings and plasma and urinary cortisol levels were estimated in student pilots and their radar intercept officers (the other member of the two-man crew) learning to land F-48 phantom fighter-bombers. Both on flying days and control non-flying days the radar intercept officers had higher anxiety ratings and hormone levels than the pilots, although the latter showed a greater increase when actually flying (Miller et al., 1970). Noradrenaline metabolite excretion also rose on flying days (Rubin et al., 1970).

The stress of long-range flying has been assessed using adrenocortical indices. An early study was inconclusive: of 2 aircrews each with 6 members and each on a long north–south flight, mean steroid excretion rose on one occasion and dropped on the other (Murphy, Gofton and Cleghorn, 1954). However, substantial increases in urinary 17-hydroxycorticosteroid levels have been reported both in pilots and in other aircrew after long flights (Hale, Ellis and Kratochvil, 1959). On training flights urinary corticosteroids were higher in inexperienced pilots than in fully trained pilots (Hale et al., 1964). In 14 B-52 bomber crew members a mean increase of 48 per cent occurred in urinary steroids during a 20-hour mission. The highest rises were noted during missions which most disrupted the normal sleep cycle (Marchbanks, 1960).

Surgical operations present a useful real-life stress for the assessment of adrenocortical responses. On the day before elective thoracic operations significant elevations in plasma cortisol levels were found at 8 a.m. (Price, Thaler and Mason, 1957). Significant relationships were found between high cortisol levels and four Rorschach variables which the authors regarded as reflecting a high degree of relatively undifferentiated 'distress-involvement'. High cortisol levels have also been found on the evening before an operation but less consistently on the morning of the operation (Thomasson, 1959). Such studies must, of course, take into account the known diurnal rhythm in cortisol levels. A further factor is the night sedation, usually a barbiturate, often given routinely the night before an elective operation; barbiturates are known to suppress hypothalamic function and the release of ACTH. In a study of 114 young adult, healthy men before dental surgery, patients with elective operations, e.g. for impacted teeth, had higher plasma cortisol levels than patients about to undergo emergency dental operations (Shannon et al., 1961).

A particularly tragic situation is that of parents of children dying of leukaemia. Twenty such parents were studied by psychometric and endocrinological means (Tecce, Friedman and Mason, 1965). The defensiveness scale of the Minnesota Multiphasic Personality Inventory and rating of anxiety symptoms proved to be important correlates of urinary 17-hydroxycorticosteroid excretion. Excretion was higher in parents with high defensiveness scores both during the chronic, ongoing stress and during any superimposed crises. The authors interpreted their results as indicating that elevated adrenocortical activity was related to curtailed verbal expression of anxiety and/or psychological inadequacy. A second study suggested, however, that the more effectively a parent defended against threat of loss, the *lower* the urinary 17-hydroxycorticosteroid excretion rate (Wolff et al., 1964). The inconsistency probably hinges on the problem of interpreting the rating scales used.

Hypnotic induction of anxiety was used by Persky, Grosz et al. (1959) in studies on adrenocortical function. Induction of the hypnotic trance significantly reduced plasma cortisol levels. Subsequent suggestion of feelings of anxiety raised cortisol levels in the female subjects but not in the men. This finding was confirmed by Grosz (1961). In another study it was noted that plasma cortisol levels dropped in some but not all subjects after 1–2 hours of trance relaxation (Sachar, Fishman and Mason, 1965). The drop in plasma cortisol (sometimes to less than 3 μg per 100 ml) was not reproducible or predictable, although it appeared that the quality of the hypnotist–subject relationship was more relevant in predicting this phenomenon than susceptibility to trance induction.

The effect of hydrocortisone infusion on hypnotically induced anxiety has also been explored (Levitt et al., 1963). Sixteen subjects were selected for hypnotisability and the suggestion of anxiety made cortisol levels rise to eight times normal. There was no evidence that an infusion of hydrocortisone (as compared with saline) caused the subject to experience more anxiety or to be more ready to experience anxiety (Weiner et al., 1963).

The factors lowering plasma cortisol levels were explored by Handlon et al. (1962). Nineteen volunteer subjects viewed two films—a Walt Disney travelogue and an exciting cowboy film. Plasma cortisol levels were maintained at about 11 μg per 100 ml from the beginning to end of the cowboy film but dropped to about half by the end of the bland film, values even lower than after a control non-film period.

Some attempts have been made to relate adrenocortical function to personality variables. Thus, in 22 male and 24 female volunteers, significant positive correlations were reported between urinary 17-hydroxycorticosteroid excretion and the Taylor Manifest Anxiety Scale and the Nowlis Hostility Score, and a negative correlation between the physiological measure and the Nowlis Social Affection Score (Curtis et al., 1970). No significant correlations were found overall between plasma cortisol and any psychometric score, although a positive correlation was found in women for the total Nowlis Score. However, as many correlations were computed in the matrix, the reported correlations could conceivably have occurred by chance. Using the Taylor Manifest Anxiety Scale, Fiorica and Muehl (1962) selected 19 subjects scoring in the upper 15 percentile and 31 scoring in the lower 15 percentile. The mean plasma cortisol level was 13 μg per 100 ml in the former group, 9·9 in the latter—a significant difference. In another study, it was reported that extraversion was related to the ratio of 17-oxogenic steroid excretion in the urine; the higher the ratio, the higher the E-score (Segraves, 1970). This suggests that extraverts have lower androgen levels than introverts.

Aldosterone excretion was measured in a group of students taking examinations. In those students who rated themselves as anxious during this time, aldosterone levels were somewhat elevated but still within the normal range (Venning, Dyrenfurth and Beck, 1957).

It would thus appear that life-situation stresses, examinations, imminent operations, dangerous activities, etc., raise both plasma cortisol levels and the amount of 17-oxogenic steroids in the urine. However, these levels are usually still within the normal range (Bliss *et al.*, 1956).

The importance of admission to hospital as a stressor procedure has been emphasised by Sachar (1967a). It was found that the urinary corticosteroid and catecholamine levels were significantly elevated on the day of admission of 60 normal adults who were to act as control subjects on a research ward (Mason *et al.*, 1965; Tolson *et al.*, 1965). These higher levels subsided within a week or two. Mixed-sex groups on the research ward seemed to have higher cortisol levels than single-sex groups (Sachar *et al.*, 1965). The implication is that hormone levels in newly admitted psychiatric patients are raised for at least a week following admission to hospital and that any elevations found cannot be ascribed to the psychiatric condition necessitating the admission (Handlon, 1962).

An interesting, pioneer study has been carried out by Persky, Smith and Basu (1971). They were able to measure plasma testosterone levels during the resting state and during a slow infusion of testosterone, the data from the latter procedure allowing an estimate of testosterone production rate to be calculated. Two groups of healthy men were studied, 18 constituting a younger group with 15 in an older group. Mean plasma testosterone levels were 686 µg per 100 ml in the younger men, 404 in the older. Ratings of aggressive feelings correlated $+0.69$ ($p < 0.001$) with testosterone production rate.

## *Adrenocortical function in patients* (Persky, 1962b)

In an early study of psychoneurotic patients, a variety of indices of adrenocortical function were measured, including lymphocyte and eosinophil counts, plasma electrolytes and corticosteroid excretion (Cleghorn and Graham, 1950). Despite the indirect nature of some of these indices a significant correlation was found between the aggregate of the indices and a rating of anxiety.

An early finding, replicated several times, was that patients rated as showing high levels of anxiety show 70 per cent higher plasma cortisol levels than normals (Bliss *et al.*, 1956). Patients rated as calm could not be distinguished from the normal control subjects. A patient who experienced a panic attack had particularly high levels. In a study carried out about the same time, Persky and his co-workers (1956) noted that morning plasma cortisol levels were 60 to 70 per cent higher in patients with acute anxiety states than in normal control subjects. Both plasma cortisol levels and urinary 17-hydroxycorticosteroid excretion levels were maintained at a high level for the four days of observation.

Stressful interviews were found to increase plasma cortisol levels even more (Persky *et al.*, 1956). In a more detailed analysis of the affective changes accompanying the raised plasma cortisol level, it appeared that the hormonal changes were concomitants of anxiety, anger or depression (Persky *et al.*, 1958). However, the closest parallel was with the total affective rating. A 'particularly striking effect' on the hormonal levels occurred when the anxiety was of a 'disintegrative' nature, e.g. fear of loss of sanity or of control. A perceptual distortion test was used as a stressful task in evaluating changes in plasma cortisol level, urinary 17-hydroxy-corticosteroid excretion and ratings of affect in 5 normal subjects and in 11 anxious patients (Persky *et al.*, 1959). The normals had significantly lower levels with respect to all these variables but responded more to the perceptual distortion stress.

Psychoneurotic patients were over-responsive to ACTH injections as evidenced by a high excretion rate of 17-hydroxy-corticosteroids (Sloan, Saffran and Cleghorn, 1958). This has been confirmed (Persky, 1957a). The cortisol turnover rate in the plasma was about 50 per cent higher in a small group of anxious patients than in a group of normal subjects (Persky, 1957b; 1962a), although this was not confirmed by Gibbons (1968). The mean ACTH level in anxious patients was more than twice as high as that in normal subjects (Persky, Maroc *et al.*, 1959).

Claims have been made that whereas urinary 17-hydroxycorti-costeroid excretion is fairly constant in normal subjects, it fluctu-ates according to the intensity of mood in psychoneurotic patients (Suwa *et al.*, 1962). Of 138 patients with various diagnostic labels, the 'patients with anxiety differed markedly . . . from the normal, with respect to plasma hydrocortisone levels' (Lingjaerde, 1964).

In an interesting and detailed study, 10 male and 10 female psychiatric in-patients were examined (Curtis *et al.*, 1966). These patients were 'judged clinically to exhibit intense, overt depression, anxiety, fear, agitation, anger, excitement, elation, or any combination of these, sustained virtually all day, every day, and who did not appear to be improving at the time of study'. They were compared with 10 male and 10 female patients with low affect levels and a group of affectively stable normal subjects. The Taylor Manifest Anxiety Scale and the Cattell Anxiety Scales were administered, plasma cortisol levels were estimated at 8.00 a.m., 11.45 a.m., 4.00 p.m. and 9.30 p.m., and 3 consecutive 8-hour urines were analysed for corticosteroid content. Significant psychometric differences were found as expected between the groups. Plasma cortisol was raised above normal levels in both the high- and the low-affect patient groups; these differences were especially pronounced in the morning. Males, especially in the high-affect group, had higher rates of corticosteroid excretion, especially in the morning. It was argued by the authors that a complex system of cortisol production and excretion is in operation and that maleness and high affect are associated with an increased disposal of cortisol. It was further suggested that plasma cortisol levels reach an asymptotic level at about 20 µg per 100 ml because at this point the transport proteins in the blood (mainly transcortin, a high-affinity cortisol-binding globulin) become saturated and any excess cortisol is rapidly metabolised, the metabolic products appearing in the urine.

It would appear that raised cortisol levels in patients with anxiety states are not specific to anxiety, *per se*. One can echo Mason's conclusion (1959):

> The pituitary-adrenal cortical system is remarkably sensitive to psychological influences in both man and monkey, and that ACTH release occurs, not in association with a specific emotional state, but rather with a wide variety of emotional disturbances which may have the relatively undifferentiated element of distress or arousal.

Certainly, the complexities of hormonal control and interaction in the pituitary-adrenocortical axis have not been fully realised by some workers in the psychiatric context. Modern assay methods have improved the techniques available in this area and further detailed evaluation of patients with anxiety states would be profitable.

*Adrenal medullary function in normals*

That adrenaline is released in states of effort and emotional arousal is now so well known as to be part of the advertising copy-writer's stock-in-trade—'this film will set the adrenaline coursing through your veins!'. Elmadjian and his colleagues, in an extensive series of studies, examined the urinary output of adrenaline and noradrenaline in various situations. They established that the day-time excretion of adrenaline was five to ten times the sleeping level whereas the excretion of noradrenaline merely doubled on waking (Elmadjian, Hope and Lamson, 1957). In professional hockey players, noradrenaline excretion rose during play in active players, whereas in reserves watching the game, adrenaline in-creased. Both hormones rose in the goal tender, neither in the coach. In boxers, adrenaline excretion levels were elevated before the bout. Of 5 basketball players, three showed very marked rises in adrenaline (Elmadjian, 1959).

Aircraft flight was studied by von Euler and his collaborators (von Euler and Lundberg, 1954). Four-hour urine samples were collected between 7 a.m. and 11 a.m. from military personnel during which time a 1–2 hour flight took place. Adrenaline ex-cretion increased with little change in noradrenaline excretion in the passengers, whereas the pilots showed an increase in the excretion of both hormones during flight.

Paratroop training has been used as a useful real-life stress situation and has the advantage that the training proceeds in easily discernible steps. Thus, during training in jumping from a tower, adrenaline and noradrenaline excretion both rose to twice those found during routine ground duties. During the period of the first jump from an aeroplane, adrenaline showed no further in-crease and noradrenaline excretion actually returned to ground duties levels. By the sixth jump, the noradrenaline had risen again to the tower training level and by the eighth jump, at night, levels appeared to have stabilised. Trained officers showed no difference in adrenaline or noradrenaline levels from the paratroop trainees during any stage. There were no consistent relationships between personality traits (as rated by each subject's peers) and catecholamine excretion (Bloom, Euler and Frankenhaeuser, 1963).

In one of Levi's studies (1967, 1972), 31 Swedish army officers and corporals undertook a 72-hour vigil during which time they performed on a simulated electronic firing range under conditions of both adequate and poor illumination and also with loud battle noises being relayed to them. Increases in catecholamine excretion were found, especially with respect to adrenaline.

Simulated weightlessness has been extensively studied in view of its relevance to the space programme. Adrenaline excretion is generally related to the intensity of the subjective emotional reactions to the stress (Goodall, McCally and Graveline, 1964). Noradrenaline excretion appears to reflect more closely the physical factors such as the cardiovascular, haemodynamic changes associated with the centrifuge used to simulate weightlessness.

Subjects who refused to continue towards the end of a scheduled week of sensory deprivation showed a significant increase in adrenaline excretion but not in noradrenaline (Zubek and Schutte, 1966). Subjects who dropped out early in the week showed no such rise.

Motion pictures have provided the stimulation situation in several experiments. In one such study (von Euler et al., 1959), 10 male medical students were shown films of fights, tortures, etc. Adrenaline excretion rose very significantly by 70 per cent and noradrenaline by 35 per cent ($p < 0.05$) over control, resting levels.

A detailed study by Levi (1965, 1972) utilised 20 healthy female office clerks who were shown four different films on four consecutive evenings. Viewing bland natural scenery films was associated with a significant increase in the rating of 'boredom', no other ratings of emotional reactions being significantly affected. Significant decreases in catecholamine excretion were found as compared with control periods. The film on the second night was Stanley Kubrick's Paths of Glory which deals with the arbitrary and unjust court-martialling and execution of three members of a French infantry regiment during the 1914–18 War. 'Fright', 'aggression' and 'despondency' ratings all increased significantly during this film; adrenaline but not noradrenaline excretion also increased significantly. The farcical comedy Charley's Aunt, shown on the third evening, was accompanied by an increase in 'amusement' and 'laughter' and by similar adrenaline increases as on the previous night. Finally, a typical horror film, The Mark of Satan, increased 'fright' and 'despondency', and rises in the excretion of both hormones occurred.

In a similar study, Levi (1972) showed a $1\frac{1}{2}$-hour film consisting of four short, silent films with a sexual content to 53 female and

50 male students, all with a medical background. Adrenaline and noradrenaline excretion increased significantly in both groups during the film period as compared with control levels before and after the film. Significant increases in sexual arousal were rated by both sexes, especially in the males. This was paralleled by greater increases in catecholamine excretion in the males.

Another stimulus found to produce increased adrenaline excretion was a series of electric shocks of increasing intensity (Frankenhaeuser, Fröberg and Mellis, 1965). This research group in Stockholm also investigated catecholamine excretion in 110 college students carrying out coding and copying tasks requiring sustained concentration (Frankenhaeuser and Patkai, 1964). The amount of noradrenaline excreted correlated positively with the improvement in performance as the task continued ($r = +0.4$; $p < 0.001$).

In another of this series of experiments, Levi (1963) used as a stressful task the sorting of steel ball-bearings of four very similar sizes in the presence of a loud noise and variations in the intensity of a bright light. Soldiers were used as experimental subjects, 20 rated as tolerant of stress, 20 rated as having low tolerance to stress. Adrenaline and noradrenaline excretion both rose during the task period, adrenaline especially so. There was no overall difference between the groups.

An extension of this type of task to an everyday industrial situation was carried out (Levi, 1964, 1972). Twelve young, healthy, female invoicing clerks undertook their normal work under two conditions of pay, salaried and piece-work. On the salaried days, 155 invoices per hour per clerk were processed; on piece-work days, the figure was 331 and the error rate remained low. Subjective reports of discomfort increased on piece-work days. Excretion of adrenaline and noradrenaline were 3·5 ng per minute and 18·5 ng per minute on salaried days, 7·7 and 23·5 on piece-work days. It is not known whether the doubled output could have been maintained for long.

A mental task under harassment constituted the stressful task for 110 male students who also rated each other for several personality traits. Adrenaline but not noradrenaline excretion rose during the stress. The personality variables were factor-analysed and it seemed possible that subjects with depressive tendencies responded to the task with a relatively smaller adrenaline output than did their more cheerful colleagues (Frankenhaeuser and Patkai, 1965). As a longer-term stimulus, it has been reported that the admission to hospital for research purposes of normal young adults is attended by a rise in urinary catecholamines on the initial day (Tolson *et al.*, 1965).

Inevitably, examinations have been used as real-life stressful situations. For example, urinary adrenaline levels increased in every member of a group of twenty students taking an important examination. Urinary noradrenaline changes were less consistent. Some relationship was detected between self-rating of affect and adrenaline increases (Bogdonoff *et al.*, 1960).

Socio-economic background has been implicated as correlating with catecholamine excretion. Three consecutive 24-hour urine samples were collected from 27 volunteer recruits into the USA army. Individuals with a low socio-economic background had a higher noradrenaline/adrenaline ratio than subjects from upper socio-economic grades. It was hypothesised that these physiological differences reflected class differences in the socialisation of children with respect to aggressiveness (Fine and Sweeney, 1967).

Indirect measures of catecholamine release such as blood pressure, pulse rate, plasma free fatty acids, cholesterol and triglycerides were estimated in normal subjects after a series of stressor stimuli such as an electric shock (Gittleman *et al.*, 1968). The rise in free fatty acid levels occurred 15 to 30 minutes after the stimulus.

Several studies have approached the problem of the relationship between catecholamines and emotions by examining the effects of these compounds given by injection (Breggin, 1964). For example, Basowitz and his colleagues (1956) interviewed 12 normal subjects (hospital interns) to ascertain any past history of stress and to note any specific reactions to it such as palpitations, apprehensiveness, tremor and perspiration. Using double-blind procedures and a cross-over design, adrenaline was infused intravenously in a dosage of 5 µg per kg body weight per hour and its effects compared with those of saline. Measurements included physiological ones such as blood pressure and pulse rate, psychological ones including hand steadiness and digit span, physical persistence such as keeping a leg raised and subjective reports. Adrenaline produced a distinct rise in pulse pressure, averaging 20 mm of mercury, and a tachycardia, averaging 13 beats per minute. Hand steadiness and physical persistence were impaired. The commonest subjective experience was palpitations. Symptoms were reported on the saline occasions as well as on the adrenaline occasions, but only half as frequently; however, all but one of the symptoms reported on the saline occasion occurred when saline had been the first treatment given. Adrenaline produced symptoms which generally resembled those elicited at the initial interview as occurring in the subjects in response to stress. In emotionally labile subjects, excess symptoms but few cardiovascular changes were noted; in rigid personalities, no symptoms but marked physiological changes occurred.

In a similar experiment utilising medical students, an infusion of adrenaline produced a tachycardia, rise in systolic blood pressure and a drop in diastolic blood pressure. No systematic relation between the intensities of the physiological and the subjective reactions was seen. Subjective estimates of effects declined steadily as each infusion proceeded (Frankenhaeuser and Järpe, 1963). When a mixture of adrenaline and noradrenaline was infused (0·28 mg of each over 36–41 minutes), the systolic blood pressure rose and the diastolic fell, but no consistent pulse rate changes were found (Frankenhaeuser and Järpe, 1962). This suggests that the adrenaline effects predominated. Among the 11 subjects, palpitations, tremor and a general feeling of discomfort were reported by most subjects; restlessness, apprehensiveness, tenseness and dyspnoea in about one half.

It has been stated that males are more aware of the body sensations following intra-muscular injections of adrenaline than are females (Fast and Fisher, 1971).

The widely cited experiments of Schachter (1966) elucidate the interactions between cognitive factors and physiological arousal. He injected small doses of adrenaline, some subjects knowing what effects to expect, others remaining in ignorance. The subjects were then placed with a stooge who acted either in a euphoric manner or angrily. Observation of the subject and his self-report both indicated that subjects ignorant of the effects of their injection showed and felt more emotional experience (euphoria or anger) than informed subjects. In a second experiment subjects given either adrenaline, a placebo or chlorpromazine watched a comedy film. The adrenaline subjects showed more amusement than those given the sympathetic blocking agent chlorpromazine (Schachter and Wheeler, 1962). Thus, awareness of physiological arousal seems to be the substrate on which cognitive clues induce a specific emotion. Although other interpretations exist, a reasonable hypothesis is that an emotion is induced by the interaction of at least two states, high physiological arousal and appropriate sensory input.

*Adrenomedullary studies in patients* (Levi, 1969)

Surprisingly, there have been very few studies of urinary excretion or plasma levels of catecholamines in patients with anxiety states or even in patients in whom anxiety was present but not the prime symptom. In 11 of the latter type of patient, adrenaline excretion increased following a psychiatric interview while noradrenaline was unchanged (Elmadjian, Hope and Lamson, 1957). Regan and Reilly (1958) classified 60 in-patients in four different ways: (1) according to clinical diagnosis; (2) according to whether blame was externalised or internalised; (3) according to whether the patient was aware of any inner conflict; and (4) by rating the intensity of emotions such as anxiety, tension, resentment and depression. Adrenaline and noradrenaline levels in the plasma were not different from normal. There was some tendency, although not statistically significant, for catecholamine levels to be higher in those patients with high emotional ratings, and this trend was especially apparent in paranoid patients.

In a group of 13 hospitalised patients with anxiety and depression, plasma catecholamine levels correlated with anxiety ratings but not with ratings of depressive affect (Wyatt *et al.*, 1971).

Using another index of catecholamine production (normetadrenaline and metadrenaline excretion in the urine), Nelson, Masuda and Holmes (1966) reported an increase during phases of agitation in disturbed patients in a locked ward.

Regarding the injection of adrenaline, an early study is worthy of mention (Wearn and Sturgis, 1919). Adrenaline, 5 mg intramuscular, produced symptoms characteristic of their acute anxiety reactions in army recruits suffering from the 'irritable heart' syndrome—dizziness, fatigue and palpitations. Concomitant physiological changes such as tachycardia were also noted. Control subjects reported no symptoms following the injection and their physiological reactions were less pronounced.

In general, normal subjects tend to report not anxiety but 'feeling as if I were anxious'. In patients, however, the symptoms closely resemble those of spontaneous morbid anxiety. Breggin (1964) regards two factors as crucial in the interpretation of such data:

firstly, the strength of the subject's previously learned association between psychological feelings of acute anxiety and sympathomimetic symptoms such as palpitations; secondly, the degree of current anxiety engendered by the experimental setting. He suggested that the sympathomimetic symptoms produced by the adrenaline further reinforced the subject's anxiety induced by the experimental situation.

An indirect measure of catecholamine release is the plasma-free fatty acid level. A significant correlation ($r = 0.49$; $p < 0.02$) was found between free fatty acid levels and anxiety content of speech in a small group of patients. There was no significant correlation with hostility scores (Gottschalk et al., 1965).

## Thyroid function in normals

Several studies have suggested that there is a slight but nonetheless significant increase in thyroid function in response to physical stress, such as undergoing a major operation. However, such studies are complicated by the tissue damage which occurs and some patients show very little response (Gibson, 1962). Even venepuncture raises the metabolic rate more than 10 per cent (Coppen and Mezey, 1960b).

The evidence with respect to emotional stresses is even more equivocal. Using measures of protein-bound iodine (PBI) before and after a stressful laboratory situation, Hetzel and his colleagues (1956) found an increase in 5 out of 14 'euthyroid' patients, but a fall in one and very little alteration in the remainder. In a study involving eleven junior medical students tested on a control day and on a day when they took oral examinations, PBI levels were estimated in samples of blood taken at 7 a.m., 1 p.m. and 5 p.m. (Tingley, Morris and Hill, 1958). On the stressful day, levels were the same as on the control day for the first two samples but a significant increase was found for the 5 p.m. samples.

Various subjects were studied by Volpé, Vale and Johnston (1960): 11 medical students preparing for annual examinations, 11 candidates for the Royal College of Physicians' examinations, 7 professional footballers, 8 patients prior to and following major operations and 9 patients after heart attacks. The PBI fluctuations were all within the normal range and the authors conclude:

Within the limits of this study, however, it is obvious that the concentration of serum protein-bound iodine in the various groups of patients and healthy persons was not significantly affected by stress and strains of examinations, athletic contests, major surgical procedures or myocardial infarcts.

Levi (1967, 1972) exposed a total of 31 Swedish army officers and corporals to a vigil lasting 75 hours, starting with a 3-hour control period and continuing throughout with a task which involved shooting on a specially designed rifle range with electronic rifles producing light beams at small targets (tanks) containing photodiodes. The tanks moved across the field of vision at a randomly varying speed, disappeared out of sight and reappeared after a random interval. Two conditions of illumination were used, one bright and adequate, the other dim. Loud battle-noises were relayed over a loudspeaker. The mean level of PBI before the ordeal was 6·1 µg per 100 ml of plasma and rose to 7·9 µg per 100 ml by the end of the study ($p < 0.001$).

A variety of psychological, physiological and endocrine measures were carried out on 14 subjects exposed to two situations, one of perceptual isolation (sensory deprivation) and a control one of social isolation with adequate sensory input (Zuckerman et al., 1966). The mean PBI level was 6·45 µg per 100 ml in the perceptual isolation situation as compared with 6·38 in the control situation; the thyroxine levels were 4·53 and 4·71 µg of iodine per 100 ml. Neither of these differences is significant. However, the mean thyroid stimulating hormone level was 27·5 mU per 100 ml of plasma in the perceptual isolation situation and 22·7 mU per 100 ml in the control situation, a difference significant at the 0·01 level of probability.

Continuous counting of radioactive iodine taken up into the thyroid gland was carried out in subjects shown two films—a bland travelogue and Wages of Fear (Alexander et al., 1961). Decreases in count were noted during the melodramatic incidents in the latter film and were interpreted as indicating 'discharge of labeled hormone into the circulation'.

## Thyroid function in patients

Heightened thyroid function, as in thyrotoxicosis, presents many of the features of anxiety states such as sweating, tachycardia and agitation. The peripheral circulation, however, is hyperdynamic, patients having hot, moist palms as compared with the cold, clammy handshake of the patient with an anxiety state. In thyrotoxicosis, the sleeping pulse rate generally remains high whereas it drops to normal levels in anxious patients. Finally, the biochemical indices are abnormal in thyrotoxicosis. Nevertheless, the two conditions commonly co-exist and the relationship between them is complex.

There is a dearth of studies on thyroid function in anxious patients. Using the radioactive iodine uptake method, it was found that 83 per cent of anxious male patients had a tendency towards reduced thyroid function; conversely, 79 per cent of the anxious females had a tendency towards heightened thyroid function (Reiss *et al.*, 1951). Whether this is a chance finding is not known and the implications of this curious disparity have not been followed up. In another study, no relationship was found between thyroid function and degree of anxiety in a group of 71 patients, nor did a stressful interview alter thyroid function in any discernible way (Dongier *et al.*, 1956).

## Lactate studies

A number of research workers have found that patients with anxiety states show a less efficient exercise response than normal controls (McFarland and Huddleson, 1936; Jones and Mellersh, 1946; Holmgren and Ström, 1959). In response to a standard exercise task, the patients show a greater rise in heart rate and in blood lactate level, and following the exercise they take up oxygen more than normals, suggesting the repayment of a larger oxygen debt (see also p. 105).

From this, Pitts and McClure (1967) developed the idea that perhaps the lactate ion itself could produce anxiety attacks in susceptible persons. To test this hypothesis they carried out a double-blind controlled experiment in which the following were infused in random order intravenously into a group of 14 patients with anxiety neurosis and into a group of 10 normal controls: 500 millimols sodium (DL) lactate, 500 millimols sodium (DL) lactate with 20 millimols calcium chloride and 555 millimols glucose in 167 millimols sodium chloride. These solutions, of similar osmolarities, were given as 20 ml per kg body weight during a 20-minute period to each subject. Symptoms were rated.

The infusion of sodium lactate produced symptoms which 'were markedly similar or identical' to those experienced in their 'worst attacks' by the anxious patients. Such reports were fewer from normal subjects. The symptoms were much less frequent when the lactate plus calcium chloride was infused, and the glucose in saline infusion produced almost no symptoms in either patients or controls.

The authors suggested that anxiety symptoms were related to hypocalcaemia produced by lactate infusion and that

> . . . anxiety symptoms could occur in the normal person under stress as a consequence of marked increase in lactate production in response to increased epinephrine release; the patient with anxiety neurosis would be someone especially subject to this mechanism because of chronic overproduction of epinephrine, overactivity of the central nervous system, a defect in aerobic or anaerobic metabolism resulting in excess lactate production, a defect in calcium metabolism or some combination of these.

These suggestions were trenchantly criticised by Grosz and Farmer (1969) who pointed out how tenuous the link was between anxiety symptoms and hypocalcaemia. Anxiety can occur without high blood lactate levels and high blood lactate levels without anxiety. An infusion of sodium lactate produces a metabolic *alkalosis* whereas the endogenously produced lactate ion shifts the acid–base balance of the body towards metabolic *acidosis*. Sodium bicarbonate levels rise with sodium lactate infusion and the compensatory respiratory acidosis (adaptive hypoventilation) could be accompanied by feelings of discomfort. Grosz and Farmer further point out that the rise in lactate produced by the infusion would cause only a trivial change in the ionised calcium level in the blood. They concluded that the hypothesis 'as a generalised explanation for anxiety neurosis seems to be incompatible or irreconcilable with many and diverse physiological and biochemical findings and considerations'.

In a further study, Grosz and Farmer (1972) repeated Pitts and McClure's experiment but included a control infusion of sodium bicarbonate. They found little difference in the symptoms produced by the bicarbonate and the lactate infusions; nor was the onset of symptoms with either infusion associated with a rise in blood lactate levels. The authors point out that the association of lactate production and anxiety is not upheld by either their evidence or other clinical evidence, e.g. 'anxiety neurosis is not typically present in patients with lactic acidaemia, that is, with very marked and chronic blood lactate elevations'.

Although it would appear that the lactate ion is not the important factor, the infusion of alkalinising solutions does seem to induce feelings of anxiety, especially in patients with anxiety states. The original findings of Pitts and McClure have been replicated several times, with EEG changes (Fink, Taylor and Volavka, 1969) and alterations in forearm blood flow (Kelly, Mitchell-Heggs and Sherman, 1971), confirming objectively the reports of subjects of infusion-induced arousal states. However, the mechanism of induction of symptoms may be related to adrenaline release. In the accounts of lactate-induced symptoms, one is struck by the similarity of the symptoms produced to those following the infusion of adrenaline (Hawkins et al., 1960) (see p. 121). There is often a marked 'as if' quality to the emotion engendered. It is known from animal studies that lactic acid causes a marked release of adrenaline and noradrenaline from the adrenal medulla (Cannon, Linton and Linton, 1924; Woods et al., 1956). Thus, the lactic acid infusions might release catecholamines and indirectly produce peripheral changes and symptoms. In anxious patients, there will have been a learned association of such symptoms with anxiety and these subjects might be more stressed by the non-specific aspects of the experimental situation anyway. The relationship between anxiety, lactate, glucose and adrenaline release would appear to be a fruitful area of research (Stanaway and Hullin, 1973).

## General considerations

From this review of the many psychophysiological studies of anxiety, certain common threads can be discerned. Differentiation between normal subjects and patients with anxiety states at rest is best seen with cardiovascular and sweat gland measures. Electromyographic and EEG measures are less consistent in this respect.

With stimulation of some kind, more clear demarcation of the groups is obtained but directly conflicting results arise. With some measures, patients are significantly less responsive than calm subjects; with other measures, patients are more reactive than normal subjects. The measures in which patients show less reactivity tend to be those in which the resting levels are higher in the patients. It is thus possible that reactivity is lowered because

*

the patients are already responding to the experimental situation in general. With many of these measures, a 'ceiling' effect occurs because the measure cannot increase indefinitely with further stimulation, e.g. forearm blood flow will not increase to levels at which the maintenance of blood pressure is jeopardised. Other measures, the electromyogram being a good example, are not dissimilar in patients and controls under resting conditions and are capable of pronounced increases with stimulation, the 'ceiling' effect being less important. With these measures, reactivity is greater in the patients. However, it is not possible to make firm predictions regarding the reactivity of patients since this will depend on the particular measure, the type of 'rest' period and stimulation, the test-sophistication of the subject, and so on. Consequently, it is a gross oversimplification to make general assertions such as that neurotic patients are over-reactive.

There is one aspect of the psychophysiology of anxious patients which has yielded consistent and important results. Patients with anxiety states adjust much more slowly than normals to the contingencies of the experimental situation as shown in two different but related ways. First, patients are slow to adapt to a changing stimulation situation. For example, it has been shown that EMG levels remained high in patients during a series of stimulation procedures whereas it diminished in controls (Martin, 1956). Similarly, anxious patients after exposure to a stimulation procedure are slower to return to pre-stimulation levels as monitored by the blood pressure, electromyograph, forearm blood flow, skin conductance and pupil size. Thus, if one wants to maximise differences between anxious and calm subjects, a stimulation procedure should be applied but particular attention be paid to the immediate post-stimulation period.

Secondly, if subjects are exposed to a repetitive series of identical stimuli, normals will usually show a marked decrement in responses whereas anxious patients tend to maintain their responses, i.e. they show impaired habituation. This is another aspect of the generally maladaptive response systems which anxious subjects have and the further implications of this are explored in the final chapter.

# Depression 5

## Introduction

The psychophysiology of depression has tended to concentrate on endocrine measures, especially cortisol, and among the autonomic measures salivation has been most studied. In a topic as little explored as this, such concentration is inevitable. As will be seen in this review, the data-gathering has been much more empirical than with schizophrenia where many heuristic hypotheses have been put forward. Nor has there been a concise unifying concept such as that of over-arousal in anxiety states. Much of the problem lies in the protean nature of depressive illness, its great clinical variety, its ubiquity in psychiatry, the lack of consensus regarding its sub-classification and its close links with other affective disorders such as anxiety (Beck, 1967; Grinker et al., 1961). Nevertheless, the bulk of clinical evidence favours the distinction between anxiety and depression (Gurney et al., 1972; Kerr et al., 1972; Mendels, Weinstein and Cochrane, 1972; Roth et al., 1972; Schapira et al., 1972). The psychophysiological literature favours such a distinction but only if particular care with sub-grouping of patients is exercised.

A classical association is that between mania and depression, the archetypal patient being the one who alternates from one state to the other (Roth, 1960a). Earlier ideas that the two affective conditions lay either side of normal with respect to a wide variety of variables as well as with mood have now been generally discounted. The two conditions are closely related and may even co-exist as the mixed affective state. Surprisingly, little work has been done on manics although they are by no means rare. The recent interest in lithium therapy has revived interest in this condition, but few psychophysiological studies have been published.

## Autonomic measures

*Sweat gland activity*

Studies of skin conductance levels, responses and spontaneous activity in depressed patients have been few and often carried out on relatively small numbers of patients or on heterogeneous groups. Richter (1928) recorded the skin resistance of a group of mentally ill patients and found that those who felt 'definitely depressed' had high resistance levels (low sweat gland activity). Sweating was measured more directly using a plastic paint technique by Bagg and Crookes (1966). Eighteen female patients, all depressed and mostly with 'endogenous' features, were studied before a course of ECT and after recovery. The mean sweat gland count rose from 21·9 per 9 mm² to 36·9 on recovery ($p < 0.01$).

Studies on GSR reactivity have not yielded consistent results. In one, twenty depressed patients and twenty normal controls were rated on a depressive scale derived from the MMPI. Subjects with higher depressive scores showed a reduction in GSR response to auditory stimuli (Greenfield *et al.*, 1963). Similarly, although many physiological measures were reported as being more responsive in depressives, examination of the results presented suggest that skin conductance was an exception (Goldstein, 1965). Gilberstadt and Maley (1965) studied seventy-three male patients admitted to the psychiatric wards of a general hospital and subjected them to skin conductance recordings at rest, during and after a noise session. Conductance was highest in those categorised as anxious, less high in patients with anxiety and depression and below normal in the depressed patients. GSR amplitude was reduced in the last group and the response in basal level to the noise stress was also small.

Lader and Wing (1969) made physiological and clinical observations on 35 patients with the diagnosis of primary depression of moderate or severe degree. Seventeen patients were predominantly agitated clinically, 13 were mainly retarded and 5 showed neither feature. The depressed patients were compared with normal subjects matched for age and sex with respect to skin conductance levels, reactivity and habituation to a series of repeated auditory stimuli. Clear-cut differences were found between the two major groups of depressed patients; agitated patients failed to show any habituation of the GSR while all but one of the retarded patients showed so little reactivity that habituation rates could not be estimated. In these measures, the normal values lay between those for the two major groups of depressives. The size of the first GSR was diminished in all the depressives as compared with normal values. Discrimination between the agitated and retarded patients was complete with respect to habituation rate and spontaneous fluctuations.

In a further study (Noble and Lader, 1971a), skin conductance data were obtained on 34 depressed in-patients prior to a course of ECT. Thirty-one subjects were re-tested when clinically improved two weeks subsequent to the ECT. Conductance levels did not change following ECT. Prior to ECT, low skin conductance correlated significantly with severity of depression and high scores on ratings for depressed mood, retardation, gastro-intestinal somatic symptoms and weight loss. Spontaneous fluctuations were reduced in the more depressed and retarded patients.

To further evaluate the relationship between retardation and physiological measures, the patients were divided on the basis of their scores on the appropriate sub-scales of the Hamilton Scale into 'retarded' and 'agitated' patients, 10 in each group, with 14 being excluded as neither feature predominated . The agitated patients had significantly more fluctuations than the retarded patients. The less clear results in this study as compared with that of Lader and Wing (1969) probably reflects the fact that the earlier study was restricted to markedly depressed patients while the depressed patients in the later study formed a consecutive series about to be given ECT, not necessarily an indication of severity.

## Salivation

Salivary investigations of depression started with the work of Strongin and Hinsie (1938b) who used a parotid duct suction cup and found that depressed patients secrete less saliva than normal subjects and less than their own levels of salivation when they are in a manic phase. In a further study, they differentiated accurately between manic-depressive depressed patients and other depressed patients, using a salivary flow rate of $0.01$ ml per 5 minutes as the discriminator (Strongin and Hinsie, 1939). This was confirmed by Eysenck and Yap (1944) who noted that salivation was less in depressed patients than in non-depressed, but psychiatrically ill, control subjects. Using the simpler dental roll method, Peck (1959) also found a lowered rate of salivary secretion in depressed patients, although the reduction in salivation was not related to the severity of the depression. These findings were soon confirmed by Busfield and Wechsler (1961) who studied forty-five depressed patients and forty-two non-depressed normal control subjects; again, the diminution in salivation was unrelated to the severity of the depression. They also found that salivary secretion in non-depressed in-patients was less than that of non-hospitalised control patients, suggesting that some of the reduction in salivary flow ascribed to depression might be due to hospitalisation and associated changes in diet and activity. In a further study (Busfield, Wechsler and Barnum, 1961), a hundred severely depressed patients were examined and the 'endogenous' and 'involutional' depressed patients had lower secretion rates than females but there was no relationship between the severity of depression within any diagnostic group and salivation rate. An interesting finding was that the subjective complaint of dry mouth was not correlated with the diminution in salivation.

Several other studies have shown that depressed patients secrete less saliva than normals (Altschule, 1964; Davies and Gurland, 1961; Gottlieb and Paulson, 1961). If depression diminishes salivary flow, then salivation of depressed patients should increase with clinical improvement; however, the results of longitudinal studies have been inconsistent. In some, salivation of depressed patients was unchanged in spite of clinical improvement (Gottlieb and Paulson, 1961; Hemsi, Whitehead and Post, 1968). Conversely, Palmai and his co-workers reported an increase in the salivation of depressed patients to normal levels before discharge from hospital (Davies and Palmai, 1964; Palmai and Blackwell, 1965; Palmai et al., 1967). In the Palmai and Blackwell (1965) study, an interesting finding concerned the reversal of salivary diurnal rhythm: in normal subjects salivation rate was highest in the morning; in depressed patients it was highest in the evening. As the depressed patients recovered clinically the diurnal pattern of their salivation returned to normal. Early morning wakening and diurnal mood variation were the clinical features particularly associated with the abnormal salivary flow diurnal pattern (Palmai and Blackwell, 1965; Palmai et al., 1967).

Loew (1965) found that patients categorised as 'agitiert' (agitated) or 'angstlich aggressiv-depressiv' (anxious depressive-aggressive) had lower salivary secretion than those who were 'gehemmt apathisch-depressiv' (inhibited apathetic-depressive), who in turn secreted less saliva than control subjects.

In a preliminary report, Brown (1970) reported that salivary inhibition was most pronounced in depressive patients with psychomotor retardation as compared with patients in which depression was a secondary symptom. However, when salivation was stimulated by the injection of a weak acid solution into the mouth, the increased quantities of reflex salivation were not significantly different from normals under the same conditions.

Thus, it is well established that depressed in-patients secrete less saliva than normal controls, but other findings regarding change with recovery are equivocal. The inhibition of resting flows in the depressive is a functional disturbance which can be overcome by stimulation.

In the study outlined earlier, of physiological measures in depressed patients about to undergo ECT, salivation was also measured (Noble and Lader, 1971b). Correlations were computed between the Hamilton Depression Scale items and salivary secretion. Significant correlations were found between salivation and retardation, gastro-intestinal somatic symptoms and weight loss. The relationship between salivary secretion and retardation was studied further using Hamilton Scale Retardation Item Scores to identify the ten least and the ten most retarded patients. The retarded group had a significantly lower salivary secretion rate than did the non-retarded group. All the patients received electroconvulsive therapy: the salivary secretion of the retarded group increased significantly after the course of treatment, whereas that of the non-retarded group decreased significantly. This difference in change in salivary flow rates with treatment might explain the discrepancies in the literature. In any group of depressives the mean change with treatment would depend on the composition: a group of predominantly retarded depressives would show an increase in salivary flow after clinical improvement (Peck, 1966), whereas a group of non-retarded patients would show little change or a mean diminution.

*Cardiovascular measures*

There have been few studies of pulse rate in depressives. Lader and Wing (1969) reported an increase in pulse rate over normal values in agitated but not retarded patients. Similar results were described by Kelly and Walter (1969). Increased pulse rates were found in a mixed group of patients (mainly depressives and anxiety states)

133

about to undergo leucotomy; the rate was lower after the operation, especially in those patients who showed clinical improvement (Kelly, Walter and Sargant, 1966).

Kelly and Walter (1969) also reported the blood flow rates of a large number of patients. Non-agitated depressives had a mean blood flow of 2·1 (ml per 100 ml of arm volume per minute), similar to that of normal subjects (2·2) but lower than that of both agitated depressives (3·2) and patients with anxiety states (4·4). However, the non-agitated depressives had an anxiety level (self-rating 3·8) close to that of the anxiety state group (4·1), although the high anxiety rating of the non-agitated depressives was not associated with an elevated blood flow. The agitated depressives had higher anxiety levels (5·0) and significantly lower blood flows than the anxiety state groups. Thus the blood flow levels of both the agitated and non-agitated depressives were substantially lower than their high anxiety levels would predict. Anxiety states are thus associated with an increase in forearm blood flow, but the relationship between depression and forearm blood flow is far less clear. It may well be that depressive illness, particularly in conjunction with retardation, is associated with a diminution in muscle blood flow below normal values.

Noble and Lader (1971c) also recorded forearm blood flow in their depressed patients before and after ECT, using venous occlusion plethysmography. The blood flow rate rose significantly after ECT. For pre-ECT readings, high scores for retardation correlated significantly with low blood flow rates.

Kielholz and Beck (1962) reported that the skin temperature of patients with 'exhaustion depression' was slow to return to normal after a cool bath.

Systolic blood pressure, both at rest and during a noise stress, was raised in depressed patients as compared with normals (Goldstein, 1965).

## Somatic measures

### Respiration

Psychoneurotic but not depressed patients showed an abnormal respiratory response to a painful stimulus (Finesinger and Mazick, 1940a, 1940b).

*Electromyogram*

Studies of EMG levels in depression are not consistent but there is some evidence that depressive illness, especially if severe, is associated with increased levels of muscle activity.

Whatmore and Ellis (1959) claimed that the EMG levels in depressed patients were markedly raised, particularly in conjunction with retardation. Subsequently, they studied the EMG in severe recurrent depressive illness (1962). EMG levels were elevated both during the depressive episodes and prior to relapse, but dropped temporarily in response to treatment.

Goldstein (1965) found raised EMG levels in depressed out-patients when compared with normal controls. These patients also showed a greater EMG response to noise. Similarly, Martin and Davies (1965) found higher frontalis EMG levels in depressed patients than controls. The forearm EMG levels were only raised in the more severely ill depressed patients.

Rimón, Stenbäck and Huhmar (1966) attempted to correlate EMG levels with the severity of depression. Mildly depressed subjects had higher masseter EMGs and severely depressed males had raised forehead and forearm EMG levels. An attempt to correlate EMG levels in depressed and non-depressed patients with assessments of the subjects' personality and experimental situation failed to yield clear or repeatable results (Goldstein *et al.*, 1964; Heath, Oken and Shipman, 1967). Also, Lader and Wing (1969) found no difference between the forearm extensor EMG activity of 35 depressed patients and 35 normal controls. In Noble and Lader's study (1971d), EMG levels subsequent to ECT were lower than those before ECT, and EMG reactivity to stress increased after ECT. Prior to ECT, high EMG levels correlated with severity of depression. High basal EMG levels and diminished reactivity also correlated with high anxiety scores, gastro-intestinal somatic symptoms, loss of libido and weight loss. It was suggested that depressive illness, especially with symptomatology of a biological type, is associated with raised forearm extensor EMG activity.

*Vascular responses to methacholine*

A prolonged and excessive drop in blood pressure in depressive patients following the intra-muscular administration of methacholine has been claimed (Funkenstein, 1954; Funkenstein, Greenblatt and Solomon, 1948, 1949, 1951). This excessive response was reported in 90 per cent of involutional and manic depressive patients. It was claimed that the methacholine test distinguished between endogenous depression and other psychiatric categories. The drop in blood pressure was attributed to a postulated excessive secretion of noradrenaline in endogenous depression. Subsequent workers (e.g. Feinberg, 1958; Rose, 1962; Sloane and Lewis, 1956) were generally unable to replicate these findings. Davies and Palmai (1964) measured the blood pressure response of 22 female depressed patients to the injection of methacholine and the data suggested that the more depressed patients showed a more pronounced drop in blood pressure.

Hamilton (1960) noted an association between a marked response to methacholine and age. In several of the studies, the depressed patients were appreciably older than the control subjects which could account for inter-group differences. The evidence is so inconsistent that the Funkenstein Test is little used nowadays.

*Sedation and sleep thresholds*

The sedation threshold is the amount of barbiturate (in mg kg$^{-1}$) needed on slow intravenous injection to produce a characteristic EEG change or slurring of speech (Shagass and Naiman, 1956). Shagass and Jones (1958) reported that the sedation threshold was low in psychotic depression and high in neurotic depression and anxiety. Although some replication of this early work has been forthcoming (Perez-Reyes, 1968; Perez-Reyes and Cochrane, 1967; Perris and Brattemo, 1963), other subsequent workers have found it difficult to obtain a reliable end-point—either of the EEG change or of any behavioural criterion—for either the sedation threshold or the sleep threshold (Boudreau, 1958) and have failed to confirm any clear-cut distinction between psychotic and neurotic depression (Ackner and Pampiglione, 1959; Martin and Davies, 1962; Nymgaard, 1959).

One possible explanation for the finding that more barbiturate is required for sedation sleep in anxious or agitated patients than in calm ones (Shagass and Naiman, 1955; Shagass, Naiman and Mihalik, 1956) lies in peripheral mechanisms and not in differences in central nervous system arousal. High muscle blood flow facilitates the uptake of barbiturate from the circulation in the muscles (Balasubramanian, Mawer and Simons, 1970). Thus, after a standard dose, barbiturate plasma levels are likely to be inversely related to muscle flow. As blood flow is raised in anxious and agitated patients more barbiturate will be extracted from the circulation per unit time and more will need to be injected before the CNS is affected. Thus, it is entirely possible that the sedation and sleep thresholds are little more than indirect measures of the state of the vascular system. Estimations of plasma barbiturate levels during the injection would help to settle this question.

As with the methacholine test, age has been found to be an important factor, the correlation between sedation threshold and age being $-0.49$ ($p < 0.01$) in one study (Fenton, Hill and Scotton, 1968). This is to be expected from the general rule in clinical pharmacology that the elderly are more sensitive to drug effects than younger adults. As psychotically depressed patients tend to be older than neurotic depressions, this is yet another possible explanation for any differences in sedation threshold found between the two groups.

*Electroencephalogram* (Hill, 1963; Shagass, 1966)

The electroencephalogram has been far less intensively studied in depressed patients than in schizophrenics. This reflects in part the relative neglect of the psychophysiology of depression in general and in part the lack of any theoretical suppositions regarding depression and its possible psychophysiological correlates. The EEG has been evaluated in purely empirical terms and in view of the heterogeneous clinical nature of depression it is hardly surprising that no clear results have emerged (Ellingson, 1954; Itil, 1964).

Davis (1941) found little difference in the EEGs of patients in manic as compared with depressive phases. Some patients had EEGs with erratic slow wave disturbances and these patients tended to be those whose behaviour was unpredictable. Another early study (Lemere, 1941) described above-average alpha activity in patients with affective reactions but little else of note. Psychotic depressions have been found to have much high-frequency activity which lessened as the symptoms remitted (Finley, 1944).

The importance of age was stressed from quite early on. Thus, Greenblatt (1944) found 31 per cent of patients with depression and 42 per cent with mania to have EEG records 'abnormal' in some respect; the percentage in normal subjects was 10. However, most of the difference in incidence could be attributed to the different age structures of the groups. In another study, EEG changes indicative of drowsiness were sought and were present in over half of a group of depressed patients. An even higher proportion (70 per cent) of such records were obtained from manic patients and 'insomniacs' (Liberson, 1944).

An extensive study involving 117 manic depressive patients (mean age 55) and 160 normal subjects (mean age 22) was reported by Hurst, Mundy-Castle and Beerstacher (1954). Patients in manic phases had a mean alpha frequency of 10·4 Hz as compared with 9·7 for depressed patients. More of the manic depressive patients had records characterised by low-voltage fast activity than the normals and this difference remained even when the age differences of the two groups were allowed for.

Another large-scale study examined elderly depressives with respect to whether they had had their first attack before the age of 60 (group A; $n = 47$) or after the age of 60 (group B; $n = 49$). An age-comparable group of 82 normal subjects was also studied. The EEGs were divided into three types: (1) normal; (2) borderline abnormal, i.e. excess beta activity, diminished or absent alpha; and (3) definitely abnormal with slow wave activity or paroxysmal activity. The patients in group B had significantly more abnormal records than the patients in group A. However, as the normal subjects also had appreciable numbers of abnormal and borderline records the authors conclude that the abnormalities reflect aging rather than any specific symptom complex or disorder (Maggs and Turton, 1956).

Using a wave analyser, EEG differences were claimed between depressives and schizophrenics, the latter having more slow wave and less fast wave activity. However, these findings were attributable to the age differences between the groups (Fink, Itil and Clyde, 1966). Conversely, increased slow wave activity has been described in manic depressive patients (Assael and Winnik, 1970). A longitudinal study of 8 female patients suffering from endogenous depression indicated that the alpha and beta wavebands were more abundant during depressive episodes than during remission (Volavka, Grof and Mrklas, 1967).

Broad-waveband analyses, both at rest and during a reaction-time task, were carried out on the EEG recordings of 20 severely depressed patients and 20 normal subjects closely matched for age and sex (Julier and Lader, unpublished data). The patients had lower mean amplitude values for the 2·3–4·0 Hz wavebands and considerably higher values for the 7·5–13·5 and 13·5–26·0 Hz wave-bands for the EEG recorded under resting conditions and during the response task. However, one factor which it was found impossible to control for was night sedation, practically all the patients having received a barbiturate or benzodiazepine hypnotic during the previous 24 hours. Single doses of hypnotics have been found to have appreciable electroencephalographic effects the following morning, the 2·3–4·0 Hz waveband showing a diminution and the 13·5–26·0 Hz waveband an increase in activity (Bond and Lader, 1972). Thus, the differences between the depressed patients and the normal subjects with respect to these wavebands could be attributable to differences in drug status. Hypnotics tended to decrease the 7·5–13·5 Hz waveband activity, so the increase in this waveband in depressed patients is most probably a genuine difference from normal.

In view of the hypothesis that schizophrenic psychopathology is associated with dysfunction of the dominant cerebral hemisphere whereas affective symptoms are related to dysfunction of the non-dominant hemisphere (see p. 163 for a fuller account), the results of D'Elia and Perris (1973) are of interest. The mean integrated amplitude of the EEG was found to be lower on the dominant than on the non-dominant side in a group of 18 depressed patients. On recovery, no differences between the two sides were apparent.

## Sleep studies

Disturbance of sleep is one of the commonest complaints of depressed patients. Although early morning wakening is generally regarded as the commonest sleep abnormality, especially in 'endogenous' depressives, broken, disturbed sleep and wakening unrefreshed can be elicited as symptoms even more frequently. The nature of sleep patterns is an obvious field for study in depression.

Hinton (1963) compared 34 depressed patients with 16 recovered patients with respect to the duration of sleep as observed by a specially trained night nurse and bodily motility measured mechanically by a transducer under the bed-springs. Depressed patients slept significantly less than their recovered colleagues (5·5 hours versus 7·2 hours). Sleep periods in the former group diminished throughout the night and motility was increased. No differences in the nurse's observation of sleep patterns nor in patients' self-reports were found between 27 patients diagnosed as reactive depressions and thirteen endogenous depressions (Costello and Selby, 1965). In an early study, the sleep EEG was recorded in six depressed patients who were drug-free and who had difficulty in falling asleep and/or early or frequent wakenings. An abnormally high proportion of sleep was in the lighter stages with more frequent oscillation from one level of sleep to another (Diaz-Guerrero, Gottlieb and Knott, 1946). Contrary findings were reported by Oswald and his colleagues (1962) who compared 6 patients with 'autonomous melancholia' with 6 age- and sex-matched controls, 5 nights of recording being obtained from each subject. Although the patients spent significantly more of the night awake, when they did sleep they spent a significantly larger proportion of the time in *deep* sleep. This was regarded by the authors as a form of compensation for sleep deprivation. The percentage of time spent in paradoxical REM sleep and the frequency of shifts between the various stages of sleep did not differ between the two groups.

In another study, 21 depressed patients and 15 age-comparable control subjects were studied for 3 consecutive nights. The depressives took an average of 31 minutes to fall asleep as compared with 11 minutes for the controls, and total sleep period was shorter — 6 h 28 min as compared with 7 h 11 min. The controls were awake for only 1 per cent of this time, the depressives for 11 per cent. Contrary to Oswald and his colleagues' findings, depressives spent proportionately less of their time asleep in Stage IV—45 per cent versus 20 per cent (Hawkins and Mendels, 1966). The patients' sleep was particularly disturbed during the latter third of the night (Mendels and Hawkins, 1967a; Lowy, Cleghorn and McClure, 1971). On clinical recovery, the sleep of the depressed patients improved considerably but Stage IV sleep was still subnormal and more time than normal was spent awake (Mendels and Hawkins, 1967b). Much individual variation among patients was noted (Mendels and Hawkins, 1971).

In a small-scale study, noteworthy for the care with which it was carried out, eight patients were compared to eight control subjects matched for sex, age, height, weight, marital status and socioeconomic status. The patients were selected for the presence of depressive symptoms and not for 'pathologic category', so they may have been heterogeneous from the viewpoint of standard clinical psychiatric practice. Four nights of recording were carried out, the first night's records being discarded. The duration of sleep was slightly longer in the controls and time to fall asleep slightly shorter. The patients spent 12 per cent of the time awake, the controls only 3 per cent, and the patients had less deep-stage sleep (Gresham, Agnew and Williams, 1965).

Treatment of depression by electroconvulsive therapy has been reported to decrease REM time and increase total sleep time (Zarcone, Gulevitch and Dement, 1967).

The time spent in REM sleep can be greatly reduced by wakening patients whenever REM sleep is identified in sleep records. This was done for from seven to fourteen nights in five severely depressed patients. Following this, two patients improved clinically and showed a decrease in the time from falling asleep to the first REM period (an increase in 'REM pressure'). Three patients neither improved clinically nor demonstrated a change in REM pressure (Vogel et al., 1968).

*Evoked responses* (Begleiter, Porjesz and Gross, 1967; Shagass, 1972)

Several methods of evoking responses in the EEG are available, such as photic stimulation, blocking of alpha rhythm and the averaged evoked response. The last technique, in particular, has become increasingly used but only too often technical sophistication has outstripped clinical rigour with respect to patient selection and control.

One form of EEG arousal response has been assessed by measuring the latency and duration of alpha-blocking in response to single light flashes in 11 depressed patients after admission to hospital and immediately prior to discharge (Paulson and Gottlieb, 1961). There was no change in the mean latency of alpha blocking on clinical recovery; nor did these values differ from normal values. With clinical recovery, there was some tendency for more stimuli to be followed by a response but for the response to be shorter. The authors regarded their results as consistent with the hypothesis that during depressive illnesses the attentional threshold is higher and central integrative processes slower than the patient's norm. Consistent results were obtained by Wilson and Wilson (1961) who found that the duration of alpha-blocking was longer in patients than controls and that habituation of the response was delayed in the patients. The patients were older (mean of 49) than the controls (27) which may possibly be a complicating factor.

Responses may also be elicited during sleep and depressives appear to be more responsive during all stages of sleep than controls and than themselves when recovered (Zung, Wilson and Dodson, 1964). The photo-convulsive threshold of the EEG did not change following ECT-induced clinical change (Driver and Eilenberg, 1960).

Several studies have examined the relationship between stimulus intensity and size of the averaged evoked response in depressed patients and normal controls (Shagass, 1972). In an initial report, a positive relationship was found between evoked response magnitude (of a component with a latency of about 50 ms) and intensity of somatosensory stimulation in 42 psychiatric patients and 24 normals (Shagass and Schwartz, 1963a). The mean slope for the 11 'dysthymics' (patients with psychoneurotic disorders characterised by anxiety, depression and somatic complaints) did not differ from normal. In an extension of this study, psychotically depressed patients, but not dysthymics, had steeper slopes (i.e. amplitude increased more rapidly as the stimuli were made more intense) and larger responses than normal (Shagass and Schwartz, 1963b; Shagass and Schwartz, 1964). However, these findings were not confirmed when the responses (up to about 120 ms latency) to just one stimulus intensity were analysed in a large group of 178 psychiatric patients and 89 non-patient controls. The meagre results which did reach significance might well have arisen by chance in view of the large number of statistical comparisons made (Shagass, 1968). Various technical differences could explain this discrepancy (Shagass, 1972).

Further work along these lines has categorised the depressive patients as bipolar, i.e. with a history of or current evidence of hypomania and mania, and unipolar depressive episodes only. Four intensities of visual stimulation were used and a component with a latency of 100–200 ms analysed. Patients with bipolar illnesses showed an increase in evoked response amplitude with increasing flash intensity ('augmenting'); unipolar patients showed the converse ('reducing'). High depression ratings were associated with reducing and treatment with lithium carbonate produced a drop in augmentation (Borge et al., 1971; Buchsbaum et al., 1971). No differences with respect to the latencies or amplitudes of the evoked response were found between the groups or in comparison with normals.

Visual and auditory responses were smaller in psychotic depressive patients than in normal control patients matched for age, sex, socio-economic status and emotional level (Levit, Sutton and Zubin, 1973). Similarly, auditory responses were smaller in severely depressed patients than closely matched controls (Julier and Lader, unpublished data). In both these studies, however, some of the patients were receiving drugs (chlorpromazine in the first study, hypnotics in the second) and this might have accounted in part for the results (Bond and Lader, 1972; Sakalis *et al.*, 1972). However, in Julier and Lader's study, several inter-stimulus intervals were used, namely 1, 3 and 10 s. It is known that the amplitude of the auditory evoked response increases with increasing inter-stimulus interval up to a plateau at intervals of 8 s and above. The mechanism for the diminution in response at inter-stimulus intervals below 8 s is unclear. Julier and Lader's results could be interpreted in at least two ways: (1) the evoked response is smaller in depressed patients and/or (2) the evoked response does not reach its maximum in depressed patients until inter-stimulus intervals greater than 10 s are used.

The latter explanation would suggest that the brains of depressive patients take longer to recover their 'excitability' than normal, and this can be related to the mass of work which has been carried out on the 'cortical recovery cycle'. This technique consists of presenting paired stimuli, the interval between the stimuli being varied from, typically, 2·5 to 200 ms. The response to the second stimulus is compared with that to an unpaired stimulus. This ratio is above 1 if 'cortical excitability' is above normal, below 1 if cortical excitability is sub-normal. Thus, by plotting this ratio against inter-stimulus interval a cortical recovery cycle can be described. There are many technical complications to this method concept and it must be emphasised that its theoretical basis is also unestablished.

In the early studies, it was found that whereas a group of thirteen non-patients had a phase of supranormal excitability with inter-stimulus intervals between 2·5 and 20 ms, a heterogeneous group of ninety-two patients showed no such facilitation (Shagass and Schwartz, 1961; Shagass and Schwartz, 1962). One obvious criticism of this study concerns the small size of the control group. In a subsequent report involving a further 27 controls and 75 patients of various types, it was again found that the peak recovery ratios during the first 20 ms were higher in the non-patients.

Patients with psychotic depression were compared with matched controls. The results were complicated in that the cortical recovery cycles varied among evoked response components, some components showing greater recovery in the patients, others less recovery (Shagass and Schwartz, 1966). In the most recent study, various technical and statistical refinements were introduced. Many components were analysed with respect to 8 latencies and 8 amplitudes and their recovery function, and some significant differences were found between patients and normals (Shagass, 1968). However, as no differences could be discerned among the various patient groups, the significance of this study remains unclear. Nevertheless, other studies have also suggested that recovery function is abnormal in psychiatric patients. Visual stimulation was used in one study and psychiatric patients showed impaired recovery of the second response. Again, the abnormality was noted among all groups of psychiatric patients and no abnormalities specific to one diagnostic group were apparent (Speck, Dim and Mercer, 1966). Another study using visual evoked responses revealed possible differences between endogenous depressives on the one hand and neurotic depressives and normals on the other (Vasconetto, Floris and Morocutti, 1971).

## Contingent negative variation

There appears to have been no systematic study of the CNV in depression. One study makes the claim that manic depressives have 'practically no Contingent Negative Variation (CNV) responses' (Small and Small, 1971; Small, Small and Perez, 1971).

## Endocrine measures

*Adrenocortical function* (Mason, 1968a; Michael and Gibbons, 1963; Rubin and Mandell, 1966).

The relationship between depression and adrenocortical function has been extensively evaluated. In this complex field, experimental approaches have been limited by the availability of techniques for the estimation of adrenocortical activity in the intact human. About twenty years ago methods for urinary steroid quantification were developed and the 1950s saw great activity in relating steroid excretion to depressive conditions.

The search for some meaningful relationship between depressive and other morbid affective states, on the one hand, and some aberration of adrenocortical function on the other, originated in the clinical observations of psychiatric symptoms accompanying gross disorders of the adrenal cortex. Addison (1855), in his description of the disease which bears his name and which is due to hypofunction of the adrenal cortex, mentioned anxiety, insomnia and confusion as symptoms commonly present. For example, one of his cases (Case V) was 'occasionally wandering a little in her intellects'. Other symptoms listed by later observers include apathy, mild depression, irritability and tiredness. Treatment of the hypofunction with cortisone and aldosterone usually results in improvement of these symptoms. Hyperfunction of the adrenal cortex (Cushing's Syndrome) is also accompanied by psychiatric disturbances (Michael and Gibbons, 1963). Appreciable affective symptoms are noted in about half of the patients with this condition; in 15 to 20 per cent the psychiatric symptoms are quite marked. The most frequently noted condition is depression, but anxiety, paranoid states and acute, confusional excitement may also be seen. In patients administered large doses of cortisone for rheumatoid arthritis or collagen diseases, psychological symptoms are quite commonly found. These may take the form of acute psychotic episodes with delusions, hallucinations, excitement or stupor, but usually with some clouding of consciousness. Euphoria is the commonest symptom, however, and may occur either in an acute episode or more chronically. Thus, there is a paradox in that naturally occurring hyperfunction of the adrenal cortex, as in Cushing's Syndrome, is associated with depressive symptoms, whereas a high level of administered hormone is accompanied by euphoria. Furthermore, the administration by injection of adrenocorticotrophic hormone (ACTH), which induces overproduction of cortical secretions, is also accompanied by symptoms of euphoria in some patients. The mechanism for the production of the psychiatric abnormalities is unclear (Quarton et al., 1955) but it would seem useful to examine the patterns of hormones in these various conditions (Fawcett and Bunney, 1967).

*Urinary excretion*

Studies of adrenocortical function in patients have either concentrated on urinary excretion of cortical hormones and their metabolites or on plasma levels of cortisol. Twelve male and 12 female patients with endogenous depression were examined with respect to urinary 17-oxosteroid and 17-hydroxycorticosteroid excretion, both under resting conditions and following an injection of 50 units of ACTH: the values obtained were all in the normal range (Brambilla and Nuremberg, 1963).

Very detailed examinations of this topic have been carried out by Bunney, Mason and Hamburg (1965) who studied 17 drug-free depressed patients admitted to a research metabolic ward. Serial 24-hour urine samples were analysed for 17-hydroxycorticosteroid content. In 12 out of the 17 patients, significant correlations were found within each patient between ratings of the intensity of the depressive affect and urinary steroid excretion. However, in 10 patients, similar correlations were found with respect to anxiety ratings, in 6 patients for psychotic behaviour, in 6 for physical activity and in 5 for somatic complaints and for ratings of anger. As might be expected, the patients showing these correlations tended to be the more emotionally volatile. Factor analysis of the data showed that depression and anxiety ratings loaded onto the same factor, and the authors point out the close relationship between these two affective components. There was no significant relationship between urinary steroids and severity of depression. It appeared that two sub-groups of the depressed patients could be distinguished. One group was characterised by high depression ratings but low and stable 17-hydroxycorticosteroid excretion levels; these patients had elaborate psychological defences, often with marked denial of their illness. The other patients also had high depression ratings but their high and fluctuating steroid excretion levels were accompanied by awareness of and involvement in a struggle with their illness.

A similar study by these authors demonstrated in seven patients that behavioural deterioration and rise in urinary 17-hydroxy-corticosteroids occurred on the same day rather than one preceding the other (Bunney et al., 1965). 'Crisis days' could be identified behaviourally and physiologically and it was estimated that a period of heightened environmental stress existed for an average of 13 days prior to the crisis. Three aspects of psychological threat were identified for these stressful events: (1) an environmental challenge to the patient's concept of his own mental health; (2) loss of ego support; and (3) involvement of a pivotal area of psychological conflict. In three patients who eventually committed suicide, steroid excretion was particularly elevated and it was tentatively suggested that potentially suicidal patients might be identifiable using physiological criteria (Bunney and Fawcett, 1965).

In a similarly careful study, Sachar (1967b) examined urinary 17-hydroxycorticosteroid excretion in 17 female and 3 male depressed patients, drug-free for at least three weeks after admission to hospital. As expected, admission to hospital itself produced an increase in steroid excretion of about 20 per cent. No patient had values grossly outside the normal range but small and significant drops in steroid excretion of about 10 per cent were found on recovery. Patients in episodes of psychotic turmoil had high levels of urinary steroids; withdrawn patients had low levels. Another interesting study by Sachar and his co-workers (1967) involved the estimation of daily urinary 17-hydroxycorticosteroid excretion in six female in-patients receiving psychotherapy for reactive depression. It was based on the hypothesis that the loss precipitating the depression is not acknowledged affectively and that, therefore, the patient undergoing psychotherapy must 'work through' that loss. The authors found that urinary corticosteroid levels were not elevated except during the transient periods in psychotherapy when there was confrontation of the loss. Otherwise, ratings of affective symptoms which made no allowance for such dynamic factors failed to correlate with steroid excretion. Emphasis was placed on the importance of distinguishing between affects associated with loss and mourning and the organised syndrome of melancholia.

Stenbäck, Jakobson and Rimón (1966) studied urinary 17-hydroxycorticosteroid excretion in 28 hospitalised depressed patients before and after one month's treatment with antidepressive drugs or electroconvulsive therapy. They did not find raised steroid levels before treatment and, despite appreciable falls in psychometric ratings on the Beck Depression Inventory and the Taylor Manifest Anxiety Scale, there were negligible drops in steroid excretion after treatment. However, those patients with the highest pre-treatment psychometric ratings tended to show the largest falls in corticosteroid excretion following treatment. The authors suggested that their patients were, in general, more mildly depressed than in-patients in other countries.

Another essentially negative study was that of Gibbons et al. (1960) who could find no relationship between urinary corticosteroids and severity or course of illness in 17 depressed male patients followed from admission to discharge. Other studies have examined different components of urinary steroids. Correlations were found between the severity of depression and the excretion of 17-oxogenic (ketogenic) steroids (Kurland, 1964); 17-oxosteroids (ketosteroids) (reflecting adrenal androgens) and 17-hydroxy-corticosteroids were raised in episodes of intensified depressive symptoms but then dropped again even if the exacerbation continued. Conversely, Rey and his associates (1961) were unable to find any consistent relationships between 17-oxosteroid excretion and the mental state in 3 patients. Using paper chromatographic separation of urinary steroids, 10 separate compounds were assayed in 5 female patients within 3 days of admission and again after treatment with electroconvulsive therapy (Ferguson *et al.*, 1964). In general, the 17-hydroxycorticosteroids elevated during stress were raised in these patients, presumably because of the hospitalisation, and these compounds dropped on recovery. Conversely, the 11-deoxy-17-oxosteroid compounds were depressed on admission to hospital and rose to normal values by the time the patient was discharged. Unfortunately, the patients were not uniformly drug-free.

Cycling manic depressive patients have received attention as some endocrinological contrasts between the manic and depressive phases might reasonably be expected. In an early study of a 39-year-old manic depressive patient with regular cycles, steroid excretion was found to be increased during depressive phases and lowered during manic episodes (Bryson and Martin, 1954). In a more recent study extending over two years, a patient with a 48-hour cycle showed elevated 17-hydroxycorticosteroid excretion rates on depressed days as compared with manic days (Bunney, Hartmann and Mason, 1965). Episodes of mania were associated with intense denial of any illness, depressive interludes with feelings of suffering, pain and awareness of illness; the results were interpreted in accord with the psychoanalytical hypothesis that mania is a defence against depression. There was no consistent relationship either in this patient or in some others between urinary corticosteroid excretion and physical activity. This possibility has been looked at in some detail by obtaining objective estimates of gross movement patterns. Motility could actually be higher in depressed patients than in manic patients in the depressed phase than in the manic phase (Schwartz *et al.*, 1966). No differences were found in steroid excretion levels in mania and depression, but when crisis days occurred steroid levels rose. Rubin (1967) reported no changes with mood in urinary corticosteroid excretion in two patients with manic depressive illnesses but, in a later study, he noted that steroid excretion was higher in the depressive phases than the hypomanic in a female patient, but only after she had become acclimatised to the hospital (Rubin, Young and Clark, 1968).

Recently, Dunner *et al.* (1972) divided their depressed patients into two groups—31 with bipolar illnesses and 49 with unipolar illnesses. The excretion of 17-hydroxycorticosteroids was lower in the bipolar depressed patients and these patients also tended to be more retarded.

That mania is accompanied by lowered steroid output confirms the early observations of Rizzo and associates (1954) in a 50-year-old cyclothymic patient who showed consistently low levels over a period of 5 months of manic overactivity. Levels rose to normal with the patient's recovery. The adrenal cortex remained normally responsive to ACTH throughout.

*Plasma levels*

One of the first studies of plasma 17-hydroxycorticosteroid levels in depressive patients was carried out by Board and his colleagues (Board, Persky and Hamburg, 1956). Their study was carried out in 30 newly admitted patients and in 24 normal controls. Detailed ratings were made of the quality, intensity and duration of the current emotional distress and of the mode of psychological defence. The plasma cortisol level averaged 12·3 μg per 100 ml in the normals and was significantly higher in the patients, the mean level being 19·8. Very high cortisol levels were associated with 'very intense distress (especially of a depressive affect in the presence of retarded behavior)' and with the development of extensive personality disintegration, especially depressive psychoses. One possible confounding influence was that of barbiturates as the 11 patients receiving hypnotics on the night before the tests had distinctly lower cortisol levels than the remainder of the patients. Fourteen patients were re-tested 17 days after the first test and, although their cortisol levels had fallen, they were still above normal. In a confirmatory study, cortisol levels were found to be significantly higher in the retarded (25·3 μg per 100 ml) than the non-retarded patients (18·3): intense suffering and inability to cry were also associated with high cortisol levels (Board, Wadeson and Persky, 1957).

In an extensive study of 50 normal females and 138 female patients with a variety of diagnoses, Lingjaerde (1964) described moderate elevations in plasma cortisol levels in depressed patients.

In a longitudinal study of 17 patients, Gibbons and McHugh (1962) found a mean plasma cortisol level of 20·8 μg per 100 ml soon after admission which decreased significantly to 10·8 μg per 100 ml immediately prior to discharge. Cortisol levels were highest in the most severely ill patients, whether they were retarded or depressed. Quite appreciable daily variations in cortisol levels have been reported (Anderson and Dawson, 1965) so it would appear important to take several plasma samples to obtain a representative figure.

Cortisol (and corticosterone) levels were estimated in plasma samples taken between 9 and 10 a.m. (Hullin *et al.*, 1967). The mean values for 6 normal subjects on successive weekly occasions were 13·2, 16·9, 15·2 and 16·0 μg per 100 ml, i.e. there was no drop attributable to habituation to the venepuncture. In 6 depressed patients, the mean value on the first occasion was 30·5 μg per 100 ml and this rose slightly to 31·5 μg per 100 ml during a course of electroconvulsive therapy; following the course of ECT the mean level showed a significant decrease to a figure of 25·0 μg per 100 ml. One patient who showed no such drop subsequently relapsed.

Plasma cortisol levels show a pronounced diurnal rhythm with maximal levels in the early morning. Brooksbank and Coppen (1967) were unable to find any significant drop in 8 a.m. plasma corticosteroid levels from admission to discharge in 29 depressed patients. However, the evening (9 p.m.) plasma samples did show a significant fall in corticosteroid content. Similarly, the relationship between hormone level and clinical state was not significant for the morning sample but reached significance for the evening sample. In McClure's study (1966a), 7 depressed patients were compared to 7 normal subjects with respect to cortisol levels in plasma samples taken at 7 a.m., 12 noon and 12 p.m. The mean levels were significantly higher in the depressives, 27·8 μg per 100 ml as against 11·8, and this difference was most marked at 7 a.m. McClure draws attention to the evidence that some cortisol-like steroids in large amounts increase brain excitability and puts forward the interesting suggestion that early morning wakening in depressives might be related to elevated cortisol levels. Five of the patients were re-tested after a month's treatment with amitriptyline or imipramine. Plasma cortisol levels decreased, especially at 7 a.m. (McClure, 1966b). In a similar study, plasma samples were taken at 12 midnight, 3 a.m. and 6 a.m. in 10 depressive patients and 9 control patients, hospitalised for minor operations.

The depressive patients had higher plasma cortisol levels at 6 a.m. only (Doig *et al.*, 1966). Bridges and Jones (1966) also used patients recovering from operations as controls but found depressive patients to have *lower* cortisol levels. Presumably the operations were sufficiently major and recent for plasma cortisol levels to be elevated in response to this stress.

In a recent very detailed study, plasma cortisol was analysed every 20 minutes throughout the 24 hours in 8 normal subjects and 6 severely depressed patients, 2 men and 4 women (Sachar *et al.*, 1973).

The depressives when ill secreted substantially more cortisol in more secretory episodes, each lasting longer than normal. Throughout the 24 hours cortisol levels were markedly higher throughout the secretory episodes. Cortisol was secreted during the late evening and early morning hours when in the normal subjects secretion was minimal. On recovery, the cortisol secretory patterns became normal. The biological half-life of cortisol remained normal throughout, suggesting that the utilisation of cortisol was normal but that there was an abnormal disinhibition of the neuroendocrine centres regulating ACTH release during depressive phases.

Diurnal patterns are also altered in manic patients: the cortisol level is often *higher* at midnight than at 8 a.m.; on recovery, the normal pattern of a peak level in the morning is re-established (Platman and Fieve, 1968; Carpenter and Bunney, 1971). However, one study showed no abnormality in cortisol production in manic patients (Sachar *et al.*, 1972).

Gibbons (1964) measured the secretion rate of cortisol by administered $0.2$ microcuries of $C^{14}$-labelled cortisol by mouth and measuring plasma and urinary radioactivity. Fifteen depressed patients aged 22–63 were studied and the mean rate of cortisol secretion was found to be $26.1$ mg in 24 hours. Seven patients were rated 'severely depressed', 8 moderately depressed: the cortisol secretion rates were 33 and 20 mg in 24 hours respectively ($p < 0.01$). After recovery or improvement, the value dropped to $14.1$ mg. Plasma cortisol level and cortisol secretion rate were estimated simultaneously in 19 instances and the encouragingly high correlation of $+0.81$ was computed.

In a second study, the secretion rate of corticosterone as well as that of cortisol was estimated in 6 depressed patients (Gibbons, 1966). Before treatment, the corticosterone production rate was $3.5$ mg in 24 hours, that of cortisol $23.0$ mg in 24 hours. After treatment both hormone secretions dropped significantly to values of 2·4 and 14·4 mg in 24 hours respectively, both lying within the normal ranges.

Another approach has been to block the synthesis of cortisol from its precursors by administration of the drug metyrapone. The effects of this drug on the pattern of urinary steroids was less marked in depressives than in non-depressed control patients, which led to the suggestion that a partial block of cortisol synthesis may already be present in depressive patients (Jakobson *et al.*, 1966).

The integrity of hypothalamic–pituitary–adrenal cortex feed-back control has been evaluated using the dexamethasone suppression test. A total of 27 depressed in-patients was studied, all patients being drug-free apart from amylobarbitone. For comparison, 22 non-depressed in-patients were also investigated and 14 of the depressed patients were re-tested immediately before discharge from hospital. Plasma cortisol levels did not differ among the depressed patients, recovered depressives and non-depressed patients. However, following dexamethasone, most of the non-depressed patients showed the expected suppression of cortisol in the blood, whereas only half the depressives did so. Only one of the 14 recovered depressives failed to suppress normally (Carroll, Martin and Davies, 1968; see also Butler and Besser, 1968).

A similar insensitivity to insulin was found in depressed patients, the plasma cortisol response to hypoglycaemia being significantly impaired (Carroll, 1969).

The raised cortisol levels in depressive patients are not associated with abnormal glucose tolerance (Pryce, 1964). Nor can the therapeutic effectiveness of ECT be ascribed to elevations in plasma cortisol induced by the treatment (Bliss *et al.*, 1954).

Finally, cortisol has been estimated in the cerebrospinal fluid of 23 depressed patients, 16 manic patients and 18 controls (in-patients with neurological illnesses) (Coppen *et al.*, 1971). A somewhat inaccurate competitive protein-binding assay was used and no differences were found between the groups. The authors conclude that the 'physiologically active level of cortisol in the brain as a whole is unlikely to be grossly abnormal in affective illness'.

*Aldosterone*

The rates of excretion of aldosterone excretion have been measured in manic depressive patients. In one study (Murphy, Goodwin and

Bunney, 1969), lower rates of excretion were found in depression than in mania; conversely, in another study (Jenner *et al.*, 1967), a cycling manic depressive patient had higher excretion rates in the depressive phases. Aldosterone production rates have been found to fall when patients swing from mania to depression (Allsopp *et al.*, 1972). These changes are obviously important when considered in relationship to the electrolyte changes in manic and depressed patients (Coppen, 1970).

*Adrenal medullary function* (Mason 1968b)

Most studies in this area have been directed towards responses to stress accompanied by anxiety and relatively few have examined adrenaline and noradrenaline levels in the urine or plasma. High correlations were found in normal subjects and depressive patients between adrenaline and noradrenaline excretion and between noradrenaline and corticosteroid excretion, but not between adrenaline and corticosteroid excretion. In affective states of depression, the excretion of noradrenaline tended to rise; in anxiety states adrenaline and corticosteroid output both showed rises; in mixed affective states of anxiety and depression, adrenaline and noradrenaline excretion increased more than did corticosteroid excretion (Curtis, Cleghorn and Sourkes, 1960).

Conversely, several studies have suggested that adrenaline and noradrenaline excretion are lowered in depressive patients (e.g. Lovegrove *et al.*, 1965). In manic patients, catecholamine excretion is higher than in depressive patients and in cyclic manic depressive patients, excretion is higher in the manic phases than in the depressive phases (Ström-Olsen and Weil-Malherbe, 1958). This has been confirmed in an extensive Scandinavian study (Bergsman, 1959). The mean value for manic patients was 21 ng per minute of adrenaline excreted as compared with the mean normal value of 7. The corresponding figures for noradrenaline excretion were 39 and 22 ng per minute. For patients with depressive psychoses the excretion rates for adrenaline and noradrenaline were 6·5 and 25 ng per minute respectively, values which do not depart from normal. Shinfuku, Omura and Kayano (1961) reported a co-relationship between noradrenaline output and mania in a cycling female manic depressive patient, but none between mood and adrenaline output. A catecholamine metabolite, vanillyl mandelic acid, was found in larger quantities in the urine in a hypomanic patient but only during bouts of physical overactivity (Rubin, Young and Clark, 1968).

## Thyroid function (Mason, 1968c)

In contrast to the extensive work on pituitary–adrenal function in depressives, there have been few studies of pituitary–thyroid function in such patients. Board, Persky and Hamburg (1956) measured the PBI levels in 30 acutely admitted psychiatric patients and found a small but non-significant elevation (mean value— 5·88 μg per 100 ml) as compared with normal control subjects (mean—4·86). This was confirmed in a second study (Board, Wadeson and Persky, 1957). In contrast to the findings with plasma cortisol, no significant relationship was found between PBI levels and the amount of distress experienced by the patients. However, in the patients rated most depressed, the mean PBI was 6·7 μg per 100 ml compared with a mean of 5·7 for the whole group. Similarly, the 7 patients rated most retarded had significantly higher PBI levels (7·2 μg per 100 ml) than the non-retarded patients (5·1). PBI levels tended to drop as the patients improved. These changes with remission were confirmed by Gibbons and his colleagues but they emphasise that the PBI levels were generally within the accepted normal range and that the drop with recovery, of the order of 0·5 μg per 100 ml, was hardly of much clinical significance (Gibbons et al., 1960; Michael and Gibbons, 1963).

In a very extensive study involving 222 in-patients who had been off all medications for at least a month, no relationship was found between thyroid function, as assessed by the radioactive iodine uptake test, and diagnostic category (Blumberg and Klein, 1968). There was some tendency for retarded patients to have higher rates of uptake than non-retarded patients.

Gibbs and Willcox (1957) noted phasic changes in PBI levels in 3 depressive patients, the fluctuations often being over 2 μg per 100 ml. No close relationship with the clinical state was found, nor was there any evidence of an interaction with the pituitary–adrenal axis.

Using the short-lived isotope $^{132}$I, it has been reported that a patient in a 6-day manic depressive cycle showed no difference in rate of iodine uptake with respect to the mood changes (Crammer and Pover, 1960).

Levels of thyroid-stimulating hormone have been reported as

abnormally high in the plasma of depressed patients (Dewhurst *et al.*, 1969), although it was concluded that this could well represent a non-specific response to stress.

Interest in the relationship between depression and thyroid activity has been revived by the observation that a combination of imipramine and thyroid hormone produced a more prompt response than with imipramine alone (Coppen *et al.*, 1972; Prange *et al.*, 1969). Patients with low normal thyroid function before treatment appeared to respond most to the combination (Wheatley, 1972).

## General considerations

As adumbrated earlier, psychophysiological research in depressed patients has proceeded in an empirical, almost haphazard, way. One major problem has been the lack of a working nosology of depression. With schizophrenia the allocation into acute and chronic has sufficed to systematise laboratory work and the further division into paranoid and non-paranoid proved fruitful. With depression no such useful sub-division has been generally accepted.

The commonest division into endogenous and reactive has been the source of controversy, often acrimonious, in the British and American literature (Kiloh and Garside, 1963; McConaghy, Joffe and Murphy, 1967; Mendels and Cochrane, 1968; Kendell, 1968). Sophisticated statistical techniques have been used (and sometimes misused) to support or refute the validity of this dichotomy. When psychophysiological data have been examined in the light of this distinction, little of use has been obtained. For example, Noble and Lader (1972) found that the distribution of their EMG, skin conductance level, skin conductance fluctuations, forearm blood flow and salivation data all followed unimodal normal distributions. Categorising their patients into 'endogenous' and 'reactive' groups using the Carney, Roth and Garside Scale, only the conductance variables were significantly different between the groups.

The distinction into bipolar and unipolar, depending on whether or not manic episodes have previously occurred, has been advocated (Perris, 1973) but its validity has not been established.

Lader and Wing (1969) and Lader and Noble (1974) advocate the clinical evaluation of depressed patients in terms of agitated and retarded. Agitation may be defined as an excess of *purposeless* activity, movement and speech. Both are observable in the patient, can be rated and make no assumptions regarding aetiology or pathological mechanisms. This dichotomy seems as useful as any. However, the two conditions can occur together and the clinical picture may alternate between them.

Nevertheless, the equating of retardation with lowered arousal is not justified. There is much evidence, reviewed in this chapter, that glandular, cardiovascular and hormonal function is lowered in retarded patients. It often appears that there is a lowering of resting levels of activity with reactivity sometimes diminished, sometimes unimpaired. The peripheral expression of many autonomic functions, e.g. salivation and sweat gland activity, appears sluggish. Yet although behaviourally depressed patients are often slow and 'inhibited', there is no evidence of inhibition centrally. Phenomenologically these patients often state that they have an excess of thoughts, ideas, fears, etc., and that it is only the verbal expression of this activity which is impaired. If the peripheral effectors by which central processes are detected are altered in function or impaired, no inferences about the level of central activity can be drawn. It is possible that such a state of affairs exists in retarded depressives.

One hypothesis that evaluates depressive illness in a biological light is the following. The basic pathological mechanism in depression is 'biological retardation'. This manifests itself as poverty of speech and movement, loss of appetite, weight and libido, amenorrhoea, constipation, and as depression of glandular function such as salivation and sweating. Retardation of affect is experienced first as depression and then, as the retardation increases, as absence of affect, characteristic of deeply depressed patients. The retardation can be 'endogenous', i.e. cause unknown, or in response to external events ('reactive') or, most commonly, an interaction between external events and a pre-disposition towards 'retardation' in the individual. As a response to the general bodily and affective changes, anxiety is engendered which may reach the dimensions of agitation but which is superimposed on and may completely mask the retardation. Psychophysiological indicators then reflect an amalgam of the retardation and agitation. The further implications of this theory, e.g. in biochemical terms, lie outside our present scope, but do allow an integration between the various biological approaches to depression.

# Schizophrenia

6

## Introduction

Many studies have examined a variety of physiological measures in schizophrenic patients; the earlier studies have been reviewed by Altschule (1953) and Shattock (1950). In these earlier studies, the techniques were unsophisticated and, together with the undoubted heterogeneity of the clinical entity, led to a welter of confusing and initially contradictory findings. Thus, Mednick (1958) postulated that schizophrenia represented a learned response to overwhelming anxiety, a concept similar to the drive state of increased arousal, which develops within the individual as a consequence of over-reactivity to repeated external stimuli. Conversely, other theorists have regarded lessened autonomic reactivity as a hallmark of schizophrenia (Gellhorn, 1953). As clinical views of schizophrenia also vary and distinctions are made between acute and chronic schizophrenia, some clarification of this issue would be most illuminating. Hypotheses involve both basal levels and amplitude of responses, and there is often a relationship between the two. The disentanglement of these relationships in normal control subjects and in schizophrenics has proved difficult but, as will be seen in the following, some pattern, at least with respect to skin conductance, has emerged in the past few years.

## Autonomic measures

### Sweat gland activity

As in so many other areas of psychophysiology, one of the most interesting of the earlier studies was carried out by Darrow (Darrow and Solomon, 1934). Small GSRs to stimuli were associated with lack of 'contact with reality' in schizophrenics. Similar results were reported in another study (Koltuv et al., 1959), and in

157

a third study clinical improvement was reflected by larger, more normal responses (Hoch, Kubis and Rouke, 1944). In a small group of paranoid schizophrenics, the skin resistance was high (little sweating) and responses small (Jurko, Jost and Hill, 1952), and similar findings were reported in a group of 60 'mixed' schizophrenics (Howe, 1958).

One investigation, carried out over 20 years ago, provided most interesting data (Williams, 1953). Eighteen chronic schizophrenics (1–3 years' hospitalisation) were compared with 18 age-comparable normal controls with respect to skin conductance, pulse rate and respiration recorded at rest, during 'impersonal stress' (an up-setting film), 'personal stress' (a free-association test) and an 'interpersonal stress' (mental arithmetic under harassment). The skin conductance level was increased in the schizophrenics at rest as compared with the normal group. However, no differences in GSR reactivity were found between the groups, although re-covery in skin conductance level following the stress procedures was somewhat delayed in the patients.

Habituation of the GSR was found to be slowed in 52 chronic schizophrenic patients, essentially drug-free at the time of testing (Zahn, Rosenthal and Lawlor, 1968). Skin conductance levels and frequency of spontaneous fluctuations were increased in the patients. In a similar study, 28 drug-free chronic schizophrenic patients, mean age 32, who had been ill for at least 2 years were compared with 18 normal controls, mean age 28 (Ax et al., 1970). Orienting responses to tones and unconditioned responses to pain stimuli were assessed. The basal skin conductance was increased in the patients. Orienting responses (GSRs) were initially smaller in the patients but, as the normals habituated to the repeated tones and the patients did not, later mean responses were of equal magnitude in the two groups. Unconditioned responses were similar in the two groups but conditioned responses were dimin-ished in the patients. In a further examination of the tracings, the recovery function of the GSR was measured as the time between the maximum point of response of the GSR and the point where the skin conductance had returned half-way to its pre-stimulus level. The mean recovery time for the normal subjects was 20·4 seconds; for the patients only 13·0 seconds ($p < 0.01$) (Ax and Bamford, 1970).

A direct and detailed examination of skin conductance levels, responses and the relationship between them was carried out by

Thayer and Silber (1971). Firstly, in a pilot experiment, they established the need to study only patients who had been drug-free for at least two weeks; tranquillisers attenuated or completely suppressed the orienting GSR. In the main study, 32 hospitalised schizophrenic patients and 32 normal control subjects were recorded from during a 20-minute rest period followed by the presentation of 85 db, 300 Hz tones, the inter-trial interval averaging 60 seconds. Normal subjects and patients were categorised as high tonic or low tonic depending on whether their basal levels were above or below the median for their group. There was no difference between the controls and the patients for mean level. The amplitudes of the GSRs, expressed in log conductance, were larger for the high tonic groups but diagnostic status was not related to the amplitude. Habituation to repeated stimulus presentation was slower in the high tonic groups; again, there was no difference between patients and normals. Similarly, high tonicity, but not diagnostic status, was associated with shorter latency of the GSR and increased frequency of spontaneous fluctuations. Thus, it appeared that 'the dimension of tonic arousal was more important in determining response strength to discrete stimuli than the dimension of psychiatric status, which accounted for no significant differences'. The authors regard their data as providing no support for the widely held hypothesis that schizophrenics have low arousal and increased reactivity during acute phases, and high arousal and low responsiveness during more chronic phases (Crooks and McNulty, 1966; Lang and Buss, 1965; Venables, 1964). The schizophrenics showed as wide a range of physiological activity as the normal subjects and separation of the patient sample nto acute and chronic conditions did not reveal two groups separate with respect to tonic level.

The responsivity of two groups of chronic schizophrenics, remitted and regressed, was compared to that of a group of normals (Bernstein, 1964). Of the regressed patients only half gave a GSR to the initial stimulus (a light), as compared with 90 per cent of the other two groups. In this study, no difference in reactivity was found between the patients receiving drugs and those not so treated. In a later investigation, Bernstein (1970) divided his chronic schizophrenic patients into 'confused' and 'non-confused' categories and reported that the former had diminished reactivity to stimuli of low and moderate intensity.

The most thorough and penetrating series of studies into the

*

psychophysiology of schizophrenia has been carried out by Venables and his associates during 20 years. Venables (1960) examined the skin potential responses to auditory and visual stimuli of male schizophrenics described as acute or chronic and active or withdrawn and of a group of normal male controls. The frequency of response was less in the withdrawn group than the other groups and the response amplitudes of all schizophrenic groups were greater than those of the control subjects.

Venables has been particularly concerned with the relationship between skin potential and the two-flash threshold. To estimate the latter a series of paired flashes are presented, the inter-pair interval varying. The subject states when he can just distinguish between the component flashes of the pair. The more alert the subject, the closer together can be the two flashes before they appear to have fused, i.e. the lower the threshold in milliseconds. A correlation of $-0.79$ ($p < 0.001$) was found in normal subjects between skin potential and the two-flash threshold, i.e. the lower the threshold, the higher the potential (and sweat gland activity). Skin potential correlated with ratings of social withdrawal in drug-free chronic schizophrenic patients: high arousal was associated with withdrawal in non-deluded patients and in deluded patients with incoherent speech, but not in coherent deluded patients (Venables and Wing, 1962). Similarly, the two-flash threshold correlated positively with a measure of selective attention; also the selective attention measure correlated positively with the degree of withdrawal in non-paranoid patients, but not in paranoid patients (Venables, 1963a). Further experiments were performed to replicate such results: negative correlations between the two-flash threshold and skin potential in normals and coherent paranoid schizophrenics; positive correlations in non-coherent paranoid schizophrenics (Venables, 1963b).

An extension of this work examined the relationship between the two-flash threshold and two-click threshold, the auditory analogue (Venables, 1966a). The mean two-flash threshold for the normals was 86 ms and for the schizophrenic patients, 84 ms; the corresponding values for the two-click threshold were 34 and 52·5. The schizophrenics had significantly smaller differences between their visual and auditory thresholds than the normal subjects. The prolongation of the auditory but not the visual thresholds suggests auditory but not visual dysfunction and accords with the frequency of auditory hallucinations in such patients in contrast to the paucity of visual hallucinations. The earlier work on this topic is well summarised in Venables (1966b).

Both flash and click thresholds were obtained in a further study on 35 drug-free schizophrenics who had been hospitalised for more than 2 years. They were rated for degree of withdrawal, paranoid tendency and incoherence by senior nurses. The non-paranoid and incoherent paranoid patients showed similar results and their pooled data yielded a correlation of +0·64 between the two-flash threshold and rating of withdrawal and +0·68 for that with the two-click threshold. The corresponding correlations for the coherent paranoid patients were also significant but in the opposite direction, —0·67 and —0·68 respectively. In other words, the former groups of patients were more withdrawn, the more aroused they were, whereas the latter patients were more withdrawn, the less aroused they were (Venables, 1967).

However, an attempt to replicate Venables' findings that the two-flash threshold is negatively related to skin potential levels in normal subjects but positively related in most schizophrenic subjects was unsuccessful (Lykken and Maley, 1968). As this was an American study the patient groups may have differed from their UK counterparts.

The latest of the studies on this topic examined two-flash thresholds, skin conductance and skin potential levels in paranoid and non-paranoid schizophrenics and controls, under non-activated conditions and activated by exercise on a bicycle ergometer (Gruzelier, Lykken and Venables, 1972). In control subjects with low levels of skin potential and conductance, a positive relationship with the two-flash threshold was discerned. In controls with high levels of sweat gland activity and in activated controls, a negative relationship obtained. The schizophrenic groups, even when non-activated, showed a negative relationship. When activated, the paranoid patients showed the same changes as the normal controls whereas the non-paranoid patients actually had a lowered skin conductance and raised thresholds. The last result was interpreted as showing that inhibitory processes, consistent with the concept of protective inhibition, are elicited as somatic arousal increases in non-paranoid but not paranoid schizophrenics. Both groups appear to be aroused in non-activated conditions, approximating to the normal control subjects when activated.

A more recent approach by Venables and his colleagues has been to study orienting responses, and the lack of them, in schizophrenics (Gruzelier and Venables, 1972). Of the 80 schizophrenics tested, 50 had been hospitalised for less than 5 years (non-institutionalised) and 30 for more than this period (institutionalised). A small group of normals and a small, highly heterogeneous group of non-psychotic patients constituted the rather inadequate controls. An habituation procedure—a series of 15 1 kHz, 85 db tones presented at intervals of 30–60 seconds—was presented while skin conductance was recorded. In 43 patients no responses at all were elicited, whereas almost all the remainder showed responses but failed to habituate to criterion (three successive failures to respond). The patients with orienting responses had higher skin conductance levels than the controls, whereas the non-responding patients had lower levels of sweating. The responses of the patients were larger, with shorter latencies and faster recovery times than the control group. Spontaneous fluctuations were frequent in the responding group, almost absent in the non-responders. There were few major differences between institutionalised and non-institutionalised patients.

Unfortunately, the patients were receiving one or more phenothiazine drugs which might have produced the phenomenon of non-response by direct, peripheral blockade of the autonomic nervous system. An analysis of the responders versus non-responders showed no difference in mean daily dosage of phenothiazines between the groups. The metabolism of phenothiazines is complex and one group could have been metabolising the drugs slowly resulting in marked pharmacological effects such as GSR suppression, the other group breaking down the drugs rapidly with little effect on the body.

That this unresponsiveness could be a genuine phenomenon is suggested by two lines of evidence. Firstly, Lader has found almost identical tracings in retarded depressives (see p. 130) and in some patients with depersonalisation (see p. 192). Both these groups of patients were drug-free at the time of testing. The second consideration comes from a further study of Gruzelier and Venables (1973). Thirty-eight schizophrenics and 20 non-schizophrenic psychiatric patients were tested. Two types of stimuli were used, neutral stimuli to which no responses were required and signal stimuli to which the subjects had to respond. Twenty of the schizophrenics showed no responses to the neutral stimuli yet all but one *did* show GSRs to the signal stimuli. It is just possible but rather unlikely that any drug blockade could be overcome by the sympathetic response to a signal stimuli but not by that to a 'weaker', neutral stimulus; the lack of response to neutral stimuli would thus appear to be a real finding.

In this study, bilateral recordings were made. This followed from the observations of Flor-Henry (1969) who examined the location of the epileptic foci in psychotic patients with temporal lobe epilepsy and found that patients with schizophreniform symptomatology had a high incidence of foci involving the temporal lobe of the dominant hemisphere, whereas foci in the non-dominant hemisphere were associated with manic depressive mood changes. Patients with bilateral foci had schizo-affective clinical pictures. As the central representation of sweat gland activity is probably ipsilateral, it was hypothesised that dextral schizophrenic patients would have impairment of left brain function and hence abnormalities in the GSR of the left hand. Such indeed was found, responses tending to be larger from the right hand than from the left.

Another report by Gruzelier (1973) showed that the asymmetry in response was present in the institutionalised patients only, fewer responses being present on the left. In general, response amplitudes were higher on the right and response recovery times faster.

These reports of asymmetry are very interesting, especially as there is confirmatory evidence from the EEG studies in depressive patients (see p. 139). Further studies of this type should be carried out, if possible using patients who are drug-free, at least with respect to phenothiazines.

In the study by Spohn, Thetford and Cancro (1970), a group of 32 male schizophrenics were compared with normal subjects with respect to skin conductance recorded during a tachistoscopic task. Basal conductances at rest were the same in both groups. During the task the mean conductance of the normal group showed a characteristic rise and then a gradual adaptation return down to resting levels. In the patients, the skin conductance first dropped and then rose *up* to resting levels. However, the patients were being treated with phenothiazines; when these were withdrawn, both resting and task conductance levels were significantly higher than in the patients before withdrawal and than in the normal subjects when re-tested. This study emphasises the need for caution in interpreting results when patients are tested while they are on drugs with known autonomic as well as central effects.

The prognostic value of skin conductance estimations in

schizophrenic patients has also been explored. Forty-four acutely ill patients underwent an habituation procedure before treatment and then five weeks later while on phenothiazine therapy (Stern, Surphlis and Koff, 1965). There was no difference on first testing between patients who later responded to treatment and those who did not. However, on re-testing, the good prognosis group habituated more rapidly than the group who had not improved. This, of course, probably reflects the central effect of the phenothiazines which were exerting a general effect, including a therapeutic one, in one group but were generally inefficacious in the other.

Another intriguing set of studies is that of Mednick and Schulsinger (1966 (Mednick), 1968, 1974). In 1962, Mednick and Schulsinger began a longitudinal study of children aged 10–20 who had a severely schizophrenic mother. This sample of 207 was compared with 104 children of normal parentage. By 1967, twenty of the high-risk subjects had suffered some sort of psychiatric illness (not necessarily schizophrenia). All the children had had psychophysiological recordings in 1962 and these records were examined to see if there were any differences then between the subsequently sick group, the high-risk but as yet well children and low-risk controls. The sick group had shown shorter GSR latency, increased stimulus generalisation and, in particular, a very fast GSR recovery time. The GSRs were larger in the sick group and took longer to habituate. The birth of members of the sick group was attended by more complications and there was more separation from their parents during childhood.

In a more detailed analysis, groups were selected on the basis of high risk and low risk but equated for parental separation, and for high and low separation but equated for risk. Both high risk and high separation were associated with shorter GSR latency and larger GSR amplitude, but not with GSR recovery rate. In a similar way, a high incidence of perinatal complications was correlated with short GSR latency and increased amplitude, and also with fast recovery rate.

## Salivation

This measure appears to have been little used in the investigation of schizophrenic patients in contrast to its widespread use in depressive patients. The pioneers with this technique, Strongin and Hinsie (1938a), described late psychotics as having raised salivary flow rates. In comparison with depressed patients, schizophrenics have been reported to have higher salivation rates (i.e. near normal values) in some studies (Peck, 1959; Busfield, Wechsler and Barnum, 1961), but equally low values have been claimed in other studies (Davies and Gurland, 1961; Giddon and Lisanti, 1962; Palmai and Blackwell, 1965).

## Heart rate

It has been reported that, whereas normal subjects show a decrease in pulse rate over a recording period, schizophrenic patients show no such decline (Cohen and Patterson, 1937). The patients' pulse rates were also more variable. In another study, the heart rate at rest appeared raised in a group of schizophrenics as compared with neurotic patients and normal controls; when a task was commenced the rise in pulse rate was much less in the schizophrenics than in the other two groups (Jurko, Jost and Hill, 1952).

In the study of Williams (1953) cited earlier (see p. 158) in which 'impersonal', 'personal' and 'interpersonal' stresses were used, the resting pulse rate was higher and more variable in the schizophrenic patients. During impersonal stress the pulse rate increased equally in both groups. During both personal and interpersonal stress, the pulse rate increased more in the patients than in the control subjects.

Kelly and Walter (1969) reported the resting pulse rate of chronic schizophrenics to be elevated compared with normal (88 and 73). With the onset of a stressful task—mental arithmetic carried out under harassment—the pulse rate rose 9 per cent in the patients but 34 per cent in the normals.

## Blood pressure

Schizophrenic patients with lack of contact with reality have been reported to show minimal blood pressure responses to stimuli (Darrow and Solomon, 1934). In paranoid schizophrenics, the blood pressure appeared below normal levels (Jurko, Jost and Hill, 1952).

## Blood flow

In an early study, the blood flow in the hand was reduced in schizophrenic patients as compared with normal controls (Abramson,

Schkloven and Katzenstein, 1941). Vanderhoof, Clancy and Engelhart (1966) examined blood flow in the calf of various groups of patients. Schizophrenic patients had significantly lower blood flows than patients with the diagnosis of personality disorder, neurosis or situational reactive symptoms. A similar study was carried out in London by Kelly and Walter (1969). Twenty chronic schizophrenic patients with process symptoms (average duration 5·6 years) were compared with a group of normal subjects and with various groups of patients. The resting forearm blood flow of the patients was 3·31 ml per minute per 100 ml of arm, significantly greater than the normal value (2·21). A mental arithmetic task induced an increase of 70 per cent in blood flow in the patients as compared with 312 per cent in the normals.

## Pupil size

Marked variability in pupillary responses have been reported in schizophrenic patients (McCawley, Stroebel and Glueck, 1966; Rubin and Barry, 1972).

## Somatic measures

### Respiration

Like heart rate, respiration is reported to be more irregular than normal in schizophrenic patients (Jurko, Jost and Hill, 1952). In normal subjects, the respiration rate increased slightly from resting to task conditions, whereas in the patients the rate dropped markedly. In Williams's study (1953), respiratory rate was increased at rest in the group of early, chronic schizophrenics as compared with the normal subjects. During the 'impersonal' and 'interpersonal' stress situations, respiratory rate rose more in the patients than in the control subjects. Recovery after the stresses was also slower in the patients.

### Electromyogram

Psychotic patients, early schizophrenics, had significantly more muscle tension than normal subjects at rest but not during stress periods (Martin, 1956). Whatmore and Ellis (1958) reported higher EMGs in the forehead, jaw, forearm and leg muscles of a group of schizophrenic patients at rest than in normal subjects. Similarly raised muscle activity was found in depressives but, in remission, the schizophrenics had labile muscle tension in contrast to the sustained high levels of depressives in remission (Whatmore, 1966).

One study, limited to a single co-operative psychotic patient, has evaluated the muscle activity accompanying hallucinations (McGuigan, 1966). Just prior to reported hallucinations, there were significant increases in EMGs recorded from the chin with lesser increases in tongue EMGs, and no change in arm muscle activity.

Motor control appears to be disrupted in chronic schizophrenics: they exerted excessively high pressures on the response button during a rapid discrimination test (Malmo et al., 1951).

## Electroencephalogram

The earlier work concerning electroencephalography in schizophrenic patients has been extensively reviewed by Hill (1957), who points out that the early workers were greatly limited by their relatively primitive techniques. On the other hand, the widespread development of complex mathematical analyses of the EEG have 'resulted in the danger that the worker will be overwhelmed by his data'. In general, the early investigators reported that the EEG was normal in schizophrenia. For example, Davis and Davis (1939), from their examination of 232 patients in mental hospitals, concluded: 'The fundamental patterns of these patients cannot be distinguished from those of our control series of 500 "normals".' Nevertheless, a large proportion of the patients' records lay outside the normal range of variability. Among the abnormalities reported was the presence of slow delta waves in the frontal areas and a 'delta index' was developed which represented the proportion of the time occupied by such activity (Hoagland, Cameron and Rubin, 1937). The claim was made that this index was significantly higher in untreated than in treated schizophrenics. Soon after, it was shown that these delta waves were related to rhythmic eye movements which were greater in schizophrenic patients and which declined as the patient recovered (MacMahon and Walter, 1938).

Another characteristic of the EEG in schizophrenia was described as 'choppy rhythm' (Davis, 1942). This consisted of an EEG with little or no alpha rhythm or slow rhythm, but low-voltage fast random frequencies between 26–50 Hz. This pattern was found in 61 per cent of schizophrenics and 39 per cent of manic depressive patients, and the suggestion was made that it reflected overstimulation of the cortex. This choppiness of the EEG is probably a real phenomenon and not due solely to the technical limitations of the earlier workers; however, it is probably not characteristic of schizophrenia *per se*.

Another type of pattern which has been described in schizophrenic patients is the so-called 'mitten' pattern (Gibbs and Gibbs, 1963). These patterns are apparently much more common in Parkinsonian patients (Lyketsos, Belinson and Gibbs, 1953). More recently, the mitten patterns have been divided into A and B. The latter is a sharp transient wave followed by slow waves (like the thumb and hand of a mitten), and it occurs in the frontal areas bilaterally and synchronously in moderately deep sleep. The A mitten pattern, occurring in Parkinsonism, differs slightly (Struve and Becka, 1968). Nineteen out of fifty-eight patients diagnosed as reactive schizophrenics showed the B mitten pattern, whereas only two out of twenty-seven labelled processed schizophrenics had this phenomenon in their EEGs (Struve, Becker and Kline, 1972). The significance of these findings is still not established.

Lester and Edwards (1966) described an increase in the amount and amplitude of pre-central EEG fast activity in patients with diagnoses of schizophrenic reactions. However, there seems to be no specificity about these findings as similar activity was noted in many patients with chronic alcoholism (especially if there was a history of hallucinosis), some neurological patients and some asymptomatic relatives of schizophrenics. In nuclear, process-type schizophrenics an absence of alpha activity has been claimed (Kortchinskaïa, 1965), and similar findings were mentioned by Bruck (1964). In a study relating prognosis in schizophrenics to the type of EEG, 46 per cent of a group of sixty-nine female schizophrenics showed records described as normal with alpha activity and neither fast nor theta waves: the prognosis of these patients was poor. The remainder of the patients had dysrhythmic EEGs with little alpha activity and either fast or theta waves superimposed, or the EEG was abnormal with slow-wave foci and paroxysmal activity. The more variable the EEG initially and the greater the change with treatment the better was the general prognosis (Igert and Lairy, 1962). The association of a persistent regular alpha rhythm and an unfavourable outcome was also found by Small and Stern (1965). The monotonous regularity of the alpha in patients with schizophrenic illnesses has been remarked on and the resistance of this alpha to stimulation is pronounced (Salamon and Post, 1965). As will be seen later, the regularity of the EEG in many schizophrenics has been confirmed using quantitative techniques (Golstein and Sugarman, 1969).

As well as general abnormalities such as the invariant alpha activity, more specific and localised abnormalities have been described (Tucker *et al.*, 1965). These results can often be attributed to the inclusion of patients with schizophrenia-like illnesses associated with epileptic phenomenon. In a survey of twenty-five Dutch Mental Hospitals carried out in 1964, Beek and his associates described very few differences between 114 patients with schizophrenia and eighty-seven controls of a similar age distribution. Indeed, the controls had a higher incidence of frontal temporal foci.

*Quantitative Measures* Using automatic analysis of the EEG, several interesting findings have been described. In one study, theta activity was more abundant and beta activity less abundant in schizophrenics than in depressives (Fink, Itil and Clyde, 1965). However, these differences could have reflected the possible effects of age differences between the two patient groups. In another study, forty-two schizophrenic patients aged between 18 and 47 and drug-free for at least two weeks were compared with forty-two controls (a factory population), age- and sex-matched. Unfortunately, the schizophrenics were tested lying quietly in an EEG laboratory while the recordings from the controls were made with a portable EEG machine and analogue tape recorder. Visual evaluation suggested that only eighteen of the schizophrenics had normal records as compared with thirty of the controls. Both the theta and alpha activities were significantly raised in the schizophrenics and the schizophrenic patients also showed a greater range of amplitudes for these wavebands. Although these results could have been due to the different recording conditions, other results are less likely to have been contaminated by this factor. Thus, there were no differences in EEG patterns between the younger and the older schizophrenics whereas slow-wave activity was significantly greater in the younger controls than the older controls.

The authors suggest that a maturation defect may exist in schizophrenic patients (Volavka, Matoušek and Roubíček, 1966). Another study using automatic frequency analysis showed no difference between mental hospital patients and normal controls (Kennard and Schwartzman, 1957). A large-scale study compared one hundred chronic schizophrenics with an equal number of age- and sex-matched normal volunteer subjects (Itil *et al.*, 1972). The patients had lower EEG amplitudes and less alpha and slow-beta activity.

Some interesting laterality differences have been tentatively reported (Rodin, Grisell and Gottlieb, 1968). Twenty-five drug-free male chronic schizophrenics in the age range 20–40 were compared with age-matched control subjects with respect to the frequency patterns of the EEGs recorded from the two sides of the head. No differences between the groups were found with respect to the EEG patterns on the left. However, the power in the 14–33 Hz waveband on the right side of the head was significantly lower in the patient group. The authors regard this as evidence that the right hemisphere is more involved than the left in the pathological process. This is inconsistent with other hypotheses regarding laterality and schizophrenia (see p. 163).

Another method of analysis which has been used, especially by Goldstein's group, comprises amplitude analysis in which the total rectified amplitude of the EEG is measured. Both the mean energy content of the EEG and its variability can be estimated. In one study 101 chronic male schizophrenics, drug-free for at least a month, were compared with a control group of thirty-three laboratory staff and fifty-one prisoners with respect to the integrated amplitude of the EEG recorded from the left occipital region. No difference was found in the overall amplitude levels between patients and normals. However, in patients the variability was about half that of the controls. The schizophrenics were also divided into the usual subgroups: the catatonics had even lower EEG variability than the other schizophrenics. Neither age nor duration of hospitalisation was related to the variability of the EEG (Goldstein *et al.*, 1965).

Using a similar technique, sixteen male chronic schizophrenics were studied over the course of one year and the EEG variability related to psychiatric ratings of psychopathology and ward behaviour. Although various drugs were given, a relationship was discerned: worsening of schizophrenic behaviour was associated with a decrease in variability and an increase in mean energy level

(Sugarman *et al.*, 1964). A third study using different techniques confirmed the findings of lower variability in patients (Burdick, Sugarman and Goldstein, 1967). More recently in Canada, the mean integrated EEG and its variability were recorded in twenty-eight chronic schizophrenics (mean duration of hospitalisation, 17·5 years; mean age 48), sixty acute schizophrenics (mean age 36) and twenty-five normals (staff members, mean age 34). No significant differences were found between the groups with respect to mean energy levels but the variability of the EEG in chronic schizophrenics was less than that in both acute schizophrenics and normal subjects. There were no correlations with age, drug intake or psychopathology severity. A recent study has again confirmed the constancy of the EEG in chronic schizophrenics (Lifshitz and Gradijan, 1972). Acute schizophrenics who were hallucinated during the recording had lower EEG variability (Marjerrison, Krause and Keogh, 1968).

The interpretation of such studies is no further advanced than that of Goldstein *et al.* (1963), namely that such data 'would suggest that the cerebral cortex of chronic schizophrenic patients is in a sustained state of excitation or even hyperexcitation'.

It must also be remembered that schizophrenic patients tend to be disturbed and their EEGs to show many artifacts. In one study, the proportion of the EEG record taken up with artifacts was almost a third greater for schizophrenics (26 per cent) than for controls (20 per cent) (Bruck and McNeal, 1964).

The transcephalic direct current potential is the slowly changing potential difference recorded from front to back of the head. Changes in this voltage have been claimed to reflect alterations in attention and some emotional states. Schizophrenic patients have significantly more negative values than non-schizophrenic patients or controls, this phenomenon being more marked in hallucinating patients (Cowen, 1968).

*Catatonic stupor* During catatonic stupor slow-wave patterns have been described together with fast spike and waves and groups of spikes. These patterns are not consistent nor is there any clear correlation between the development of the EEG abnormalities and the clinical stage of the stupor (Hill, 1952).

*EEG responses*

Photic stimulation has been used to produce EEG responses. In one study (Blum, 1956), alpha activity in normal subjects tended to drop with photic stimulation (as expected), but in patients with organic states or schizophrenia the alpha activity tended to rise. In a follow-up study (Blum, 1957), twenty-four normal subjects, twenty schizophrenic patients on tranquillisers, twenty drug-free schizophrenics and twenty brain-damaged patients were compared with respect to their alpha activity both at rest and in response to photic stimulation at 10, 20 and 40 flashes per second. No significant differences between the groups were seen with respect to the resting activity, but the normal subjects were significantly more responsive to the photic stimulation than were either the schizophrenics or the brain-damaged patients. There was no apparent effect of the drugs. In a Russian study (Féigenberg, 1964), it was claimed that alpha activity was widespread and very clearly shown in patients with 'nuclear schizophrenia'. No differences in photic responses or auditory responses were noted between the usual sub-groups of schizophrenia. This latter result was also noted by Hein and his colleagues (Hein, Green and Wilson, 1962) who found the latency and duration of photically elicited arousal responses to be similar in drug-free patients with hebephrenic, catatonic or simple schizophrenia.

More complex results were obtained in a study involving a total of 241 subjects. Schizophrenic patients from a university psychiatric service, schizophrenics from state hospitals, psychopaths and controls (medical and surgical patients and healthy subjects) were compared with respect to habituation of the alpha attenuation response: 50 light flashes were presented at intervals of 5–20 seconds when alpha activity was apparent. No differences were found between most of the groups, but the state hospital schizophrenics differed from the control subjects and from the other schizophrenics in showing shorter latency of alpha-blocking and more persistent responses, i.e. less habituation (Milstein, Stevens and Sachdev, 1969). The possible role of drugs in influencing this result is unclear.

EEG responses during sleep were studied in schizophrenic patients (Passouant, Duc and Minvielle, 1961). There was hyperreactivity to auditory stimulation in 17 per cent of the cases studied, but the authors are careful to point out that they do not believe that this is specific to schizophrenia but probably depends on the anxious state of the patients. A study with a rather different conclusion was that of Wilson and Parker (1957) who compared eighteen drug-free schizophrenic patients with four students and nine neurotic patients of similar age range. The EEG was monitored during the intravenous injection of noradrenaline and fewer schizophrenic patients were aroused than non-schizophrenics.

*Evoked potentials* (Begleiter, Porjesz and Gross, 1967)

One group of studies which has produced a great deal of interest was that of Callaway and his co-workers in San Francisco. They developed a technique in which tones of different frequency (600 Hz and 1,000 Hz) were presented to subjects and the evoked responses to these tones were derived separately. The similarity between the evoked responses to the two sets of tones was then estimated (Jones *et al.*, 1965). Three groups of patients were compared—paranoid schizophrenics, non-paranoid schizophrenics and non-schizophrenics; most were being currently treated with phenothiazine drugs. The correlation between the evoked responses to the two-tone frequencies was high in the non-schizophrenic and the paranoid schizophrenic patients (and also in a separate group of normals). However, the non-paranoid schizophrenics had a significantly lower correlation coefficient. This was interpreted as meaning that normal subjects, non-schizophrenic patients and paranoid schizophrenic patients soon stopped distinguishing between two 'irrelevant' tones whereas non-paranoid schizophrenics continued the discrimination despite its irrelevance. The finding was confirmed in a further group of schizophrenics in which some relationship was found between lower inter-evoked response correlations and clinical features such as thought disorder (Jones, Blacker and Callaway, 1966).

More recently a more detailed analysis of this interesting finding has been carried out (Callaway, Jones and Donchin, 1970). It is pointed out that the dissimilarity between the evoked responses in schizophrenics as compared with the greater inter-evoked response similarity in other patients and normals could be due to one or more of three possibilities:

(1) Schizophrenic patients have consistently different evoked responses to differing tones.
(2) Schizophrenics have more variable evoked response to tones.
(3) There is a more variable background EEG.

Using more detailed analyses, including the variability of the evoked response and of the preceding background EEG, it was found

that the variability of the EEG responses was greater for schizophrenics than for normal subjects but that there was no difference
in the variability of the background EEG, i.e. possibility (2) was the
most likely. This study shows the necessity for very careful controls
and for detailed analysis of data where powerful techniques such
as averaging are carried out. It also shows, as have many other
studies (e.g. Inderbitzin *et al.*, 1970), that the characteristic above
all else which distinguishes schizophrenics from normals is the
variability of response.

Another study using detailed analysis of auditory responses also
divided the schizophrenic patients into those with thought disorder
and those without thought disorder. The auditory evoked responses to a 1,000 Hz tone presented at 2-second intervals were
most variable in thought-disordered schizophrenics, less so in the
other schizophrenics and least in normals. The latencies of the
evoked response components were shortest and the amplitudes
smallest in thought-disordered schizophrenics (Saletu, Itil and
Saletu, 1971). This study again demonstrates the variability of
responses, especially in the more ill schizophrenics. Diminution in
amplitude and shortening of latencies of visual evoked responses
have also been described in schizophrenic patients (Vasconetto,
Floris and Morocutti, 1971).

The influence of drugs on the auditory evoked response of
schizophrenics was more pronounced on the $P_2$ than on the $P_3$
wave (Roth and Cannon, 1972).

The recovery cycle of somatosensory evoked responses has been
evaluated in a large group of patients by Shagass (1968). In this
technique stimuli are paired, the interval between the stimuli being
varied, and the ratio of the two responses computed. It is assumed
that if the second response is diminished this provides some index
of the degree of cortical recovery from the first response. No
group-specificity was found for the recovery cycle in the psychiatric patients. Visual evoked responses have also been used in a
similar manner (Heninger and Speck, 1966). Cortical recovery
appeared to be impaired in schizophrenic patients before treatment
as compared to normal controls. With treatment with phenothiazines this abnormality was lessened. Some abnormalities in the
recovery cycle of the visual evoked potential in paranoid schizophrenics have also been reported (Floris *et al.*, 1967).

A recent study has evaluated visual and auditory evoked potentials recorded from the scalp under complex psychological con-

ditions such as stimulus uncertainty and changes in the modality of stimulation. Schizophrenic patients and normal controls matched for age, sex and race, socio-economic status and educational level were studied, but the patients were on chlorpromazine medication. The schizophrenics had smaller evoked responses ($N_1$–$P_3$ complex) than the normals. Both groups had larger amplitudes under conditions of stimulus uncertainty than under conditions when they knew when to expect the stimulus. However, the effect of uncertainty was greater in the normal group than in the schizophrenic group (Levit, Sutton and Zubin, 1973).

The contingent negative variation (CNV) has been studied in a presumably heterogeneous group of forty-five psychotic patients and compared with that from forty-five hysterics, twenty-five obsessionals and forty-five normal subjects (Timsit *et al.*, 1970). The amplitude of the CNV was similar in all groups but its duration appeared prolonged in psychotic patients. This suggested that the second imperative stimulus failed to terminate the state of expectancy. CNVs have been described as more variable than normal in schizophrenics (Small and Small, 1971).

## Sleep studies

There are especial problems with carrying out studies of sleep patterns in schizophrenic patients (Feinberg and Evarts, 1969). For example, many patients refuse to participate in such studies, especially if they necessitate transfer to a research laboratory. Severely ill negativistic schizophrenic patients are particularly difficult to study, and the selection of co-operative patients only must inevitably bias the sample of patients studied. A second problem stems from the use of drugs such as hypnotics and major tranquillisers. These are often given quite routinely and are well known to have effects on sleep patterns. Again, as it is the more severely disturbed patients who require treatment, a bias in selection towards the less ill patients may ensue. As well as these factors, the technical problems of a sleep laboratory are such that only a limited number of readings can be economically taken from any subject. Because of the fluctuating mental state of acutely schizophrenic patients an unrepresentative sample of sleep recordings might be obtained.

Despite all these difficulties, useful information concerning sleep and dreaming in schizophrenic patients has been obtained.

In one study the sleep of seventeen chronic schizophrenic patients was compared with that of thirteen medical students (Dement, 1955). No differences were found between the groups with respect to the number, quality and duration of REM periods.

In elderly deluded patients, the lighter stages of sleep are difficult to distinguish and Stage III contains long runs of delta waves (Ridjanović, 1964).

Further observations of schizophrenic patients were carried out by Feinberg and his co-workers (1964, 1965). The sleep patterns of twenty-two drug-free schizophrenic patients were determined from 154 nights of recording: eighteen patients were acutely ill whereas four were in remission. A control group consisting of four hospitalised patients with personality disorders and six non-hospitalised control subjects was used. The total sleep time of the actively ill schizophrenic patients was similar to that of the control subjects although the patients took a longer time to fall asleep and showed greater variability in the length of sleep prior to the onset of the first dream. During REM periods the schizophrenics had less eye movement activity than controls. The acutely ill patients showed less dream time than the chronic patients and the control subjects.

Caldwell and Domino (1967) studied twenty-five male chronic schizophrenics and compared them with ten control subjects of slightly younger mean age. In ten schizophrenics, no Stage IV sleep was apparent and there was a significant diminution in Stage III sleep. Stage I and REM stages showed no difference.

In thirteen chronic male schizophrenics entering periods of remission, the REM time was increased in comparison with control subjects. Eye movement was increased during REM sleep and there was a failure to suppress tonic muscle activity during these periods. The authors believe that their results suggest either that such patients are REM-deprived or that there is an innate abnormality of sleep patterns in schizophrenic patients (Gulevich et al., 1967).

The effects of REM phase deprivation on schizophrenics and controls has been studied (Zarcone et al., 1968). Groups of acutely ill schizophrenics, remitted schizophrenics and non-schizophrenic controls underwent two nights of partial REM deprivation. The normal subjects made up 60 per cent of their lost REM time on succeeding nights; the schizophrenics in remission showed a markedly exaggerated REM-deprivation compensation, 'making up' 215 per cent of their lost REM time. Conversely, acutely ill patients

showed no compensation at all. The authors suggest that schizophrenia is an active process associated with a decreased need for
REM sleep, perhaps because certain essential components are discharged while awake instead. A further study did not, in fact, confirm these findings as there was no evidence of any differences in
REM-deprivation 'make up' between schizophrenics and normals
(Vogel and Traub, 1968). In a review of this subject, Vogel (1968)
could find no conclusive evidence that in schizophrenic patients
dreams or REM states erupt into wakefulness.

The effects of sleep deprivation on chronically catatonic patients
has also been assessed (Luby and Caldwell, 1967). Sleep deprivation lasting 85 hours produced a marked decrease in the catatonic
features. When allowed to sleep the amount of slow-wave sleep
hardly increased. The authors regard their findings as suggesting
'an irreversible defect in brain synchronising mechanisms'.

Recently a report on computer-analysed all-night sleep EEG
patterns has appeared (Itil *et al.*, 1972). Thirty-one chronic
schizophrenics (mean age 40) were compared with thirteen
normals (mean age 34). All the patients had been drug-free for at
least four weeks. The schizophrenic patients showed significant
diminution in the deep sleep stages, more light sleep stages and
awakening periods, a later onset of 'spindle' sleep and marked
variability in sleep patterns, both within a single night and from
night to night. There was no difference between patients and
controls for either the duration of REM sleep periods or their
number. There was some tendency for hallucinating schizophrenics
to have longer REM periods than non-hallucinating schizophrenics.

Spontaneous skin potential fluctuations diminished in REM sleep
in normal subjects but increased in acutely ill schizophrenic
patients; this might imply that the boundaries between REM
sleep and waking is less distinct in schizophrenics (Wyatt *et al.*,
1970).

## Dreams and hallucinations

Aristotle (edition 1941) commented on the similarity between
hallucinations, dreaming and madness. Many studies have examined this relationship, and based on the ideas of William James
and Hughlings Jackson three hypotheses associating dreams and
hallucinations have recently been formulated (Feinberg and
Evarts, 1969):

177

(1) Neurophysiological processes associated with dreams are also associated with hallucinations occurring in the waking state.

(2) Those mechanisms underlying normal vision will be active in the course of dreams and visual hallucinations.

(3) Dreams and hallucinations result from the elimination of an inhibitory process.

However, there is little direct experimental support for these propositions. For example, there was no difference in the dream time and REM time between hallucinating and non-hallucinating patients (Koresko, Snyder and Feinberg, 1963). However, in another study, hallucinating schizophrenics showed more eye movements during dream periods than non-hallucinating schizophrenics (Feinberg, Koresko and Gottlieb, 1965). In five schizophrenic patients, the waking EEGs, eye movements and EMG activity bore no convincing resemblance to the patterns occurring during REM stages of sleep. The results fail to support the hypothesis that the schizophrenic stage has any obvious physiological similarity to normal dreaming (Rechtschaffen, Schulsinger and Mednick, 1964).

The reaction time is prolonged and the visual evoked response is diminished during episodes of auditory hallucinations (Inouye and Shimizu, 1972).

The relationship between REM sleep abnormalities and serotonin imbalance has been explored, but lies outside the scope of this book (Wyatt, Termini and Davis, 1971).

## Endocrine measures

### Adrenocortical function (Mason, 1968a)

The investigation of adrenocortical function in psychiatric patients was first systematically pursued by Pincus, Hoagland and their associates during the decade from 1945 onwards. The interest of this research group lay in attempting to find biochemical abnormalities in schizophrenic patients rather than in relating adrenocortical functioning to the psychological status of the patients. In the early studies, groups of chronic schizophrenic patients were compared with groups of normal subjects with respect to lymphocyte levels and urinary 17-oxosteroid excretion levels, both at rest and following stressful stimuli. Such stimuli included heat, cold, anoxia, and psychological tests and also physiological stimuli such as an ACTH injection. The general conclusion reached was that psychotic patients fail to show normal adrenocortical responses to stress (Elmadjian and Pincus, 1946; Pincus and Elmadjian, 1946). Confirmatory experiments were carried out and interpreted as supporting the conclusion that chronic schizophrenic patients displayed a type of 'hypoadrenalism' (Pincus, Hoagland et al., 1949). Giving patients dietary supplements with vitamins and protein did not rectify the deficient responses to ACTH (Pincus, Schenker et al., 1949). Differences in the steroid excretion pattern led to the suggestion that some form of steroid dysgenesis occurred in schizophrenia (Mittelman et al., 1952).

The influence of age was examined in some later studies. Groups of normal men and schizophrenic men were further sub-divided into those aged 20–39 and those aged 40–60. Under resting conditions the schizophrenic patients had higher 17-oxosteroids but lower 17-hydroxycorticosteroid urinary excretion rates than the normals. The older patients showed less response to ACTH than both the older normals and the younger patients (Hoagland et al., 1953). This was confirmed in more elderly patients (Freeman et al., 1955).

From their work, Faurbye and his co-workers (1951) concluded that there was a 'slight relative adrenal insufficiency in chronic schizophrenia', but few clear-cut results were obtained in another study (Friedlander et al., 1950).

Other studies have failed to support the conclusions of Hoagland's group. Changes in a variety of adrenocortical indices (including eosinophil count, uric acid levels, 17-oxosteroid excretion and sodium concentration in sweat) after injection of ACTH were not diminished in psychotic patients as compared with the changes in non-psychotic subjects. Indeed, schizophrenic patients appeared to show greater than normal changes in carbohydrate metabolism after such an injection (Altschule et al., 1950). The eosinopenia after ACTH was normal in twenty-five out of thirty patients with long-standing schizophrenia (Hiatt, Rothwell and Horwitt, 1952).

Using techniques for estimating plasma cortisol, the responses to ACTH, to a pyrogen and to a subcutaneous injection of insulin were monitored. No difference was found between a group of chronic schizophrenic patients and a normal group, and it was concluded that there was 'no evidence of any impairment of adrenocortical physiology in the chronic schizophrenic patient' (Bliss et al., 1955). Using modern techniques, eleven urinary steroids were quantified and no differences were found between schizophrenics and normals (Coppen *et al.*, 1967). It must be concluded that the assertion that chronic schizophrenic patients show less adrenocortical responsivity than normal subjects is not proven.

Another approach to the evaluation of adrenocortical function in schizophrenic patients has been in longitudinal studies. In one patient with catatonic schizophrenia, plasma cortisol levels were found to rise immediately prior to episodes of catatonic excitement (Gunne and Gemzell, 1956). Similar results with respect to urinary 17-oxosteroids have been reported (Batt *et al.*, 1957) and a relationship claimed between the severity of the illness and the urinary steroid excretion (Eiduson, Brill and Crumpton, 1961).

Very detailed longitudinal studies of several months' duration were carried out by Sachar and his associates (1963) in four young soldiers during their first episode of acute schizophrenia. During psychotic phases with high levels of anxiety or depression, there were marked increases in urinary 17-hydroxycorticosteroid levels, often as much as two or three times normal. A drop towards normal levels occurred at times of 'psychotic equilibrium' and on recovery. It was suggested from the detailed clinical observations that corticosteroid excretion 'may not be influenced by the *type* of psychological defenses employed by the patient in protecting himself from anxiety and depression, but rather by the *effectiveness* of the defenses, whether they be psychotic or neurotic'. Later studies confirmed that urinary steroid excretion increased during times of psychological 'turmoil' (Sachar *et al.*, 1971) and that the meaning to the patient and the effectiveness of his defensive systems were important factors (Wohlberg, Knapp and Vachon, 1970).

Upsets in the circadian rhythms of plasma cortisol concentrations were noted in patients with acute psychotic symptoms and in chronic deteriorated subjects. In the former patients, the disturbances were transient, in the latter the abnormalities were constant (Suwa and Yamashita, 1972).

Acute schizophrenics have higher 17-hydroxycorticosteroid excretion levels than normal (Lovegrove *et al.*, 1965) and even higher relative levels of 17-oxosteroid excretion (Matsumoto *et al.*, 1966). Schizophrenic patients also have a wider range of excretion than normal—2–48 mg in 24 hours as compared with 7–18 mg in 24 hours (Batt *et al.*, 1957).

It has been claimed that aldosterone excretion is low in patients with chronic schizophrenia, but the evidence is unconvincing (Elmadjian, 1962).

## Adrenomedullary function

In one of the earliest studies of plasma catecholamine levels, Weil-Malherbe (1955) found no appreciable differences between schizophrenic patients and other patients or normal subjects. This finding was confirmed with respect to urinary catecholamine output by Bergsman (1959). However, when chronic schizophrenic patients had emotional outbursts, concomitant rises in adrenaline excretion were noted.

In the longitudinal study of acutely schizophrenic patients cited earlier, Sachar et al. (1963) reported that urinary adrenaline output tended to follow similar patterns to those of cortisol excretion, i.e. it was raised in periods of affective distress such as 'turmoil' and 'depression'. When patients became extremely disturbed, adrenaline excretion could be up to eight times that during non-disturbed phases. There was no obvious relationship between catecholamine excretion and motor activity. The rise in adrenaline and noradrenaline excretion during phases of disturbed behaviour was noted in another study (Pscheidt et al., 1964); the closest relationship was between anxiety and increased catecholamine output.

In a third study (Lovegrove et al., 1965), a marked but not significant drop in both adrenaline and noradrenaline output was noted in acute schizophrenic patients on recovery.

## Thyroid function

Interest in thyroid function in schizophrenic patients has occurred in successive waves as more and more refined tests of thyroid activity have been introduced. Initial studies used estimates of basal metabolic rates in schizophrenic patients with scant success, although occasional reports of low metabolic rates in these patients appeared. Brody and Mann (1950) reported no difference in serum precipitable iodine values between fifty-seven schizophrenic patients and normals, but claimed that low basal metabolic rates characterised such patients and were a function not of low thyroid activity but of defective responsivity of the schizophrenic organism to circulating thyroid hormone. [131]I uptake, protein-bound iodine levels, basal metabolic rate and plasma cholesterol levels were estimated in twenty-four schizophrenic patients and twelve control subjects; a wider range of values occurred in the patients (Bowman *et al.*, 1950).

The use of single estimations in heterogeneous groups of schizophrenic patients has been criticised (Batt *et al.*, 1957). The careful sub-division of schizophrenic patients in clinical categories, longitudinal studies with several estimations on the same individual and observations on patients in several hospitals over long periods of time were suggested as desirable. These authors described their male schizophrenic patients as having some tendency to lowered thyroid functioning but this was not apparent in the female patients.

The importance of dietary control has been stressed (Kelsey, Gullock and Kelsey, 1957). The high radioactive iodine uptakes observed in a large proportion of psychotic in-patients were corrected by the introduction of iodised salt to the diet. A further factor was emphasised by Lingjaerde, Skaug and Lingjaerde (1960). They pointed out that schizophrenic patients are often asthenic and undernourished so that the calculated 'normal' basal metabolic rate may be too high. This could well account for the sporadic reports of lowered metabolic rate in schizophrenic patients. The suggestion that schizophrenic tissues are in some way less responsive to thyroid hormone than normal tissues has been refuted by Faurbye, Munkvad and Pind (1958) who found that chronic hebephrenic schizophrenics showed the expected biological response to treatment with thyroid hormones. No psychological effects were apparent.

The suggestion has been made that schizophrenic patients resemble the elderly in having decreased radioactive iodine uptake in conjunction with normal PBIs (Simpson, Cranswick and Blair, 1963, 1964). This fits in with evidence from adrenocortical studies, but there are many alternative explanations such as inadequate diet.

Little change has been reported in thyroid indices with differing phases of catatonic illnesses (Gjessing, 1964). Thyroxine turnover rate (estimated by injecting [131]I-labelled thyroxine) was more variable in a group of schizophrenic patients than in a group of normal subjects, but the mean values were similar (Reichlin, 1959).

No clear conclusions can be reached regarding thyroid function in schizophrenic patients. Most of the reported abnormalities in schizophrenia have not been confirmed or can be attributed to such factors as body build, diet and living conditions.

## General considerations

There have been many formulations of the psychological deficits in schizophrenic patients (Shakow, 1963, 1971). The various theories and areas of investigation may be roughly divided into the following categories: (1) affect and reinforcement, (2) concept attainment, (3) attention, (4) set, (5) associative interference, and (6) drive (Buss and Lang, 1965; Lang and Buss, 1965). As some of these considerations are relevant in interpreting the psychophysiological studies of schizophrenic patients, a brief outline will be given.

Certain 'affective' stimuli are disturbing to some patients but the stimuli are so varied and the responses of the patients so unpredictable that little additional precision is imparted to any study by attempting to distinguish such stimuli. Stimuli denoting censure seem especially disturbing. Schizophrenics benefit more from feedback of information during a task than do normals and seem to lack self-guidance during the task. Punishment such as shocks seems sometimes to assist the schizophrenic by breaking up a perseverative tendency.

The attainment of concepts is disordered in many schizophrenics. Rather than having especially concrete concepts, these patients tend to have eccentric or bizarre concepts. Nor are the concepts necessarily child-like or 'regressed'. Lack of ability to communicate also handicaps schizophrenic patients. Schizophrenics have broad, overinclusive concepts and they suffer from the interference of extraneous and irrelevant elements.

Attention is certainly an important aspect of psychological deficit in schizophrenics (Kornetsky, 1964; Silverman, 1964). McGhie and Chapman (1961; Chapman and McGhie, 1962) attributed this deficit to a disturbance of selective attention. Distractibility is also heightened in the patients (McGhie, Chapman and Lawson, 1965a, 1965b; Venables, 1963c). Because attention is so inconstant, schizophrenics are less flexible in their perceptual monitoring (Venables, 1964). Thus, the deficit in the patient is greatest when he must attend to several inputs, switch his attention from one input to another or cut out irrelevant stimuli in favour of less powerful stimuli in physical terms. Deficit is least when the irrelevant stimuli are few, the task stimulus is powerful and unambiguous and no switching is called for.

Schizophrenics are also less able to carry out tasks in which a response has to be made at some pre-determined time in the future, e.g. in carrying out a reaction time response after a long fore-period. In other words, the 'set' of a schizophrenic is easily disrupted.

The disturbance in association is a fundamental one in schizophrenia, being manifested as bizarre ideas, fragmented thinking, thought-blocking and loose associations of ideas. This looseness of associations can interfere with the performance of a task. In doing a task a subject must be free of as many distractions as possible. He must suppress responses to inappropriate external stimuli and to inappropriate internal stimuli such as extraneous thoughts and associations which may distract his attention. Not only does the schizophrenic have difficulty in sustaining his attention to the relevant external stimuli but also he cannot prevent his idiosyncratic associations intruding. Schizophrenics have unusual associations and are unable to inhibit them, thus displaying impaired performance (Shakow, 1963). Response disorganisation characterises both acute and chronic schizophrenics, the chronic patients attempting to cope by observing fewer stimuli, both external and internal, wherever possible (Broen, 1966).

Drive theories of schizophrenia have centred around two aspects, negative drive theory, inhibition during conditioning and reminiscence being implicated, and positive drive theory, which allocates anxiety the key role (Epstein and Coleman, 1970). The negative drive theory stems from Pavlov's (1941) postulate that schizophrenics have an excess of inhibition which protects them against sensory overload (Lynn, 1963). Further developments of this theory have been forthcoming (e.g. Claridge, 1960, 1967; Eysenck, 1961). Thus, schizophrenics are supposed to accumulate reactive inhibition more rapidly than normals and to dissipate it more slowly. Accordingly, they should learn more slowly than normals and show a greater increment in performance after a rest period (reminiscence). Neither prediction is supported by much experimental evidence and interpreting behavioural changes in ambiguous terms such as 'reactive inhibition' is unprofitable.

The anxiety drive theories of schizophrenia deserve closer attention. Intense anxiety is experienced by the early schizophrenic as the breakdown in perceptual and cognitive processes proceeds (Chapman, 1966). However, there are many theorists who see a more fundamental role for anxiety: they hypothesise that there is a continuum of neurosis to psychosis and that schizophrenia ensues when the individual's neurotic defences against social or personal anxiety finally succumb (Fenichel, 1945). Mednick (1958) assumes anxiety to be intense in the pre-schizophrenic individual resulting in excessive stimulus generalisation and high drive. The increase in drive leads to more reactivity so that stimuli produce more response causing in turn higher drive: a positive feedback system ensues. In later stages of schizophrenia the looseness of association directs the patient from anxiety-provoking stimuli and the resulting drop in anxiety then acts as a positive reinforcer. Eventually, the schizophrenic becomes unresponsive, the chronic stage.

Mednick's theory makes essentially four assumptions: (1) schizophrenics acquire classical conditioned responses faster than normal controls, (2) schizophrenics learn slower in more complex situations, (3) schizophrenics overgeneralise, and (4) high anxiety is associated with overgeneralisation and faster conditioning. Support for these assumptions is not strong and the link between anxiety and schizophrenia may not lie in the causal chain. Thus, it is uncommon for patients with anxiety states, however severe, to develop schizophrenia. What is seen clinically is a patient with 'angst-psychose', but this is an uncommon schizophreniform psychosis which occurs as the anxiety level rises. Complete recovery is the rule. Secondly, many schizophrenic patients are anxious as an understandable reaction to the profound disruption in mental processes. Therefore, any abnormalities of perception, cognition, etc., or of psychophysiological variables could be secondary to the anxiety and not to the schizophrenic 'process'. It is instructive to compare the findings in schizophrenics outlined in this chapter with those in anxiety states (chapter 4). Practically all the positive findings in schizophrenics have also been described in anxiety states whenever direct comparisons have been made. It is not defeatism but realism to suggest that no psychophysiological property of schizophrenics has been unequivocally demonstrated. Until patients with anxiety states are routinely included as an additional control in studies of schizophrenic patients no real scientifically sound conclusions can be drawn. Thus, the raised autonomic and endocrine variables, the lack of reactivity, the slowness to adapt and habituate, the poor stimulus discrimination and the generally impaired performance of the schizophrenic are found to a greater or lesser extent in the morbidly anxious patient and can often be induced by stressful procedures in the calm normal.

## Problems of diagnosis

So far the psychophysiology of schizophrenia has been discussed as if 'schizophrenia' was a disease as well defined as pneumococcal pneumonia and a group of schizophrenics as homogeneous as Huntington's choreics. There are two aspects to this: firstly, the problems of diagnosing schizophrenia as opposed to other psychiatric conditions and, secondly, the sub-categories of schizophrenia (Silverman, 1967).

The criteria for the diagnosis of schizophrenia vary from country to country or even from centre to centre within a country. The Scandinavian and British concepts of schizophrenia are quite similar although several Scandinavian centres lay emphasis on the schizophreniform psychoses. The rest of Western Europe tends to take a Bleulerian view of schizophrenia and approximates to the British concept although a variety of sub-groups are often distinguished. It is the marked differences between the European and the American concepts which leads to major problems in interpreting experimental results. In the majority of American psychiatric institutions (and in the USSR), the diagnosis of schizophrenia is much more readily made than in European hospitals and clinics. In some hospitals in the USA, as many as half the patients diagnosed as schizophrenic would be regarded as manic, depressed or suffering from a personality disorder in Europe. Thus, the American psychophysiologist will often be studying a group of patients grossly heterogeneous by European standards. Conversely, patients labelled manic or depressive in Europe will be suspect to American eyes. However, in many cases the experimenters are well aware of this problem and they confine their attentions to unequivocal cases of so-called 'core' schizophrenics.

The usual sub-categories used are hebephrenic, catatonic, paranoid and simple. The last category is difficult to define and rather suspect in that definite symptoms are often absent. The catatonic variety is now uncommonly seen in its full-blown picture although catatonic features may be encountered in some patients. Similarly, paranoid features are common in schizophrenic patients. However, there is a definite sub-group in the form of the paranoid schizophrenia of later onset. The symptoms tend to come on in middle age and the personality and mental functions remain relatively intact. Venables has shown the great usefulness of distinguishing such patients from the remainder of the general schizophrenic category.

The other major distinction is between 'process' and 'reactive' schizophrenics. This is probably a useful distinction in that the latter group is heterogeneous, and therefore confining a laboratory study to process patients should result in a reasonably well-defined group. Furthermore, if only patients with Schneiderian first-rank symptoms are included, almost all psychiatrists would agree that a group of 'schizophrenics' was being studied although other patients who might well come under this rubric might be excluded. The first-rank features include hallucinatory voices commentating on the patient's actions, hearing thoughts spoken out aloud, broadcasting of thoughts, thought withdrawal, bodily feelings of influence, passivity feelings and primary delusional perceptions.

The dichotomy widely used in psychophysiological research is into acute and chronic patients, perhaps based on the notion that the former are overaroused, the latter underaroused. A time point is usually selected, say two years of continuous illness. Such an approach gainsays the variety and complexity of the natural history of the schizophrenia group of illnesses. For example, one quite common pattern is for a patient to have a series of acute episodes interspersed with several years of apparent normality. However, after each attack, the degree of recovery is a little incomplete so that eventually psychological deficits become apparent. Such a process cannot be fitted into the acute–chronic dichotomy.

A further objection to this system is that many of the features of chronic schizophrenia are a reflection of years of institutionalisation and drug therapy rather than of any disease process. Dividing patients into institutionalised and non-institutionalised is a recognition of this problem. However, it must be remembered that some schizophrenics are as effectively institutionalised by living at home as in hospital.

# Miscellaneous conditions

In this chapter a selection of other conditions frequently met with in psychiatric and medical practice will be outlined with respect to psychophysiological research.

## Hysterics

The term 'hysteria' is almost impossible to define as the processes underlying the condition are so ill-known. The entire topic is shrouded with confusing terms, vague concepts and untestable 'hypotheses' (Slater, 1965). Patients designated 'hysteric' range from histrionic adolescent girls to severely disabled older individuals whose symptoms are inexplicable in organic terms. Often the term is applied pejoratively to patients who complain. From this welter of psychopathology, one group can be distilled. These are patients with conversion phenomena which are objectively observable. Such patients have symptoms of a neurological nature —paralysis, anaesthesia, blindness, aphonia, fits, amnesia, etc.— for which there is no apparent neurological cause. There may be disagreement over whether a symptom is caused by a neurological lesion or is a conversion symptom but, usually, the diagnosis is not too difficult to make. There are other features which are less susceptible to precise observation such as a stressful precipitant, secondary gain and *belle indifférence*.

There have been relatively few studies of the psychophysiology of hysterics and they have concentrated on two aspects—the physiological characteristics of hysterics and the neurophysiological mechanisms underlying the symptoms.

### Autonomic activity

Lader and Sartorius (1968) carried out a small study on ten patients who had conversion symptoms at the time of testing. Eight were female and six were in their late teens or early twenties. All but two had been ill for more than six months. They were compared with seventy-one patients with anxiety and phobic states and seventy-five normal subjects with respect to their self-rating of anxiety, the psychiatrist's rating of overt anxiety and physiological measures such as skin conductance levels, habituation of the GSR to repeated auditory stimuli and spontaneous skin conductance fluctuations. The hysterics rated themselves significantly *more* anxious than the anxiety states; the psychiatrist rated the hysterics as significantly *less* anxious. The hysterics had higher skin conductance levels, slow or even absent GSR habituation and more fluctuations than the anxious patients. That is, the physiological measures were consistent with the patients' but not the psychiatrist's ratings. The results were interpreted as implying that in this small group of rather chronic patients high anxiety levels were experienced and were accompanied by much sweat gland activity, but that little emotional distress was conveyed to the observing psychiatrist. Similar results were found in a further ten patients of this type.

The original ten patients were followed up over the ensuing three years mainly by reference to the case notes. Several indices of anxiety such as self-rating and spontaneous sweat gland activity correlated negatively with outcome, i.e. high anxiety levels were associated with subsequent persistence of conversion symptoms (Lader, 1969).

Conversely, some other observations have supported the original early formulation by Freud (1948) that the conversion symptoms represent 'psychic energy' associated with unacceptable urges being 'converted' into somatic symptoms. In a series of unpublished case studies of Levy, two patients showed an increase in sweat gland fluctuations when the symptoms disappeared, after hypnosis in one case and natural remission in the second.

The discrepancy between Lader's work and Levy's study has been partly explained by an Australian investigation (Meares and Horvath, 1972). They distinguished two groups of hysterics: (1) six patients with acute, short-lived conversion symptoms who otherwise had normal medical histories and adequate work records; and (2) eleven patients with more chronic symptoms (more than one month), with histories of failure in the occupational, interpersonal and sexual spheres and with many medical complaints over a long period. The first group had essentially normal psychophysiological functioning whereas the chronic group had

189

significantly higher sweat gland activity, faster heart rates and higher muscle activity.

These results are not conclusive because all patients were in remission at the time of the physiological recordings. However, it might well be that patients with acute conversion symptoms show little anxiety and have low levels of physiological activity whereas chronically ill patients have consistently high levels. Consequently, the research setting is important, general and neurological hospitals tending to deal with acute cases, psychiatric departments encountering the chronic patients.

It is not known whether patients with acute symptoms who fail to respond to treatment and become chronic have high levels of anxiety and physiological activity throughout or whether low levels are superseded by higher levels as the symptoms persist. From the laboratory data and from clinical observations, there seems to be a group of polysymptomatic neurotic patients with persistently high anxiety levels who eventually develop conversion symptoms under extra stress. The conversion symptoms provide just enough secondary gain to perpetuate the illness but not sufficient to lower anxiety levels. This contrasts with the patient with a histrionic personality but no overt symptoms who develops intense anxiety with temporary stress. The anxiety level drops as the conversion symptom develops but if the stress is removed the conversion symptom remits without re-establishment of the anxiety.

*Evoked responses*

The other area in which several studies on hysterics have been mounted is evoked responses. The technique is most appropriate to investigating the mechanisms underlying the symptoms.

In one of the earliest studies, seven patients with hysterical anaesthesias were investigated using electrical stimulation of sensory or mixed nerves and of the skin. In every case the cerebral potential evoked from stimulation of the affected side was similar to that evoked from the normal side (Alajouanine *et al.*, 1958).

In contrast, Hernández-Peón, Chávez-Ibarra and Aguilar-Figueroa (1963) reported on a 15-year-old girl with glove and sleeve analgesia and thermoanaesthesia of the left arm. Short trains of electrical stimuli of just suprathreshold intensity were applied to the skin of each forearm in turn. Clear somatosensory evoked potentials were obtained over the contralateral parietal area on stimulation of the normal side. When the left, affected side was stimulated, no definite response was discernible from the right parietal area. The response was induced when the patient was put under light anaesthesia. The authors concluded: 'The presented findings fall in line with the proposed hypothesis that hysterical anaesthesia may be the result of an increased inhibition of different transmission somewhere along the somatic sensory pathway.'

More recent studies have failed to confirm these positive findings (Bergamini and Bergamasco, 1967). Halliday (1968) detailed the case of a 40-year-old man with hysterical anaesthesia of the left thumb and index finger who had normal evoked potentials. In particular, the response latencies were quite normal which was regarded as strong evidence against a possible lesion in the afferent pathways. In some otological centres, auditory evoked responses are used routinely to detect hysterical deafness (Cody and Bickford, 1965; Goldstein and Price, 1966).

A detailed analysis of the evoked responses in a 43-year-old woman with right hemianaesthesia was carried out by Levy and Behrman (1970). Stimulation at various levels of intensity was applied to both the skin overlying the ulnar nerve and to skin on the forearm not over a major nerve. When high intensity stimuli were applied to the nerve on the affected side the evoked responses were as large as those when the normal side was stimulated; with low intensity nerve stimuli the evoked response from stimulation of the affected side was definitely reduced; with skin stimulation of any intensity the response from the affected side was also diminished. The results were interpreted as implying at least two different physiological mechanisms underlying hysterical mechanisms: (1) a lowering of peripheral receptor sensitivity, and (2) a central mechanism of inhibition along the afferent pathways. Data from a further eight cases supported this conclusion (Levy and Mushin, 1973). Nevertheless, these findings may only be applicable to somatosensory stimulation as normal evoked responses to flashes were found in almost all of nineteen patients with hysterical amblyopia despite gross abnormalities of dark adaptation (Behrman, 1969; Behrman and Levy, 1970).

In view of the complex and unclear relationships between hysteria and hypnosis, it is appropriate to mention that no consistent, unequivocal effects of hypnotic suggestion on the evoked response has ever been demonstrated in an adequate number of

*

subjects (Beck and Barolin, 1965; Beck, Dustman and Beier, 1966; Halliday and Mason, 1964), although there have been interesting individual cases in which marked attenuation of the evoked response occurred when the suggestion was made under hypnosis that the stimulus was absent (Clynes, Kohn and Lifshitz, 1964; Hernández-Péon and Donoso, 1959; Satterfield, 1964).

## Depersonalisation

This interesting phenomenon is found in a wide variety of clinical syndromes, both organic and functional (Shorvon, 1946; Ackner, 1954). It is particularly associated with phobic anxiety (Roth, 1960b).

In one study, I was recording the skin resistance from an anxious female patient and a typical tracing with low resistance (high sweating rate), many fluctuations and discernible GSRs to external stimuli was being obtained. The pulse rate was high. Over a few minutes the activity in the skin resistance trace increased even further and the pulse rate rose to 140 per minute. Then, fairly abruptly, the skin resistance rose to high levels and became flat and unresponsive, and the pulse rate dropped. On questioning later, the patient described how she had been feeling more and more panicky and was about to cry out for help when the anxiety suddenly subsided to be replaced by a strange feeling of detachment. Sounds appeared distant, vision was blurred and 'swimmy' and the patient's limbs felt as if they did not belong to her. The description was of depersonalisation and derealisation. On three subsequent occasions with other patients, I have noted similar short-term changes.

In another instance, a patient, a 25-year-old girl, complained that she felt 'like a robot' and was devoid of feeling and perception. The skin resistance tracing at the time was very high (see Figure 7.1). A few weeks later the girl reverted to her usual anxious state and the recording was characterised by extreme activity.

Such data support the speculation that depersonalisation and derealisation might in some cases be linked to some emergency physiological mechanism which counteracts excess arousal from sensory input by blocking that sensory input. However, as the mechanism is unselective, all sensory input—visual, auditory, olfactory, proprioceptive and visceroceptive—is attenuated, giving rise to the characteristic perceptual changes.

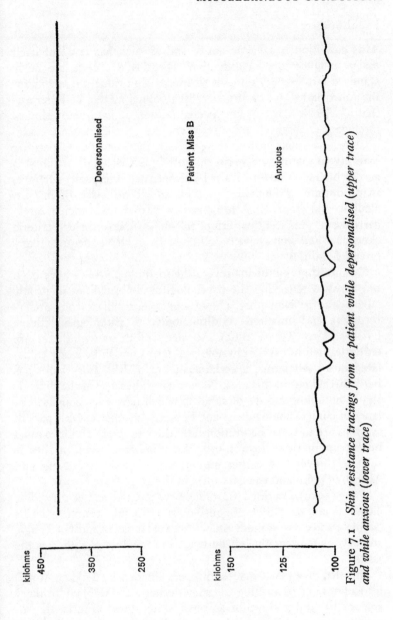

Figure 7.1  *Skin resistance tracings from a patient while depersonalised (upper trace) and while anxious (lower trace)*

## Psychopathy

This condition is a vague entity and as such has not lent itself easily to laboratory investigation. Diagnostic criteria are fairly standard but are very difficult to apply being value-judgments for the most part. The most generally accepted system of criteria is that of Cleckley (1959): unexpected failure, undisturbed technical intelligence, absence of neurotic anxiety, persistent and inadequately motivated antisocial behaviour, irresponsibility, peculiar inability to distinguish between truth and falsehood, inability to accept blame, failure to learn by experience, incapacity for love, inappropriate or fantastic reactions to alcohol, lack of insight, shallow and impersonal responses to sexual life, suicide rarely carried out, persistent pattern of self-defeat. Nevertheless, criteria check lists and scales have been drawn up and have adequate inter-rater reliabilities.

Despite these problems several heuristic hypotheses have been put forward regarding the psychological abnormalities in people labelled as psychopaths. These suggestions range from under-reactivity and impaired conditionability to pathological stimulation-seeking (Quay, 1965). As many of these hypotheses are either framed in psychophysiological terms or can be easily translated into such terms, a certain amount of laboratory work has been carried out in this area. Nevertheless, because of the difficulties of obtaining groups of subjects which have even some semblance of clinical homogeneity and because the most suitable patient samples are in penal institutions and the laboratory facilities must be set up in those institutions, the number of such studies is relatively few. The earlier studies are reviewed by Tong and Murphy (1960) and the later ones in detail by Hare (1970).

Tong (1959) described 'unstable' psychopathic subjects as being either over- or under-responsive to stressful stimuli whereas 'stable' subjects were moderately reactive. However, most of Tong's subjects were mentally sub-normal which unduly complicates the issue.

Inmates of a penal institution were divided by Lykken (1957) into a group of 19 meeting Cleckley's criteria and dubbed 'primary sociopaths' and a group of 20 not meeting these criteria, the so-called 'neurotic sociopaths'. A control group was also studied. Anxiety questionnaires and GSR conditioning were the main procedures used. The primary sociopaths had significantly less

'questionnaire anxiety' than the normals and less GSR responsiveness both to shocks and to tones signalling the shocks. The primary sociopaths were less successful at avoiding the shock during
avoidance learning. The neurotic sociopaths had distinctly more
'questionnaire anxiety' than the other groups.

Hare, working at the University of British Columbia, has carried
out an extensive series of studies examining reactivity and conditionability in psychopathic and non-psychopathic criminals. In
an early study, Hare (1965a) compared 12 psychopathic with 12
non-psychopathic institutional inmates with respect to acquisition
and generalisation of conditioned GSR responses. The psychopaths
conditioned more slowly than the non-psychopaths and showed
less generalisation to other stimuli. In a similar study comparing
psychopathic, non-psychopathic and non-institutionalised controls,
Hare (1965b) reported that the psychopaths had the lowest skin
conductance and showed the least reactivity to threat of shock.

In a larger study (Hare, 1968), the subjects were 51 inmates of
the British Columbia Penitentiary and were classified into 3 sub-
groups—primary psychopaths (21 in number), secondary (neurotic)
psychopaths (18) and non-psychopaths (12). Skin conductance,
heart rate, finger pulse volume and respiration rate were recorded
from the subjects at rest, during an habituation sequence of 15
auditory tones and during mental arithmetic. The primary
psychopaths again had lower resting skin conductance levels than
the non-psychopaths but the secondary psychopaths also had low
levels. Neither heart rate nor respiration rate differed among the
groups although heart rate variability tended to be less in the
primary psychopaths. GSR responsivity and habituation were
similar in the three groups but heart rate habituation was slowest
in the primary psychopaths and a similar tendency was noted for
vasoconstrictor responses. The results were evaluated by Hare in
terms of possible autonomic hyporeactivity in the primary psychopaths, but it was appreciated that the data were complex and not
easily interpreted.

In an experiment on similar subjects but using more complex
stimulation paradigms, Hare and Quinn (1971) confirmed that
psychopaths had low skin conductance levels and small GSRs but no
abnormalities in autonomic conditioning were apparent. A lower
frequency of skin conductance fluctuations has been found in
psychopathic criminals at rest (Fox and Lippert, 1963), during
stress and recovery periods (Lippert and Senter, 1966) and during

anticipation of stress (Schalling and Levander, 1967). Schalling and her associates (1973) administered the Gough Delinquency Scale to 25 men under arrest and divided them into 2 sub-groups—the high delinquency group (HD) and the low delinquency group (LD). The sub-groups were compared with respect to skin conductance, finger pulse volume and finger temperature during a rest period and then during and after an auditory tone habituation procedure. The HD group had significantly fewer skin conductance fluctuations during the stimulation period and the post-stimulation rest period. Skin conductance levels were also lower in the HD group. The results were interpreted in terms of lower cortical arousal in these subjects.

An ingenious study was that of Schachter and Latané (1964) who presented 15 primary sociopaths, 10 mixed (neurotic) sociopaths and 15 normal with an avoidance-of-shock learning task after injecting them with either placebo or adrenaline. The groups learnt the task at the same rate and adrenaline had no effect on the rate of learning. On the placebo occasion, the rate at which the shocks were administered dropped steadily in the mixed sociopaths and the normal subjects but remained level in the primary sociopaths, i.e. the latter group failed to improve their avoidance of shocks. On the adrenaline occasion, the primary sociopaths learnt more rapidly than the other two groups, i.e. the reverse happened. The pulse rate of the primary sociopaths rose after adrenaline but no change was observed in the others. However, this was not confirmed in two similar studies (Goldman, Lindner, Dinitz and Allen, 1971; Hare, 1972).

Electroencephalographic studies have shown a higher incidence of abnormality in subjects with psychopathic personalities than in normal subjects or patients with psychoneuroses (Hill, 1963). Estimates of the incidence of abnormality vary from 48 to 75 per cent according to different workers. The type of abnormality is generally found to be an excess of theta rhythm (4–7 Hz). The amplitude of these waves is not great and the waves are bilaterally synchronous. The abnormality is more prevalent in the younger age groups and is generally held to be a maturational defect. Its relevance to the psychological status of the subject is still unclear.

Walter (1966) has claimed that psychopaths are devoid of CNV waves. This is an interesting finding which seemed present in almost all the psychopaths tested. As psychopathy is such a heterogeneous entity and no real control groups were used it is possible that some other factor such as institutionalisation may have been operating. Replications of this study are in progress and the results are awaited with interest.

## Organic conditions

In these conditions objective physical abnormalities can be observed and interest has been concentrated on these aspects rather than on psychophysiological changes. For example, Levy, Isaacs and Hawks (1970) estimated the motor and sensory nerve conduction velocities in 28 demented patients and 19 control subjects. The motor nerve conduction velocity was reduced in the patients, especially the more demented. On re-testing a year later, a progression of the dementing process was associated with further slowing. Sensory nerve conduction was not affected although the latencies of certain components of the somatosensory evoked response on the scalp were delayed, suggesting some CNS effect (Levy, Isaacs and Behrman, 1971). Motor nerve conduction velocity was higher in agitated organic patients than in the non-agitated (Jurko, Foshee and Smith, 1964).

Studies of skin conductance variables in brain-damaged patients have shown that sweat gland activity is raised in these patients in comparison with non-brain-damaged control patients (Parsons and Chandler, 1969). In the brain-damaged patients, high arousal was associated with better psychomotor performance; the reverse relationship was found in the control patients. In patients with unilateral brain damage, the skin conductance was lower on the side of the lesion (Holloway and Parsons, 1969). This finding accords with the hypothesis of Gruzelier and Venables concerning schizophrenia and brain dysfunction (see p. 163).

Brain-damaged patients had significantly larger GSRs and smaller alpha-blocking responses than control patients. Habituation occurred for the heart rate, sweat gland and EEG responses in the controls but only for the sweat gland responses in the brain-damaged patients (Holloway and Parsons, 1971).

## Studies in children

There is a large literature on the changes in psychophysiological measures in infancy and childhood, i.e. developmental psychophysiology. Very little has been done on psychiatrically abnormal children. Hyperkinetic children were found to have below-normal skin conductance levels, fluctuations and responses. Amphetamine, often an effective treatment in such patients, increased these measures towards normal (Satterfield and Dawson, 1971).

Autistic children had smaller GSRs to novel stimuli than did normal children. There was no differential responsivity of the autistic children to different modalities of stimulation. Habituation rates did not distinguish between the groups (Bernal and Miller, 1970). During REM sleep, activity in the 10·5–15 Hz waveband of the EEG was increased in patients, although the amount of eye movement activity was below normal (Ornitz *et al.*, 1969). However, in another study no differences were found (Onheiber *et al.*, 1965).

## Psychosomatic conditions

In some ways, psychophysiology might be regarded as a science lying basic to psychosomatic conditions in the way that neurophysiology is fundamental to neurology. However, as will be seen, the concepts used in psychosomatic medicine are too imprecise to allow extrapolations from laboratory experiments.

In the halcyon days of psychosomatic medicine certain illnesses were designated psychosomatic—bronchial asthma, essential hypertension, neurodermatitis, peptic ulcer, rheumatoid arthritis, thyrotoxicosis and ulcerative colitis. Many other conditions have since been labelled psychosomatic, including diabetes mellitus, anorexia nervosa, obesity, psychogenic vomiting, abdominal pain, diarrhoea, irritable colon, coronary thrombosis, torticollis and writer's cramp. However, there is no general agreement as to which illnesses are 'psychosomatic'. No rigorous definition, or even acceptable description, of psychosomatic illness has ever been proposed, the only common characteristic being the assumption that psychological factors play an important role in their complex, obscure aetiology (Lipowski, 1968). On these grounds alone the term 'psychosomatic' has limited scientific value. Furthermore, the term is counter-productive, because designating some illnesses as psychosomatic implies that the remainder are not psychosomatic. Thus, the eclecticism of approach which is the strength of psychosomatic medicine is concentrated on only a minority of diseases and not brought to bear on the bulk of illness.

A second criticism of the concept of psychosomatic illness is that it implies more homogeneity with respect to aetiology than may be justified. Many conditions labelled psychosomatic are syndromes and represent a range of conditions, from those in which physical factors predominate almost exclusively through those in which both physical and psychological factors are important to those in which psychological factors strongly influence the clinical picture. For example, patients with torticollis range from those with obvious and constant neurological deficits to those whose condition varied with psychological factors (Meares, 1971; Meares and Lader, 1971). Furthermore, the relative contribution of physical and psychological factors may vary at different stages of a disease. Again taking torticollis as an example, it may present with marked psychological precipitants, initially pursue a fluctuating course, then become more severe and constant until finally other neurological abnormalities, such as widespread dystonias, occur.

## Psychosomatic approach

Although psychosomatic illnesses cannot be adequately defined, one could assert that the nub of the matter concerns the method of approach to ill people. Wolff (1970) has summed up this approach thus: 'The majority of illnesses are multi-factorial in origin and psychological and somatic aspects and their mutual interaction need to be taken into consideration in every patient who is ill.' These sentiments are admirable and unexceptionable but consist of little more than eclecticism regarding aetiology. Again, this could be counter-productive, since the existence of some practitioners rightly stressing such an approach could lessen the onus on other clinicians to assess all aspects of the patient.

This is only a minor criticism. The real problem is the difficulty in isolating and assessing such psychological factors, especially as the term 'psychological' is often taken to mean 'psychic' rather than 'behavioural'. Furthermore, there seems to be no unanimity about conceptualising the way in which 'psychic' factors influence somatic processes. This is essentially a philosophical problem which needs either solution or successful evasion in order that a fruitful scientific approach can be adopted. Unfortunately, many advocates of the psychosomatic approach perpetuate a Cartesian dualist model. For example, one of the leading proponents of the psychosomatic approach (Engel, 1967) states: 'The psychosomatic approach is concerned with the ways in which psychological and somatic factors interact in the whole sequence of events that constitute a particular disease experience.' Engel implies an 'inter-face' with a complex 'coding' between mind and body.

## Psychosomatic research

The basic strength of psychosomatic concepts lies not in their application to clinical treatment nor in their philosophical impli-cations but in the unique nature of the research which they foster. Lewis (1954) concluded:

> It is best to recognise that 'psychosomatic' refers to an ill-defined area of interest, with constantly changing boundaries, in which there are manifest relations between events best studied by psychological methods and events best studied by physiological methods.

That statement emphasises the research aspects of the topic: the simultaneous study of at least two major aspects of human functioning.

## A philosophy for psychophysiology and psychosomatic medicine

Graham (1971) has stated: 'Psychosomatic medicine is clinical psychophysiology, and there is no question in psychophysiology that does not have an exactly analogous counterpart in psycho-somatic medicine.' Both disciplines can adopt an identical phil-osophy with respect to the mind–body relationship, namely the assumption of psychophysical parallelism. In this epistemological model psychic events and physiological events are parallel and simultaneous, and neither can occur alone or produce direct effects one on the other. An interface between mind and body is assumed but is regarded as extensive and simple, although one cannot say whether this relationship differs fundamentally from, say, the translation of physiological events into biochemical processes. By adopting parallelism, research in this area can sidestep the issue of the mind–body relationship because it is simplified to the point where it can be ignored and research can concentrate on the relationship between behavioural and physiological events. From the scientific standpoint, there is no fundamental difference between the observation of avoidance of a phobic object, the noting of a facial expression of fear, the measurement of any increase in heart rate on a polygraph and the analysis of verbal reports. But the subjective changes presumed to underlie the verbal reports are epiphenomena not susceptible to scientific analysis, although, of course, of profound clinical significance. Therefore, anxiety can never cause tachycardia but verbal reports of anxiety are usually accompanied by tachycardia, both being produced by the same stimulus. Psychological events are regarded as responses, not as stimuli as in other psychosomatic models.

## The concept of response specificity

The experiments bearing on this and related concepts have been outlined in chapter 3. It was seen that both response specificity, i.e. a consistent pattern of response of each individual across different types of stimulus, and stimulus specificity, i.e. a consistent pattern of response to each type of stimulus across different individuals, had received experimental support: it appeared that both the stimulus and the idiosyncrasies of the individual were important.

A related principle, also of direct relevance to psychosomatic research, is that of 'symptom specificity'. This states 'that in psychiatric patients presenting a somatic complaint, the particular physiological mechanism of that complaint is specifically susceptible to activation by stressful experience' (Malmo, Shagass and Davis, 1950). A group of patients was divided into those with head and neck pains and those with cardiovascular complaints; the latter patients were found to have higher mean heart rates and heart rate variability, while the other sub-group had higher mean electromyographic levels in the neck muscles (Malmo and Shagass, 1949). Support comes from Sainsbury and Gibson's (1954) study in which they divided their anxious patients into a group complaining of headache and a group with aching of the limbs or rheumatic pains. The group with headache had higher frontalis tension, while the latter group had higher forearm muscle activity.

Specificity has been a key concept in psychosomatic medicine for a long time although the nature of the specificity has been disputed. Alexander's (1950) theory postulates that 'physiological responses to emotional stimuli, both normal and morbid, vary according to the nature of the precipitating emotional state'. When correlations between psychological events and particular psychosomatic conditions have been attempted, ambiguous aetiological theories have been constructed with subsequent disillusionment with the whole concept of 'specificity'. The psychophysiological concept of patterns of response depending partly on the stimulation situation and partly on individual idiosyncrasies allows more flexibility in the experimental approach to the whole problem of specificity in psychosomatic medicine, because the examination of the relationship between psychophysiological responses and psychosomatic illnesses can be attempted at a more fundamental level. However, it is unlikely to elucidate the psychological or personality factors (traits, emotions, attitudes, defences, ego-strength) which are supposed to relate to particular psychosomatic conditions, because the relationships between psychophysiological responses and personality factors are themselves tenuous.

So far it has been supposed that the stimulus-related parts of the response and the individual-determined parts of the response are independent and additive. However, it is very likely that the two factors interact and that this interaction determines the form of the response. Thus, physiological changes occur as concomitants to the emotion. Four factors c an be invoked to explain differing individual patterns of response.

(1) The emotion produced dep ends to some extent on the particular person's previous experiences, and physiological patterns vary according to the emotion (Ax, 1953; Schachter, 1957; Averill, 1969; Silverman *et al.*, 1961).

(2) Differences between individuals in response to affectively neutral stimuli are marked and should be no less variable than responses to emotional evocative stimuli.

(3) The intensity of the response varies from individual to individual and various systems of the body will be differentially involved at the various levels of response.

(4) Awareness of peripheral autonomic changes varies from system to system so that differential feedback could occur.

In the next section, a few of the more relevant studies in this area will be reviewed and their contribution to our understanding of psychological factors in 'psychosomatic' illnesses assessed.

*Experimental studies*

There have been many experimental studies carried out within a psychosomatic framework, but most have been concerned with the general question of whether psychosocial stimuli can produce either transiently (i.e. an emotion) or chronically (i.e. personality reactions) psychological states which are associated with physical disease. Few studies have examined psychophysiological mechanisms in psychosomatic illnesses.

In one evaluation of muscle action potentials in patients with rheumatoid arthritis, activity was higher in these patients than in a group of controls (Gottschalk, Serota and Shapiro, 1950). A detailed examination of this topic was carried out by Moos and Engel (1962) who recorded from muscles in arthritic patients in areas which had recently been painful and in symptomless regions. The comparison group were patients with hypertension. Muscle activity was higher in the arthritics for the painful area but not for the symptomless area. The activity gradually lessened over the course of the recording in the hypertensives but not in the arthritics. The blood pressure showed opposite results, adapting in the arthritics but not in the hypertensives. However, no conclusions regarding the pathogenetic role of muscle tension can be drawn from this experiment as the increased muscle activity could have been secondary to the pain.

Many studies have found that the blood pressure in hypertensives is abnormally responsive to a wide range of psychological stimuli and is slow to adapt. Again, the association allows no deductions regarding cause and effect. Attempts have been made to distinguish patterns of cardiovascular system response in association with different emotional feelings such as anger directed at others, anger directed at oneself and anxiety (Funkenstein, King and Drolette, 1957). The differences found were not marked.

Thus, abnormal patterns or amplitudes of physiological measures have been found in such patients with psychosomatic conditions, but interpretation is difficult. Pathological changes in the affected organ could be secondary to the psychosomatic condition, not causal to it. Similarly, abnormal responses in other systems could be due to emotional changes following the physical symptoms, rather than reflecting a general psychophysiological imbalance. Firm evidence of this type would only be obtained if there was an invariant relationship between the abnormal physiological measures and the degree of pathology during cycles of exacerbation and remission.

An alternative approach is the epidemiological one. The psychophysiological research approach could with advantage be combined with the epidemiological in prospective studies, such as the large-scale screening of thousands of normal people. This technique of screening 'well' populations has been used to some extent, but to be of use for psychosomatic complaints new techniques need to be developed. Thus, a range of physiological measures would be assessed in the normal population under laboratory conditions of rest and during stressful stimuli. A long-term follow-up would then be mounted to note changes in the life circumstances of the probands and to detect psychosomatic illnesses. Unfortunately, such a study would be very expensive and wasteful because of the small numbers of people falling ill with any one complaint. Despite the large amounts of useful normative information which would accrue, such a study is not economically viable.

The problem is essentially to narrow the search to the population at risk. One could concentrate on a selected group of the initially screened population, such as those with the highest gastric acidity. The probability of illness is still fairly low and one might miss important factors because present data are still so scanty.

An alternative is to study a population at risk because of changes in life-events. Such a population is immigrants and here the problems of mounting a prospective psychophysiological study are not insuperable. Immigrants to a new country should receive a health check anyway, especially if their living conditions have been sub-standard in their country of origin, and if the new country has advanced free medical services the follow-up becomes almost automatic. A study of this type would still be expensive but not prohibitively so and the results would be important.

## Psychophysiological measures in psychopharmacology

At several points we have touched on aspects of pharmacology, and the relationship between psychophysiology and psychopharmacology is a close one (Stroebel, 1972). A great deal of psychophysiology utilises autonomic measures and the pharmacology of the autonomic nervous system is both advanced and complex. Antagonists and synergists of both the cholinergic and adrenergic divisions of the autonomic nervous system are widely used in clinical practice and drugs acting more selectively at various points in the system have been developed.

Drugs can also be used as stimuli, the mecholyl test being a good example. Here the effects of a standard dose of the drug on the body are quantified using physiological measures such as pulse and blood pressure. As a corollary, the amount of drug required to attain a standard effect may be the variable of interest, as in the sedation threshold. Unfortunately, it has often been forgotten that pharmacology has its own sources of variance such as age and sex, and that dosage *per se* is not an uncomplicated independent variable.

Psychophysiological measures can be used in three ways as indicators of psychotropic drug effects. Firstly, the measure can provide an estimate of central change. For example, in the studies of Lader and Wing (1966) outlined on p. 99, GSR habituation and skin conductance fluctuations were more sensitive indicators of barbiturate and benzodiazepine effects than were clinical ratings of sedative effects. In this and many similar instances, the changes detected peripherally are presumed to be a direct result of central effects because the drugs under study have little or no peripheral effects. However, in the second way of using psychophysiological measures, the drugs administered are known to have peripheral effects. For example, chlorpromazine has alpha-adrenoceptor blocking and anticholinergic effects. Consequently, its administration will result in gross alteration in autonomic functioning such as diminution in sweating and salivation, drop in blood pressure and pupillary constriction (Sakalis *et al.*, 1972). It is impossible, therefore, to derive any information regarding the central effects of chlorpromazine by means of psychophysiological measures. The variables will reflect peripheral changes and can be used to monitor unwanted effects. In other words, as the central psychological correlate of the *psychophysiological* measure cannot be clearly determined, the measure can only be used in the more simple *physiological* context.

The third type of use is as a purely empirical indicator of central effect. For example, the benzodiazepines and the barbiturates increase fast-wave activity in the EEG. So sensitive is this measure that effects can be detected up to 18 hours after single doses of the drugs (Bond and Lader, 1973). Again, the effects cannot be equated with psychophysiological changes. Increase in fast-wave activity would normally be associated with increased alertness and these depressant drugs decrease alertness. The physiological reasons for the drug-induced changes are not known, in contradistinction to the effects of chlorpromazine mentioned above, but again the measure must be used empirically in this context and no inferences made regarding the form of the central effects.

In a few instances, drugs have been powerful tools in elucidating psychophysiological mechanisms. One example concerns the experiments of Schachter (1966) relating emotional response to an amalgam of heightened arousal and cognitive clues. To raise arousal levels, injections of adrenaline were used; to block autonomic responses, chlorpromazine was administered. Another example is the use of beta-adrenoceptor blocking agents in the evaluation of feedback hypotheses of emotional functioning (such as the James–Lange hypothesis). By blocking the autonomic expression of emotional response, the perception of such emotions should be lessened. Unfortunately, the perfect pharmacological tools have yet to be invented as drugs do not have the total specificity of action, e.g. on peripheral receptors only, to yield conclusive results.

Finally, it must be remembered that normal subjects are self-administering many drugs. Caffeine, from coffee and tea, is the most commonly used, closely followed by nicotine and alcohol. Cannabis is taken fairly widely among student populations and many other drugs with psychotropic actions are taken non-medically. By definition, such psychotropic drugs will alter psychological functioning and hence psychophysiological measures. Some, e.g. nicotine, have peripheral effects as well.

# Conclusion 8

So much of psychophysiological research in psychiatry has taken place in an empirical way and so few of the data collected have resulted in any coherent, integrated theory that it is difficult to draw together the many threads running through the previous chapters. A few topics suggest themselves as unifying and heuristic and will be outlined. No attempt will be made to present an all-embracing psychophysiological theory of mental illness because to do so would imply a homogeneity in mental illness which is belied by clinical experience. Nor will any critique of the psychophysiological approach to psychiatry be put forward as the previous chapters bear witness to the contributions which this discipline has made, to the limitations of the methods and to the danger of erecting overelaborate theoretical superstructures on the shaky foundations provided by our meagre established results.

## Theories of emotion

Of the many theories of emotion advanced at one time or another (Gardiner, Metcalf and Beebe-Centre, 1937; Götlind, 1958; Hillman, 1960), the first one to be firmly set in a physiological nexus was that of James (1884). He succinctly summarises his position thus:

> that the bodily changes follow directly the perception of the exciting fact and that our feeling of the same changes as they occur is the emotion. Every one of the bodily changes, whatsoever it be, is felt acutely or obscurely the moment it occurs.

He boldly asserts that no emotion can exist if the bodily experience of it is removed and that objectless emotion is due to derangement of bodily functions and not mental ones. Unfortunately, James's hypothesis is not susceptible to scientific disproof as it deals with the *feeling* of emotion (introspective experience) and not the expression of emotion (objectively verifiable). Thus, attempts like that of Cannon (1927) to 'disprove' the hypothesis are irrelevant (Lader and Tyrer, 1975). Even attempts to modify emotions by blocking peripheral physiological responses have not led to unequivocal results as the actions of the drugs employed are complex.

Other theories of emotion have regarded the physiological changes as secondary to emotional responses or have emphasised the association without implying any cause-and-effect relationships. Based on these various theories, and especially on the interaction between arousing stimuli and cognitive factors, a model of emotion can be suggested.

## A model of emotion

This model (Figure 8.1) is an amalgam of many authors' suggestions, especially those of Spielberger, Lushene and McAdoo (1971), Lazarus (1966), Schachter (1966) and Epstein (1967). In this formulation, external stimuli impinge on the organism. The stimuli can be physical, such as trauma and noise, or social, such as poor living conditions, inadequate nutrition, etc., or psychosocial, such as marital discord and problems at work. Internal stimuli are also

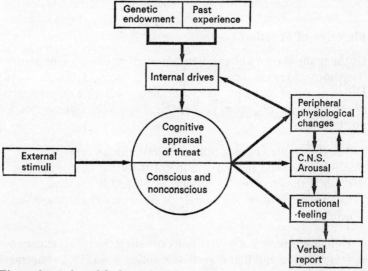

Figure 8.1  *A model of emotion*

important but they are better labelled 'drives' and
thoughts, needs, aspirations, and so on. Both external
stimuli are appraised for possible threats to the organ
vidual. The internal stimuli are modified by genetic
and past experience, nature and nurture, which them
act. The internal stimuli modify the appraisal of bot__ ___
and the external stimuli.

If either a potential advantage or potential disadvantage is
detected, two processes follow. First, the activity of certain parts
of the CNS increases but remains co-ordinated and integrated. This
is arousal. Second, an affect is experienced which is appropriate
to the stimulus in both qualitative and quantitative terms. Thus,
a dangerous stimulus would result in fear, an obnoxious one in
disgust, etc.

How is the emotional state recognised and described verbally?
Although both the development of emotional expression in children
and their acquisition of language have been carefully studied,
there have been relatively few studies on the acquisition of emotional language. It appears that a child learns to describe his feeling state appropriately as 'fear', 'anger', etc., because his mother
teaches him the correct word inferring his mental state from his
situation, his behaviour and his facial expression. Thus although
the experience of an emotion is presumed to be innate, the use of
the generally accepted words to describe the feeling is a learned
skill. Because of the rewarding properties of the mother's solicitous
attention, overt signs of the emotion may be reinforced: consequently, overdemonstrative mothers would be expected to have
overdemonstrative offspring. Nevertheless, some mothers may be
insensitive to their children's emotional feelings and diagnose them
wrongly. Thus a child may associate an inappropriate word to
his feeling and in later life may complain of anxiety when he is
depressed or vice versa.

The CNS arousal is accompanied by widespread physiological
changes (which have formed the substance of this book). These
changes are relayed back to the CNS by proprioceptive pathways
but can also be consciously perceived by the subject (Mandler
and Kremen, 1958; Mandler, Mandler and Uviller, 1958). These
may reinforce the emotion by acting as internal stimuli and may
constitute a potential positive feedback loop.

Methods for coping with heightened emotional states, especially
unpleasant ones, interact with many points of the model. Thus,

external stimuli apparently producing the emotion can be identified and removed by environmental manipulation. Appropriate coping behaviour can be learnt, thus adding to and modifying past experience; the most fundamental form of coping behaviour is adaptation or habituation. There may be re-appraisal of the properties of the stimulus. Also, there are the wide range of psychological mechanisms studied by Freud such as denial, repression, regression, projection and reaction formation.

Can such a model explain morbid emotions and their accompanying physiological changes? Firstly, pathological trait emotions such as lugubriousness or suspiciousness can be regarded as extreme deviations, as the upper end of a normally distributed continuum of personality factors, of depressive tendencies and of distrust respectively. Genetic factors are important here and interact with previous experience to render an individual particularly liable to experience certain emotions under minimal 'stress'. This forms the basis of a type of specificity in that particular emotions will be characteristic of particular individuals. (This is of course, merely re-stating the Ancients' way of classifying people into the choleric, the phlegmatic, the melancholic and the sanguine.)

A second possibility depends on invoking mechanisms occurring outside conscious control. If the transactions between the external and internal stimuli on the one hand and cognitive appraisal processes on the other take place outside consciousness, then the emotional response when it appears may seem excessive or inappropriate or both. Because of previously acquired irrational associations, the interaction assumes a critical character and gives rise to unconscious affect-formations and to conscious emotions. Psychoanalytic therapy and less intensive forms of psychotherapy attempt to bring these transactions into consciousness in order that their irrationality be appreciated and normal coping mechanisms effectively mobilised.

A third possible mechanism is physiological arousal not secondary to cognitive assessment of sensory input, i.e. of an 'endogenous' nature. This is less common but spontaneously occurring emotions may occur in temporal lobe epilepsy and in drug states such as amphetamine and LSD toxic conditions. The quality of the emotion is convincing to the subject in contradistinction to peripheral 'arousal', such as that induced by adrenaline infusions, in which the psychological state differs in subtle but crucial ways from the natural emotion. The adrenaline-induced emotion, usually anxiety, has an 'as if' quality.

A fourth possible mechanism relates to the interaction between arousal level and adaptation. Many studies (see p. 128) have shown that anxious patients adapt slowly to the changing exigencies of the experimental situation and this impairment probably exists in other states of high arousal such as ecstasy and revulsion. Thus, if the level of activity rises for any reason, adaptation will be impaired, and above a critical level of activity adaptation will be absent. Chronic or repetitive stimuli raise physiological activity levels and if these go beyond the critical level the physiological arousal would become self-perpetuating, so that cessation of the stimuli would have no effect. In clinical terms, chronic or repeated stimuli, so-called 'life-stresses', will eventually precipitate an acute emotional reaction which because of impaired adaptation might become chronic. Such a mechanism is particularly appropriate to the genesis of chronic anxiety but might also operate in chronic paranoid conditions and states of morbid ecstasy. Reactive depressions are probably more complicated in view of retardation changes (see p. 156), but might fit into a similar framework in that they often persist despite the removal of the putative precipitant.

## The problem of arousal

These models of emotion, normal and morbid, rely heavily on the unitary concept of arousal. As arousal is an hypothesised behavioural continuum with a neurophysiological substrate not easily available to direct investigation in the intact, conscious human, indirect psychophysiological measures provide the main estimates of this factor. The concept of arousal has been criticised on many grounds, but most of these criticisms reflect the indirectness and inexactitude of the psychophysiological measures rather than the deficiencies of the concept itself. Several criticisms fail to take into account the intrinsic restraints on the measures arising from their physiological nature. This point has been stressed at several points in this book. It can be illustrated diagrammatically in Figure 8.2. Each measure bears a characteristic functional relationship with arousal. Thus, the EMG hardly alters at low and moderate levels of arousal but then increases rapidly as arousal increases. Finger pulse volume is large (i.e. vasodilatation) at low levels,

**Physiological indicators of arousal**

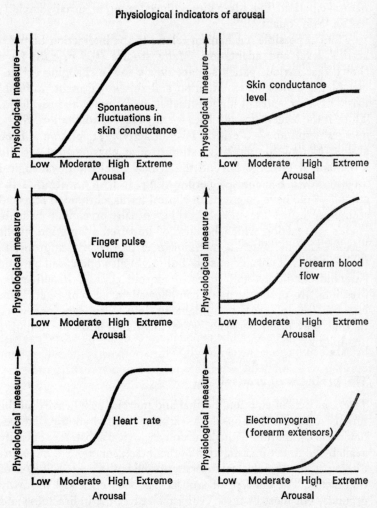

Figure 8.2 *An impressionistic view of the relationships between various physiological measures and 'arousal'*

vaso-constriction ensues rapidly at moderate levels and remains low thereafter. Consequently, few correlations would be expected between variables as each variable has its own floor, ceiling and range. With experience the psychophysiologist appreciates which measure is most appropriate for each range of arousal. For example, the EMG is useful at high levels but insensitive at low levels; with spontaneous skin conductance fluctuations the reverse is the case.

Nevertheless, the concept of arousal in its basic, unitary form is a single continuum, providing only one dimension, and this is a serious limitation. It is of most heuristic value in conditions such as anxiety states which on clinical grounds appear to be quantitatively but not qualitatively different from normal. In other psychiatric conditions, it provides one dimension among a presumed many and it may not even be an important one. Even so, it may explain some of the secondary phenomena of the illness such as agitation in depression.

## Implications of psychophysiological research for psychiatry

Psychophysiology offers novel approaches to psychiatric problems in two ways. First, it provides methods for the accurate assessment of concomitants of mental illness. For example, drug treatments can be monitored providing that the interactions between the drug and the measures are known. In this respect the psychophysiological measures are being used as extensions of clinical observations. The clinician observes furrowing of the brow in a depressed patient; the psychophysiologist records the frontalis EMG and finds it raised. The clinician notes sweating of the palms; the skin conductance level is high. This approach, especially when repeated measurements are made on each individual, is straightforward and makes no theoretical assumption except that the measure sampled is relevant to the psychopathology of interest. Some psychiatrists appreciate the value of quantitative assessments and may refer patients with particular syndromes for further investigation. A typical example concerns the patient who complains bitterly of anxiety but who appears calm. Psychophysiological assessment using measures such as the forearm blood flow or skin conductance usually reveals that the patient is overaroused, i.e. the physiological measures are consistent with his complaints.

The second approach is for psychophysiological techniques to be applied in attempts to elucidate the pathological mechanisms in mental illness. Here the bulk of research with autonomic measures, somatic measures, the EEG and endocrine indices points to a relatively non-specific heightening of general activity manifest as anxiety or agitation or other extreme emotions. Thus, anxious, depressed or schizophrenic patients may show changes which are most economically interpreted as 'overarousal'. There is also an elementary logical error in comparing one group of diagnostically labelled patients with a group of so-called normals and assuming that any difference between the groups is a function of the main diagnosis. For these reasons psychophysiological techniques should be applied to several groups of patients to ascertain whether secondary attributes such as agitation, retardation or depersonalisation are more closely related to the psychophysiological pattern than primary diagnoses such as depression or schizophrenia. Patients with anxiety states often constitute an additional useful control group when studying psychotic patients with agitation.

With this approach many interesting leads have been suggested although no 'breakthrough' in our knowledge of the pathogenesis or pathophysiological mechanisms of mental illness has occurred. These growing points have been reviewed in previous chapters and offer hope for the future.

The warnings given earlier should be repeated. Psychophysiological techniques range from the complex and difficult to the simple and routine. All must be used with full appreciation of the underlying physiological considerations and within the limits that any biological approach imposes. Psychiatry is still very inexact and rigid classificatory schema could stultify any attempts at a physiological approach because of the irrelevance of the classification in biological terms. Flexibility in approach will remain essential.

Finally, psychophysiology need not be employed in practical or theoretical isolation. Indeed, the major advances are likely to come by studying mentally ill patients from several aspects simultaneously. By evaluating the interaction between biological, social and intra-psychic factors, the problems of mental illness may be yet more efficiently tackled.

# Bibliographical index

Figures in square brackets indicate the pages in this book where these references are cited.

ABRAMSON, D. I., SCHKLOVEN, N., and KATZENSTEIN, K. H. (1941). Peripheral blood flow in schizophrenia and other abnormal mental states. *Archives of Neurology and Psychiatry*, **45**, 973-9. [104, 166]

ACKNER, B. (1954). Depersonalization: 1. Aetiology and phenomenology. *Journal of Mental Science*, **100**, 838-53. [192]

ACKNER, B. (1956a). Emotions and the peripheral vasomotor system. A review of previous work. *Journal of Psychosomatic Research*, **1**, 3-20. [104]

ACKNER, B. (1956b). The relationship between anxiety and the level of peripheral vasomotor activity. *Journal of Psychosomatic Research*, **1**, 21-48. [102, 104]

ACKNER, B., and PAMPIGLIONE, G. (1959). An evaluation of the sedation threshold test. *Journal of Psychosomatic Research*, **3**, 271-81. [77, 136]

ADAMS, T., and VAUGHAN, J. A. (1965). Human eccrine sweat gland activity and palmar electrical skin resistance. *Journal of Applied Physiology*, **20**, 980-3. [18]

ADDISON, T. (1855). *On the Constitutional and Local Effects of Disease of the Suprarenal Capsules*, Samuel Highley, London. [145]

AGRAS, W. S. (1965). An investigation of the decrement of anxiety responses during systematic desensitization therapy. *Behaviour Research and Therapy*, **2**, 267-70. [102]

ALAJOUANINE, T., SCHERRER, J., BARBIZET, J., CALVET, J., and VERLEY, R. (1958). Potentiels évoqués corticaux chez des sujets atteints des troubles somesthésiques. *Revue Neurologique*, **98**, 757-61. [190]

ALEXANDER, F. (1950). *Psychosomatic Medicine*, Norton, New York. [201]

ALEXANDER, F., FLAGG, G. W., FOSTER, S., CLEMENS, T., and BLADH, W. (1961). Experimental studies of emotional stress: I. Hyperthyroidism. *Psychosomatic Medicine*, **23**, 104-14. [124]

ALLSOPP, M. N. E., LEVELL, M. J., STITCH, S. R., and HULLIN, R. P. (1972). Aldosterone production rates in manic-depressive psychosis. *British Journal of Psychiatry*, **120**, 399-404. [153]

ALTSCHULE, M. D. (1953). *Bodily Physiology in Mental and Emotional Disorders*, Grune & Stratton, New York. [102, 157]

ALTSCHULE, M. D. (1964). Salivary changes in emotional states. *Medical Science*, **15**, 60-1. [132]

ALTSCHULE, M. D., PROMISEL, E., PARKHURST, B. H., and GRUNEBAUM, H.

(1950). Effects of ACTH in patients with mental disease. *Archives of Neurology and Psychiatry*, **64**, 641–9. [179]

ANDERSON, W. M., and DAWSON, J. (1965). The variability of plasma 17-hydroxycorticosteroids—levels in affective illness and schizophrenia. *Journal of Psychosomatic Research*, **9**, 237–48. [150]

ARISTOTLE (1941). *The Basic Works of Aristotle*, McKeon, R. (ed.), Random House, New York, p. 619. [177]

ASERINSKY, E., and KLEITMAN, N. (1953). Regularly occurring periods of eye motility, and concomitant phenomena, during sleep. *Science*, **118**, 273–4. [57, 90]

ASERINSKY, E., and KLEITMAN, N. (1955). Two types of ocular motility occurring during sleep. *Journal of Applied Physiology*, **8**, 1–10. [57, 90]

ASSAEL, M. I., and WINNIK, H. Z. (1970). Electroencephalographic findings in affective psychosis. *Diseases of the Nervous System*, **31**, 695–702. [138]

AVERILL, J. R. (1969). Autonomic response patterns during sadness and mirth. *Psychophysiology*, **5**, 399–414. [202]

AX, A. F. (1953). The physiological differentiation between fear and anger. *Psychosomatic Medicine*, **15**, 433–42. [202]

AX, A. F., and BAMFORD, J. L. (1970). The GSR recovery limb in chronic schizophrenia. *Psychophysiology*, **7**, 145–7. [158]

AX, A. F., BAMFORD, J. L., BECKETT, P. G. S., FRETZ, N. F., and GOTTLIEB, J. S. (1970). Autonomic conditioning in chronic schizophrenia. *Journal of Abnormal Psychology*, **76**, 140–54. [158]

BAGG, C. E., and CROOKES, T. G. (1966). Palmar digital sweating in women suffering from depression. *British Journal of Psychiatry*, **112**, 1251–5. [130]

BALASUBRAMANIAN, K., MAWER, G. E., and SIMONS, P. J. (1970). The influence of dose on the distribution and elimination of amylobarbitone in healthy subjects. *British Journal of Pharmacology*, **40**, 578–9P. [136]

BANCROFT, J. (1971). The application of psychophysiological measures to the assessment and modification of sexual behaviour. *Behaviour Research and Therapy*, **9**, 119–30. [39]

BARBER, T. X., DICARA, L. V., KAMIYA, J., MILLER, N. E., SHAPIRO, D., and STOYVA, J. (eds) (1971). *Biofeedback and Self-control*, Aldine, Chicago. [87]

BARCROFT, H. (1960). Sympathetic control of vessels in the hand and forearm skin. *Physiological Review*, Suppl. **4**, 81–91. [35]

BARCROFT, H., and SWAN, H. J. C. (1953). *Sympathetic Control of Human Blood Vessels*, Edward Arnold, London. [36]

BARTOSHUK, A. K. (1959). Electromyographic reactions to strong auditory stimulation as a function of alpha amplitude. *Journal of Comparative and Physiological Psychology*, **52**, 540–5. [106]

BASOWITZ, H., KORCHIN, S. J., OKEN, D., GOLDSTEIN, M. S., and GUSSACK, H. (1956). Anxiety and performance changes with a minimal dose of epinephrine. *Archives of Neurology and Psychiatry*, **76**, 98–108. [120]

BASOWITZ, H., PERSKY, H., KORCHIN, S. J., and GRINKER, R. R. (1955). *Anxiety and Stress. An Interdisciplinary Study of a Life Situation*, McGraw-Hill, New York. [111]

BATT, J. C., KAY, W. W., REISS, M., and SANDS, D. E. (1957). The endocrine concomitants of schizophrenia. *Journal of Mental Science*, **103**, 240–56. [180, 182]

BECK, A. T. (1967). *Depression: Clinical, Experimental and Theoretical Aspects*, Hoeber Medical Division (Harper & Row), New York. [129]

BECK, E. C., and BAROLIN, G. S. (1965). Effect of hypnotic suggestions on evoked potentials. *Journal of Nervous and Mental Disease*, **140**, 154-61. [192]

BECK, E. C., DUSTMAN, R. E., and BEIER, E. G. (1966). Hypnotic suggestions and visually evoked potentials. *Electroencephalography and Clinical Neurophysiology*, **20**, 397-400. [192]

BEEK, H. H., VAN BORK, J. J., HERNGREEN, H., and VAN DER MOST VAN SPIJK, D. (1964). Considerations on electroencephalography in schizophrenics with reference to a survey in 25 Dutch mental hospitals. *Psychiatria, Neurologia, Neurochirurgia*, **67**, 95-101. [169]

BEGLEITER, H., PORJESZ, B., and GROSS, M. M. (1967). Cortical evoked potentials and psychopathology. A critical review. *Archives of General Psychiatry*, **17**, 755-8. [141, 173]

BEHRMAN, J. (1969). The visual evoked response in hysterical amblyopia. *British Journal of Ophthalmology*, **53**, 839-45. [191]

BEHRMAN, J., and LEVY, R. (1970). Neurophysiological studies on patients with hysterical disturbances of vision. *Journal of Psychosomatic Research*, **14**, 187-94. [191]

BENJAMIN, L. S. (1963). Statistical treatment of the law of initial values (LIV) in autonomic research: a review and recommendation. *Psychosomatic Medicine*, **25**, 556-66. [85]

BENSON, A. J., and GEDYE, J. L. (1961). Some supraspinal factors influencing generalized muscle activity. In Turnbull, P. C. (ed.), *Symposium on Skeletal Muscle Spasm*, Franklyn, Ward & Wheeler, Leicester, pp. 31-50. [45]

BERGAMINI, L., and BERGAMASCO, B. (1967). *Cortical Evoked Potentials in Man*. Thomas, Springfield, Illinois. [191]

BERGSMAN, A. (1959). The urinary excretion of adrenaline and nor-adrenaline in some mental diseases. A clinical and experimental study. *Acta Psychiatrica et Neurologica Scandinavica*, Suppl **133**. [153, 181]

BERKUN, M. M., BIALEK, H. M., KERN, R. P., and YAGI, K. (1962). Experimental studies of psychological stress in man. *Psychological Monographs*, **76**, No. 15, Whole No. 534. [111]

BERLYNE, D. E. (1960). *Conflict, Arousal and Curiosity*, McGraw-Hill, New York. [89]

BERNAL, M. E., and MILLER, W. H. (1970). Electrodermal and cardiac responses of schizophrenic children to sensory stimuli. *Psychophysiology*, **7**, 155-68. [198]

BERNSTEIN, A. S. (1964). The galvanic skin response orienting reflex among chronic schizophrenics. *Psychonomic Science*, **1**, 391-2. [159]

BERNSTEIN, A. S. (1970). Phasic electrodermal orienting response in chronic schizophrenics: II. Response to auditory signals of varying intensity. *Journal of Abnormal Psychology*, **75**, 146-56. [159]

BICKFORD, R. G., CANTER, C. R. Q., and BICKFORD, J. A. (1966). Problems in the application of evoked potential techniques in psychiatry. *Excerpta Medica International Congress Series*, No. **117**, p. 119. [57]

BLAIR, D. A., GLOVER, W. E., GREENFIELD, A. D. M., and RODDIE, I. C. (1959).

Excitation of cholinergic vasodilator nerves to human skeletal muscles during emotional stress. *Journal of Physiology*, **148**, 633–47. [35]

BLISS, E. L., MIGEON, C. J., BRANCH, C. H. H., and SAMUELS, L. T. (1955). Adrenocortical function in schizophrenia. *American Journal of Psychiatry*, **112**, 358–65. [179]

BLISS, E. L., MIGEON, C. J., BRANCH, C. H. H., and SAMUELS, L. T. (1956). Reaction of the adrenal cortex to emotional stress. *Psychosomatic Medicine*, **18**, 56–76. [114, 115]

BLISS, E. L., MIGEON, C. J., NELSON, D. H., SAMUELS, L. T., and BRANCH, C. H. H. (1954). Influence of E.C.T. and insulin coma on level of adrenocortical steroids in peripheral circulation. *Archives of Neurology and Psychiatry*, **72**, 352–61. [152]

BLOCH, S., and BRACKENRIDGE, C. J. (1972). Psychological performance and biochemical factors in medical students under examination stress. *Journal of Psychosomatic Research*, **16**, 25–33. [111]

BLOOM, G., EULER, U. S. V., and FRANKENHAEUSER, M. (1963). Catecholamine excretion and personality traits in paratroop trainees. *Acta Physiologica Scandinavica*, **58**, 77–89. [117]

BLUM, R. H. (1956). Photic stimulation, imagery, and alpha rhythm. *Journal of Mental Science*, **102**, 160–7. [172]

BLUM, R. H. (1957). Alpha-rhythm responsiveness in normal, schizophrenic, and brain damaged persons. *Science*, **126**, 749–50. [172]

BLUMBERG, A. G., and KLEIN, D. F. (1968). Psychiatric diagnosis, activation, and radioactive iodine uptake. *Archives of General Psychiatry*, **18**, 601–4. [154]

BOARD, F., PERSKY, H., and HAMBURG, D. A. (1956). Psychological stress and endocrine functions. Blood levels of adrenocortical and thyroid hormones in acutely disturbed patients. *Psychosomatic Medicine*, **18**, 324–33. [149, 154]

BOARD, F., WADESON, R., and PERSKY, H. (1957). Depressive affect and endocrine functions. Blood levels of adrenal cortex and thyroid hormones in patients suffering from depressive reactions. *Archives of Neurology and Psychiatry*, **78**, 612–20. [149, 154]

BOGDONOFF, M. D., BOGDONOFF, M. M., and WOLF, S. G. (1961). Studies on salivary function in man: variations in secretory rate as part of the individual's adaptive pattern. *Journal of Psychosomatic Research*, **5**, 170–4. [96]

BOGDONOFF, M. D., ESTES, E. H., HARLAN, W. R., TROUT, D. L., and KIRSHNER, N. (1960). Metabolic and cardiovascular changes during a state of acute central nervous system arousal. *Journal of Clinical Endocrinology and Metabolism*, **20**, 1333–40. [120]

BOND, A. J., JAMES, D. C., and LADER, M. H. (1974). Physiological and psychological measures in anxious patients. *Psychological Medicine*, in press. [100, 103]

BOND, A. J., and LADER, M. H. (1972). Residual effects of hypnotics. *Psychopharmacologia*, **25**, 117–32. [139, 143]

BOND, A. J., and LADER, M. H. (1973). The residual effects of flurazepam. *Psychopharmacologia*, **32**, 223–35. [205]

BORGE, G. F., BUCHSBAUM, M., GOODWIN, F., MURPHY, D., and SILVERMAN, J.

(1971). Neuropsychological correlates of affective disorders. *Archives of General Psychiatry*, **24**, 501–4. [142]

BOSTEM, F., ROUSSEAU, J. C., DEGOSSELY, M., and DONGIER, M. (1967). Psychopathological correlations of the non-specific portion of visual and auditory evoked potentials and the associated contingent negative variation. *Electroencephalography and Clinical Neurophysiology*, Suppl **26**, 131–8. [109]

BOUDREAU, D. (1958). Evaluation of the sedation threshold. *Archives of Neurology and Psychiatry*, **80**, 771–5. [136]

BOWMAN, K. M., MILLER, E. R., DAILEY, M. E., SIMON, A., FRANKEL, B., and LOWE, G. W. (1950). Thyroid function in mental disease measured with radioactive iodine, I$^{131}$. *American Journal of Psychiatry*, **106**, 561–72. [182]

BOWMAN, K. M., and ROSE, M. (1951). A criticism of the terms 'psychosis', 'psychoneurosis', and 'neurosis'. *American Journal of Psychiatry*, **108**, 161–6. [97]

BRAMBILLA, F., and NUREMBERG, T. (1963). Adrenal cortex function of cyclothymic patients in depressive phase. *Diseases of the Nervous System*, **24**, 727–31. [146]

BRAZIER, M. A. B., FINESINGER, J. E., and COBB, S. (1945). A contrast between the electroencephalograms of 100 psychoneurotic patients and those of 500 normal adults. *American Journal of Psychiatry*, **101**, 443–8. [108]

BREGGIN, P. R. (1964). The psychophysiology of anxiety with a review of the literature concerning adrenaline. *Journal of Nervous and Mental Diseases*, **139**, 558–68. [120, 122]

BRIDGES, P. K., and JONES, M. T. (1966). The diurnal rhythm of plasma cortisol concentration in depression. *British Journal of Psychiatry*, **112**, 1257–61. [151]

BROCKWAY, A. L., GLESER, G., WINOKUR, G., and ULETT, G. A. (1954). The use of a control population in neuropsychiatric research (psychiatric, psychological, and EEG evaluation of a heterogeneous sample). *American Journal of Psychiatry*, **111**, 248–62. [108]

BRODY, E. B., and MANN, E. B. (1950). Thyroid function measured by serum precipitable iodine determinations in schizophrenic patients. *American Journal of Psychiatry*, **107**, 357–9. [181]

BROEN, W. E. (1966). Response disorganization and breadth of observation in schizophrenia. *Psychological Review*, **73**, 579–85. [184]

BROOKSBANK, B. W. L., and COPPEN, A. (1967). Plasma 11-hydroxy-corticosteroids in affective disorders. *British Journal of Psychiatry*, **113**, 395–404. [150]

BROWN, C. C. (ed.) (1967). *Methods in Psychophysiology*, Williams & Wilkins, Baltimore. [6, 9]

BROWN, C. C. (1970). The parotid puzzle: a review of the literature on human salivation and its applications to psychophysiology. *Psychophysiology*, **7**, 66–85. [29, 133]

BRUCK, M. A. (1964). Synchrony and voltage in the EEG of schizophrenics. *Archives of General Psychiatry*, **10**, 454–68. [168]

BRUCK, M. A., and MCNEAL, B. F. (1964). Artifacts in the EEG of schizophrenic patients. *American Journal of Psychiatry*, **121**, 265–6. [171]

BRYSON, R. W., and MARTIN, D. F. (1954). 17-ketosteroid excretion in a case of manic-depressive psychosis. *Lancet*, **2**, 365–7. [148]

BUCHSBAUM, M., GOODWIN, F., MURPHY, D., and BORGE, G. (1971). AER in affective disorders. *American Journal of Psychiatry*, **128**, 19–25. [142]

BUNNEY, W. E., and FAWCETT, J. A. (1965). Possibility of a biochemical test for suicide potential. An analysis of endocrine findings prior to three suicides. *Archives of General Psychiatry*, **13**, 232–9. [146]

BUNNEY, W. E., HARTMANN, E. L., and MASON, J. W. (1965). Study of a patient with 48-hour manic depressive cycles. II. Strong positive correlation between endocrine factors in manic defense patterns. *Archives of General Psychiatry*, **12**, 619–25. [148]

BUNNEY, W. E., MASON, J. W., and HAMBURG, D. A. (1965). Correlations between behavioral variables and urinary 17-hydroxycorticosteroids in depressed patients. *Psychosomatic Medicine*, **27**, 299–308. [146]

BUNNEY, W. E., MASON, J. W., ROATCH, J. F., and HAMBURG, D. A. (1965). A psychoendocrine study of severe psychotic depressive crises. *American Journal of Psychiatry*, **122**, 72–80. [146]

BURDICK, J. A., SUGERMAN, A. A., and GOLDSTEIN, L. (1967). The application of regression analysis to quantitative electroencephalography in man. *Psychophysiology*, **3**, 249–54. [171]

BUSFIELD, B. L., and WECHSLER, H. (1961). Studies of salivation in depression. I. A comparison of salivation rates in depressed, schizoaffective depressed, nondepressed hospitalized patients, and in normal controls. *Archives of General Psychiatry*, **4**, 10–15. [132]

BUSFIELD, B. L., WECHSLER, H., and BARNUM, W. J. (1961). Studies of salivation in depression. II. Physiological differentiation of reactive and endogenous depression. *Archives of General Psychiatry*, **5**, 472–7. [132, 165]

BUSS, A. H., and LANG, P. J. (1965). Psychological deficit in schizophrenia: I. Affect, reinforcement, and concept attainment. *Journal of Abnormal Psychology*, **70**, 2–24 [183]

BUTLER, P. W. P., and BESSER, G. M. (1968). Pituitary-adrenal function in severe depressive illness. *Lancet*, **1**, 1234–6. [152]

CALDWELL, D. F., and DOMINO, E. F. (1967). Electroencephalographic and eye movement patterns during sleep in chronic schizophrenic patients. *Electroencephalography and Clinical Neurophysiology*, **22**, 414–20. [176]

CALLAWAY, E., JONES, R. T., and DONCHIN, E. (1970). Auditory evoked potential variability in schizophrenia. *Electroencephalography and Clinical Neurophysiology*, **29**, 421–8. [173]

CALLAWAY, E., JONES, R. T., and LAYNE, R. S. (1965). Evoked responses and segmental set of schizophrenia. *Archives of General Psychiatry*, **12**, 83–9. [173]

CAMERON, D. E. (1944). Observations on the patterns of anxiety. *American Journal of Psychiatry*, **101**, 36–41. [106]

CANNON, W. B. (1915). *Bodily Changes in Pain, Hunger, Fear, and Rage*, Appleton-Century-Crofts, New York. [89]

CANNON, W. B. (1927). The James-Lange theory of emotion. *American Journal of Psychology*, **39**, 106–24. [208]

CANNON, W. B., LINTON, J. R., and LINTON, R. R. (1924). Conditions of activity in endocrine glands. XIV. The effects of muscle metabolites on adrenal secretion. *American Journal of Physiology*, **71**, 153–62. [127]

CARPENTER, W. T., and BUNNEY, W. E. (1971). Diurnal rhythm of cortisol in mania. *Archives of General Psychiatry*, **25**, 270–3. [151]

CARRIE, J. R. G. (1965). Visual effects on finger tremor in normal subjects and anxious patients. *British Journal of Psychiatry*, **111**, 1181–4. [108]

CARROLL, B. J. (1969). Hypothalamic-pituitary function in depressive illness: insensitivity to hypoglycaemia. *British Medical Journal*, **3**, 25–7. [152]

CARROLL, B. J., MARTIN, F. I. R., and DAVIES, B. (1968). Resistance to suppression by dexamethasone of plasma 11-O.H.C.S. levels in severe depressive illness. *British Medical Journal*, **3**, 285–7. [152]

CARRUTHERS, M., TAGGART, P., CONWAY, N., BATES, D., and SOMERVILLE, W. (1970). Validity of plasma-catecholamine estimations. *Lancet*, **2**, 62–7. [74]

CHAPMAN, J. (1966). The early symptoms of schizophrenia. *British Journal of Psychiatry*, **112**, 225–51. [184]

CHAPMAN, J., and MCGHIE, A. (1962). A comparative study of disordered attention in schizophrenia. *Journal of Mental Science*, **108**, 487–500. [183]

CLARIDGE, G. S. (1960). The excitation–inhibition balance in neurotics. In Eysenck, H. J. (ed.), *Experiments in Personality*, vol. 2, Routledge & Kegan Paul, London, pp. 107–54. [184]

CLARIDGE, G. S. (1967). *Personality and Arousal. A Psychophysiological Study of Psychiatric Disorder*, Pergamon, Oxford. [184]

CLECKLEY, H. M. (1959). Psychopathic states. In Arieti, S. (ed.), *American Handbook of Psychiatry*, vol. 1, Basic Books, New York, pp. 567–88. [194]

CLEGHORN, R. A., and GRAHAM, B. F. (1950). Studies of adrenal cortical activity in psychoneurotic subjects. *American Journal of Psychiatry*, **106**, 668–72. [70, 114]

CLEMENS, T. L., and SELESNICK, S. T. (1967). Psychological method for evaluating medication by repeated exposure to a stressor film. *Diseases of the Nervous System*, **28**, 98–104. [77]

CLYNES, M., KOHN, M., and LIFSHITZ, K. (1964). Dynamics and spatial behavior of light evoked potentials, their modification under hypnosis, and on-line correlation in relation to rhythmic components. *Annals of the New York Academy of Sciences*, **112**, 468–508. [192]

CODY, D. T. R., and BICKFORD, R. G. (1965). Cortical audiometry: an objective method of evaluating auditory acuity in man. *Proceedings of the Mayo Clinic*, **40**, 273–87. [191]

COHEN, L. H., and PATTERSON, M. (1937). The effect of pain on the heart rate of normal and schizophrenic individuals. *Journal of General Psychology*, **17**, 273–89. [165]

COLES, M. G. H., GALE, A., and KLINE, P. (1971). Personality and habituation of the orienting reaction: tonic and response measures of electrodermal activity. *Psychophysiology*, **8**, 54–63. [96]

CONNELL, A. M., COOPER, J., and REDFEARN, J. W. (1958). The contrasting effects of emotional tensions and physical exercise on the excretion of 17-ketogenic steroids and 17-ketosteroids. *Acta Endocrinologica (Kobenhavn)*, **27**, 179–94. [110]

COOPER, J. E., KENDELL, R. E., GURLAND, B. J., SHARPE, L., COPELAND, J. R. M.,

# BIBLIOGRAPHICAL INDEX

and SIMON, R. (1972). *Psychiatric Diagnosis in New York and London*, Oxford University Press, London. [4]

COPE, C. L., and PEARSON, J. (1965). Clinical value of the cortisol secretion rate. *Journal of Clinical Pathology*, **18**, 82–7. [68]

COPPEN, A. (1970). *The Chemical Pathology of Affective Disorders*, Scientific Basis of Medicine, Annual Review, pp. 189–210. [153]

COPPEN, A., BROOKSBANK, B. W. L., NOGUERA, R., and WILSON, D. A. (1971). Cortisol in the cerebrospinal fluid of patients suffering from affective disorders. *Journal of Neurology, Neurosurgery and Psychiatry*, **34**, 432–5. [152]

COPPEN, A., JULIAN, T., FRY, D. E., and MARKS, V. (1967). Body build and urinary steroid excretion in mental illness. *British Journal of Psychiatry*, **113**, 269–75. [180]

COPPEN, A. J., and MEZEY, A. G. (1960a). The influence of sodium amytal on the respiratory abnormalities of anxious psychiatric patients. *Journal of Psychosomatic Research*, **5**, 52–5. [105]

COPPEN, A. J., and MEZEY, A. G. (1960b). Metabolic effect of venepuncture in man. *Journal of Psychosomatic Research*, **5**, 56–9. [123]

COPPEN, A., WHYBROW, P. C., MAGGS, R., and PRANGE, A. J. (1972). The comparative antidepressant value of L-tryptophan and imipramine with and without attempted potentiation by liothyronine. *Archives of General Psychiatry*, **26**, 234–41. [155]

COSTELLO, C. G., and SELBY, M. M. (1965). The relationships between sleep patterns and reactive and endogenous depressions. *British Journal of Psychiatry*, **111**, 497–501. [140]

COWEN, M. A. (1968). Schizophrenic hallucinations and the transcephalic DC potential. *Archives of General Psychiatry*, **18**, 114–16. [171]

CRAMMER, J. L., and POVER, W. F. R. (1960). Iodine-132 uptakes by the thyroid in psychotics. *Journal of Mental Science*, **106**, 1371–6. [154]

CROOKS, R., and MCNULTY, J. (1966). Autonomic response specificity in normal and schizophrenic subjects. *Canadian Journal of Psychology*, **20**, 280–95. [159]

CURTIS, G. C., CLEGHORN, R. A., and SOURKES, T. L. (1960). The relationship between affect and the excretion of adrenaline, noradrenaline and 17-hydroxycorticosteroids. *Journal of Psychosomatic Research*, **4**, 176–84. [153]

CURTIS, G. C., FOGEL, M. C., MCEVOY, D., and ZARATE, C. (1966). The effect of sustained affect on the diurnal rhythm of adrenal cortical activity *Psychosomatic Medicine*, **28**, 696–713. [115]

CURTIS, G., FOGEL, M., MCEVOY, D., and ZARATE, C. (1970). Urine and plasma corticosteroids, psychological tests, and effectiveness of psychological defenses. *Journal of Psychiatric Research*, **7**, 237–47. [113]

DALE, H. H., and FELDBERG, W. (1934). The chemical transmitter of nervous stimuli to the sweat glands of the cat. *Journal of Physiology*, **81**, 40P–1P. [21]

D'ANGELO, S. A. (1963). Central nervous regulation of the secretion and release of thyroid stimulating hormone. In Nalbandov, A. V. (ed.), *Advances in Neuroendocrinology*, University of Illinois, Urbana, pp. 158–205. [76]

222

DARROW, C. W. (1933). Considerations for evaluating the galvanic skin reflex. *American Journal of Psychiatry*, **90**, 285–98. [97]

DARROW, C. W. (1934). The significance of the galvanic skin reflex in the light of its relation to quantitative measurements of perspiration. *Psychological Bulletin*, **31**, 697–8. [18, 22]

DARROW, C. W. (1943). Physiological and clinical tests of autonomic function and autonomic balance. *Physiological Review*, **23**, 1–36. [82]

DARROW, C. W. (1964a). Psychophysiology, yesterday, today, and tomorrow. *Psychophysiology*, **1**, 4–7. [1]

DARROW, C. W. (1964b). The rationale for treating the change in galvanic skin response as a change in conductance. *Psychophysiology*, **1**, 31–8. [22]

DARROW, C. W., and SOLOMON, A. P. (1934). Galvanic skin reflex and blood pressure reactions in psychotic states. *Archives of Neurology and Psychiatry (Chicago)*, **32**, 273–99. [157, 165]

DAVIDOWITZ, J., BROWNE-MAYERS, A. N., KOHL, R., WELCH, L., and HAYES, R. (1955). An electromyographic study of muscular tension. *Journal of Psychology*, **40**, 85–94. [106]

DAVIES, B. M., and GURLAND, J. B. (1961). Salivary secretion in depressive illness. *Journal of Psychosomatic Research*, **5**, 269–71. [132, 165]

DAVIES, B., and PALMAI, G. (1964). Salivary and blood pressure responses to methacholine in depressive illness. *British Journal of Psychiatry*, **110**, 594–8. [132, 136]

DAVIS, J., MORRILL, R., FAWCETT, J., UPTON, V., BONDY, P. K., and SPIRO, H. M. (1962). Apprehension and elevated serum cortisol levels. *Journal of Psychosomatic Research*, **6**, 83–6. [110]

DAVIS, J. F., MALMO, R. B., and SHAGASS, C. (1954). Electromyographic reaction to strong auditory stimulation in psychiatric patients. *Canadian Journal of Psychology*, **8**, 177–86. [105]

DAVIS, P. A. (1941). Electroencephalograms of manic-depressive patients. *American Journal of Psychiatry*, **98**, 430–3. [137]

DAVIS, P. A. (1942). Comparative study of the EEGs of schizophrenic and manic-depressive patients. *American Journal of Psychiatry*, **99**, 210–17. [167]

DAVIS, P. A. D., and DAVIS, H. (1939). The electroencephalograms of psychiatric patients. *American Journal of Psychiatry*, **95**, 1007–20. [167]

DAVIS, R. C. (1957). Response patterns. *Transactions of the New York Academy of Sciences*, **19**, 731–9. [86]

DAVIS, R. C. (1959). Environmental control of gastrointestinal activity. *Science*, **130**, 1414–15. [41]

DAVIS, R. C., and BERRY, F. (1963). Gastrointestinal reactions during a noise avoidance task. *Psychological Report*, **12**, 135–7. [41]

DAVIS, R. C., BUCHWALD, A. M., and FRANKMANN, R. W. (1955). Autonomic and muscular responses and their relation to simple stimuli. *Psychological Monograph*, **69**, No. 20, 1–71 (Whole No. 405). [86]

DAVIS, R. C., GARAFOLO, L., and GAULT, F. P. (1957). An exploration of abdominal potentials. *Journal of Comparative and Physiological Psychology*, **50**, 519–23. [40]

DEANE, G. E. (1961). Human heart rate responses during experimentally induced anxiety. *Journal of Experimental Psychology*, **61**, 489–93. [95]

DEANE, G. E. (1964). Human heart rate responses during experimentally induced anxiety: a follow up with controlled respiration. *Journal of Experimental Psychology*, **67**, 193–5. [95]

D'ELIA, G., and PERRIS, C. (1973). Cerebral functional dominance and depression. An analysis of EEG amplitude in depressed patients. *Acta Psychiatrica Scandinavica*, **49**, 191–7. [139]

DEMENT, W. C. (1955). Dream recall and eye movements during sleep in schizophrenics and normals. *Journal of Nervous and Mental Diseases*, **122**, 263–9. [176]

DEMENT, W. C., and KLEITMAN, N. (1957a). The relation of eye movements during sleep to dream activity: an objective method for the study of dreaming. *Journal of Experimental Psychology*, **53**, 339–46. [90]

DEMENT, W. C., and KLEITMAN, N. (1957b). Cyclic variations in EEG during sleep and their relation to eye movements, body motility and dreaming. *Electroencephalography and Clinical Neurophysiology*, **9**, 673–90. [90]

DEMENT, W. C., RECHTSCHAFFER, A., and GULEVICH, G. (1966). The nature of narcoleptic sleep attack. *Neurology*, **16**, 18–33. [92]

DEWHURST, K. E., EL KABIR, D. J., HARRIS, G. W., and MANDELBROTE, B. M. (1969). Observations on the blood concentration of thyrotropic hormone (T.S.H.) in schizophrenia and affective states. *British Journal of Psychiatry*, **115**, 1003–11. [155]

DIAZ-GUERRERO, R., GOTTLIEB, J. S., and KNOTT, J. R. (1946). The sleep of patients with manic-depressive psychosis, depressive type. An electroencephalographic study. *Psychosomatic Medicine*, **8**, 399–404. [140]

DIXON, P. F., BOOTH, M., and BUTLER, J. (1967). The corticosteroids. In Gray, C. H., and Bacharach, A. L. (eds), *Hormones in the Blood*, vol. 2, Academic Press, London, pp. 305–89. [68]

DOIG, R. J., MUMMERY, R. V., WILLS, M. R., and ELKES, A. (1966). Plasma cortisol levels in depression. *British Journal of Psychiatry*, **112**, 1263–7. [151]

DONGIER, M., and BOSTEM, F. (1967). Essais d'application en psychiatrie de la variation contingente négative. *Acta Neurologica et Psychiatrica Belgica*, **67**, 640–5. [109]

DONGIER, M., WITTKOWER, E. D., STEPHENS-NEWSHAM, L., and HOFFMAN, M. M. (1956). Psychophysiological studies in thyroid function. *Psychosomatic Medicine*, **18**, 310–23. [125]

DORFMAN, R. I., and UNGAR, F. (1965). *Metabolism of Steroid Hormones*, Academic Press, London. [66]

DREYFUSS, F., and FELDMAN, S. (1952). Eosinopenia induced by emotional stress. *Acta Medica Scandinavica*, **144**, 107–13. [110]

DRIVER, M. V., and EILENBERG, M. D. (1960). Photoconvulsive threshold in depressive illness and the effects of E.C.T. *Journal of Mental Science*, **106**, 611–17. [142]

DUDLEY, D. L., MARTIN, C. J., and HOLMES, T. H. (1964). Psychophysiologic studies of pulmonary ventilation. *Psychosomatic Medicine*, **26**, 645. [41]

DUFFY, E. (1941). The conceptual categories of psychology: a suggestion for revision. *Psychological Review*, **48**, 177–203. [89]

DUFFY, E. (1951). The concept of energy mobilization. *Psychological Review*, **58**, 30–40. [89]

DUFFY, E. (1957). The psychological significance of the concept of 'arousal' or 'activation'. *Psychological Review*, **64**, 265–75. [89]

DUFFY, E. (1962). *Activation and Behavior*, Wiley, New York. [89]

DUFFY, E. (1972). Activation. In Greenfield, N. S., and Sternbach, R. A. (eds), *Handbook of Psychophysiology*, Holt, Rinehart & Winston, New York, pp. 577–622. [89]

DUNNER, D. L., GOODWIN, F. K., GERSHON, E. S., MURPHY, D. L., and BUNNEY, W. E. (1972). Excretion of 17-OHCS in unipolar and bipolar depressed patients. *Archives of General Psychiatry*, **26**, 360–3. [149]

DUREMAN, I., and SAAREN-SEPP'A'L'A', P. (1964). Biopsychologic studies of depression. I. Electrodermal reactivity as related to self-rated and clinically rated symptoms of anxiety and depression. *Acta Psychologica*, **22**, 218–30. [101]

DYKMAN, R. A., ACKERMAN, P. T., GALBRECHT, C. R., and REESE, W. G. (1963). Physiological reactivity to different stressors and methods of evaluation. *Psychosomatic Medicine*, **25**, 37–48. [86]

DYKMAN, R. A., REESE, W. G., GALBRECHT, C. R., and THOMASSON, P. J. (1959). Psychophysiological reactions to novel stimuli: measurement, adaptation, and relationship of psychological and physiological variables in the normal human. *Annals of the New York Academy of Sciences*, **79**, 43–107. [86]

EDELBERG, R. (1967). Electrical properties of the skin. In Brown, C. C. (ed.), *Methods in Psychophysiology*, Williams & Wilkins, Baltimore, pp. 1–53. [19, 24]

EIDUSON, S., BRILL, N. Q., and CRUMPTON, E. (1961). Adrenocortical activity in psychiatric disorders. *Archives of General Psychiatry (Chicago)*, **5**, 227. [180]

ELLINGSON, R. J. (1954). The incidence of EEG abnormality among patients with mental disorders of apparently nonorganic origin: a critical review. *American Journal of Psychiatry*, **111**, 263–75. [108, 137]

ELLIOT, R. (1966). Effects of uncertainty about the nature and advent of a noxious stimulus (shock) upon heart rate. *Journal of Personality and Social Psychology*, **3**, 353–6. [95]

ELMADJIAN, F. (1959). Excretion and metabolism of epinephrine. *Pharmacological Review*, **11**, 409–15. [117]

ELMADJIAN, F. (1962). Aldosterone excretion in behavioral disorders. *Research Publications of the Association for Research into Nervous and Mental Diseases*, **40**, 414–19. [181]

ELMADJIAN, F., HOPE, J. M., and LAMSON, E. T. (1957). Excretion of epinephrine and norepinephrine in various emotional states. *Journal of Clinical Endocrinology*, **17**, 608–20. [117, 122]

ELMADJIAN, F., HOPE, J. M., and LAMSON, E. T. (1958). Excretion of epinephrine and norepinephrine under stress. *Recent Progress in Hormone Research*, **14**, 513–45. [74]

ELMADJIAN, F., and PINCUS, G. (1946). A study of the diurnal variations in circulating lymphocytes in normal and psychotic subjects. *Journal of Clinical Endocrinology*, **6**, 287–94. [68, 179]

ENGEL, B. T. (1960). Stimulus-response and individual-response specificity. *Archives of General Psychiatry*, **2**, 305–13. [86]

ENGEL, B. T. (1972). Response specificity. In Greenfield, N. S., and Sternbach, R. A. (eds), *Handbook of Psychophysiology*, Holt, Rinehart & Winston, New York, pp. 571–6. [85]

ENGEL, B. T., and BICKFORD, A. F. (1961). Response specificity. Stimulus-response and individual-response specificity in essential hypertensives. *Archives of General Psychiatry*, **5**, 478–89. [86]

ENGEL, G. L. (1967). The concept of psychosomatic disorder. *Journal of Psychosomatic Research*, **11**, 3–9. [199]

EPPINGER, H., and HESS, L. (1910). *Die Vagotonie*, Berlin. [81]

EPSTEIN, S. (1967). Toward a unified theory of anxiety. In Maher, B. A. (ed.), *Progress in Experimental Personality Research*, vol. 4, Academic Press, New York, pp. 1–89. [208]

EPSTEIN, S., and COLEMAN, M. (1970). Drive theories of schizophrenia. *Psychosomatic Medicine*, **32**, 113–40. [184]

VON EULER, U. S. (1956). *Noradrenaline: Chemistry, Physiology, Pharmacology and Clinical Aspects*, Thomas, Springfield. [71]

VON EULER, U. S., GEMZELL, C. A., LEVI, L., and STROM, G. (1959). Cortical and medullary adrenal activity in emotional stress. *Acta Endocrinologica (Kobenhavn)*, **30**, 567–73. [118]

VON EULER, U. S., and LUNDBERG, U. (1954). Effect of flying on the epinephrine excretion in Air Force personnel. *Journal of Applied Physiology*, **6**, 551–5. [117]

EYSENCK, H. J. (1961). Psychosis, drive and inhibition: a theoretical and experimental account. *American Journal of Psychiatry*, **118**, 198–204. [184]

EYSENCK, H. J., and YAP, P.-M. (1944). Parotid gland secretion in affective mental disorders. *Journal of Mental Science*, **90**, 595–602. [131]

EYSENCK, S. B. G. (1956). An experimental study of psychogalvanic reflex responses of normal, neurotic and psychotic subjects. *Journal of Psychosomatic Research*, **1**, 258–72. [98]

FAST, G. J., and FISHER, S. (1971). The role of body attitudes and acquiescence in epinephrine and placebo effects. *Psychosomatic Medicine*, **33**, 63–84. [121]

FAURBYE, A., MUNKVAD, I., and PIND, K. (1958). The thyroid function in chronic schizophrenia (hebephrenia). *Acta Endocrinologica (Kobenhavn)*, **28**, 395–409. [182]

FAURBYE, A., VESTERGAARD, P., KOBBERNAGEL, F., and NIELSEN, A. (1951). Adrenal cortical function in chronic schizophrenia (stress, adrenaline-test, ACTH-test). *Acta Endocrinologica (Kobenhavn)*, **8**, 215–46. [179]

FAWCETT, J. A., and BUNNEY, W. E. (1967). Pituitary adrenal function and depression. An outline for research. *Archives of General Psychiatry*, **16**, 517–35. [145]

FÉIGENBERG, I. M. (1964). Electroencéphalographie comparative des groupes cliniques variés de malades de schizophrénie. *Zhurnal Nevropatologii Psikhiatrii*, **64**, 567–74. [172]

FEINBERG, I. (1958). Current status of the Funkenstein test. A review of the literature through December 1957. *Archives of Neurology and Psychiatry*, **80**, 488–501. [136]

FEINBERG, I., and EVARTS, E. V. (1969). Some implications of sleep research for psychiatry. In Zubin, J., and Shagass, C. (eds), *Neurobiological Aspects of Psychopathology*, Grune and Stratton, New York, pp. 334-93. [175, 177]

FEINBERG, I., KORESKO, R. L., and GOTTLIEB, F. (1965). Further observations on electrophysiological sleep patterns in schizophrenia. *Comprehensive Psychiatry*, 6, 21-4. [176, 178]

FEINBERG, I., KORESKO, R. L., GOTTLIEB, F., and WENDER, P. H. (1964). Sleep electroencephalographic and eye movement patterns in schizophrenic patients. *Comprehensive Psychiatry*, 5, 44-53. [176]

FENICHEL, O. (1945). *The Psychoanalytic Theory of Neurosis*, Norton, New York. [185]

FENTON, G. W., HILL, D., and SCOTTON, L. (1968). An EEG measurement of the effect of mood change on the thiopentone tolerance of depressed patients. *British Journal of Psychiatry*, 114, 1141-7. [137]

FENZ, W. D., and EPSTEIN, S. (1967). Gradients of physiological arousal of experienced and novice parachutists as a function of an approaching jump. *Psychosomatic Medicine*, 29, 33-51. [96]

FENZ, W. D., and JONES, G. B. (1972). Individual differences in physiologic arousal and performance in sport parachutists. *Psychosomatic Medicine*, 34, 1-8. [96]

FÉRÉ, C. (1888). Note sur les modifications de la résistance électrique sous l'influence des excitations sensorielles et des émotions. *Comptes Rendues des Séances de la Societé de Biologie*, 40, 217-19. [19]

FERGUSON, H. C., BARTRAM, A. C., FOWLIE, H. C., CATHRO, D. M., BIRCHALL, K., and MITCHELL, F. L. (1964). A preliminary investigation of steroid excretion in depressed patients before and after electroconvulsive therapy. *Acta Endocrinologica (Kobenhavn)*, 47, 58-68. [148]

FERREIRA, A. J., and WINTER, W. D. (1963). The palmar sweat print: a methodological study. *Psychosomatic Medicine*, 25, 377-84. [18]

FINE, B. J., and SWEENEY, D. A. (1967). Socio-economic background, aggression, and catecholamine excretion. *Psychological Report*, 20, 11-18. [120]

FINESINGER, J. (1944). The effect of pleasant and unpleasant ideas on the respiratory pattern (spirogram) in psychoneurotic patients. *American Journal of Psychiatry*, 100, 659-67. [105]

FINESINGER, J. E., and MAZICK, S. G. (1940a). The respiratory response of psychoneurotic patients to ideational and to sensory stimuli. *American Journal of Psychiatry*, 97, 27-46. [134]

FINESINGER, J. E., and MAZICK, S. G. (1940b). The effect of a painful stimulus and its recall upon respiration in psychoneurotic patients. *Psychosomatic Medicine*, 2, 333-68. [134]

FINK, M. (1958). Lateral gaze nystagmus as an index of the sedation threshold. *Electroencephalography and Clinical Neurophysiology*, 10, 162-3. [77]

FINK, M., ITIL, T., and CLYDE, D. (1965). A contribution to the classification of psychoses by quantitative EEG measures. *Proceedings of the Society for Biological Psychiatry*, 2, 5-17. [169]

FINK, M., ITIL, T., and CLYDE, D. (1966). The classification of psychoses by quantitative EEG measures. In Wortis, J. (ed.), *Recent Advances in Biological Psychiatry*, vol. 8, Plenum, New York, pp. 305–12. [138]

FINK, M., TAYLOR, M. A., and VOLAVKA, J. (1969). Anxiety precipitated by lactate. *New England Journal of Medicine*, **281**, 1429. [127]

FINLEY, K. H. (1944). On the occurrence of rapid frequency potential changes in the human EEG. *American Journal of Psychiatry*, **101**, 194–200. [137]

FIORICA, V., and MUEHL, S. (1962). Relationship between plasma levels of 17-hydroxy-corticosteroids (17-OH-CS) and a psychological measure of manifest anxiety. *Psychosomatic Medicine*, **24**, 596–9. [113]

FLOR-HENRY, P. (1969). Psychosis and temporal lobe epilepsy. A controlled investigation. *Epilepsia*, **10**, 363–95. [163]

FLORIS, V., MOROCUTTI, C., AMABILE, G., BERNARDI, G., RIZZO, P. A., and VASCONETTO, C. (1967). Recovery cycle of visual evoked potentials in normal and schizophrenic subjects. *Electroencephalography and Clinical Neurophysiology*, Suppl. **26**, 74–81. [174]

FOX, R., and LIPPERT, W. W. (1963). Spontaneous GSR and anxiety level in sociopathic delinquents. *Journal of Consulting Psychology*, **27**, 368. [195]

FRANKENHAEUSER, M., FRÖBERG, J., and MELLIS, I. (1965). Subjective and physiological reactions induced by electrical shocks of varying intensity. *Neuroendocrinology*, **1**, 105–12. [119]

FRANKENHAEUSER, M., and JÄRPE, G. (1962). Psychophysiological reactions to infusions of a mixture of adrenaline and noradrenaline. *Scandinavian Journal of Psychology*, **3**, 21–9. [121]

FRANKENHAEUSER, M., and JÄRPE, G. (1963). Psychophysiological changes during infusions of adrenaline in various doses. *Psychopharmacologia*, **4**, 424–32. [121]

FRANKENHAEUSER, M., and PATKAI, P. (1964). Catecholamine excretion and performance during stress. *Perceptual and Motor Skills*, **19**, 13–14. [119]

FRANKENHAEUSER, M., and PATKAI, P. (1965). Interindividual differences in catecholamine excretion during stress. *Scandinavian Journal of Psychology*, **6**, 117–23. [119]

FREEMAN, H., PINCUS, G., ELMADJIAN, F., and ROMANOFF, L. P. (1955). Adrenal responsivity in aged psychotic patients. *Geriatrics*, **10**, 72–7. [179]

FREUD, S. (1948). *Inhibitions, Symptoms and Anxiety*, Hogarth, London. [189]

FRIEDLANDER, J. H., PERRAULT, R., TURNER, W. J., and GOTTFRIED, S. P. (1950). Adrenocortical response to physiologic stress in schizophrenia. *Psychosomatic Medicine*, **12**, 86–8. [179]

FUNKENSTEIN, D. H. (1954). Physiologic studies of depression. In Hoch, P., and Zubin, J. (eds), *Depression*, Grune & Stratton, New York, pp. 183–9. [135]

FUNKENSTEIN, D. H., GREENBLATT, M., and SOLOMON, H. C. (1948). Autonomic nervous system changes following electric shock treatment. *Journal of Nervous and Mental Diseases*, **108**, 409–22. [135]

FUNKENSTEIN, D. H., GREENBLATT, M., and SOLOMON, H. C. (1949). Psychophysiological study of mentally ill patients. Part I—The status of the peripheral autonomic nervous system as determined by the reaction to epinephrine and mecholyl. *American Journal of Psychiatry*, **106**, 16–28. [135]

FUNKENSTEIN, D. H., GREENBLATT, M., and SOLOMON, H. C. (1951). Prognostic tests indicating the effectiveness of treatment. *Research Publications of the Association for Research into Nervous and Mental Diseases*, **31**, 245–66. [135]

FUNKENSTEIN, D. H., KING, S. H., and DROLETTE, W. E. (1957). *Mastery of Stress*, Harvard University Press, Cambridge, Mass. [203]

GADDUM, J. H. (1945). Lognormal distributions. *Nature*, **156**, 463–6. [85]

GANONG, W. F. (1963). The central nervous system and the synthesis and release of adrenocorticotropic hormone. In Nalbandov, A. V. (ed.), *Advances in Neuroendocrinology*, University of Illinois, Urbana, pp. 92–149. [64]

GARDINER, H. M., METCALF, R. C., and BEEBE-CENTER, J. G. (1937). *Feeling and Emotion. A History of Theories*, American Book Co., New York. [207]

GASTAUT, H., and BROUGHTON, R. (1965). A clinical and polygraphic study of episodic phenomena during sleep. In Wortis, J. (ed.), *Recent Advances in Biological Psychiatry*, vol. 1, Plenum, New York, pp. 197–221. [92]

GEDDES, L. A., and HOFF, H. E. (1964). The measurement of physiologic events by electrical impedance: a review. *American Journal of Medical Electronics*, **3**, 16–27. [37, 42]

GEER, J. H. (1966). Fear and autonomic arousal. *Journal of Abnormal Psychology*, **71**, 253–5. [101]

GEISLER, C. D. (1960). Average responses to clicks in man recorded by scalp electrodes. *Massachusetts Institute of Technology Research Laboratory in Electronics, Technical Report*, **380**, 1–158. [55]

GELLHORN, E. (1953). *Physiological Foundations of Neurology and Psychiatry*, University of Minnesota Press, Minneapolis. [157]

GELLHORN, E., and MILLER, A. D. (1961). Methacholine and noradrenaline tests. Their reliability and physiological significance. *Archives of General Psychiatry*, **4**, 371–80. [78]

GIBBONS, J. L. (1964). Cortisol secretion rate in depressive illness. *Archives of General Psychiatry*, **10**, 572–5. [151]

GIBBONS, J. L. (1966). The secretion rate of corticosterone in depressive illness. *Journal of Psychosomatic Research*, **10**, 263–6. [151]

GIBBONS, J. L. (1968). The adrenal cortex and psychological distress. In Michael, R. P. (ed.), *Endocrinology and Human Behaviour*, Oxford University Press, London, pp. 220–36. [115]

GIBBONS, J. L., GIBSON, J. G., MAXWELL, A. E., and WILLCOX, D. R. C. (1960). An endocrine study of depressive illness. *Journal of Psychosomatic Research*, **5**, 32–41. [147, 154]

GIBBONS, J. L., and MCHUGH, P. R. (1962). Plasma cortisol in depressive illness. *Journal of Psychiatric Research*, **1**, 162–71. [150]

GIBBS, F. A., and GIBBS, E. L. (1963). The mitten pattern: an electroencephalographic abnormality correlating with psychosis. *Journal of Neuropsychiatry*, **5**, 6–13. [168]

GIBBS, J. B., and WILLCOX, D. R. C. (1957). Observations on thyroid adrenocortical relationships. *Journal of Psychosomatic Research*, **2**, 225–35. [154]

GIBSON, J. G. (1962). Emotions and the thyroid gland. A critical appraisal. *Journal of Psychosomatic Research*, **6**, 93–116. [123]

GIDDON, D. B., and LISANTI, V. F. (1962). Cholinesterase-like substance in the parotid saliva of normals and psychiatric patients. *Lancet*, **1**, 725–6. [165]

GILBERSTADT, H., and MALEY, M. (1965). GSR, clinical state and psychiatric diagnosis. *Journal of Clinical Psychology*, **21**, 233–8. [98, 130]

GITTLEMAN, B., SHATIN, L., BIRENBAUM, M. L., FLEISCHMAN, A. I., and HAYTON, T. (1968). Effects of quantified stressful stimuli on blood lipids in man. *Journal of Nervous and Mental Disease*, **147**, 196–201. [120]

GJESSING, L. R. (1964). Studies of periodic catatonia. I. Blood levels of protein-bound iodine and urinary excretion of vanillyl-mandelic acid in relation to clinical course. *Journal of Psychiatric Research*, **2**, 123–34. [182]

GLENN, E. M., and NELSON, D. H. (1953). Chemical method for the determination of 17-hydroxycorticosteroids and 17-ketosteroids in urine following hydrolysis with β-glucuronidase. *Journal of Clinical Endocrinology*, **13**, 911–21. [68]

GLICKSTEIN, M., *et al.* (1957). Temporal heart rate patterns in anxious patients. *Archives of Neurology and Psychiatry (Chicago)*, **78**, 101–6. [102]

GOLDMAN, H., LINDNER, L., DINITZ, S., and ALLEN, H. (1971). The simple sociopath: physiologic and sociologic characteristics. *Biological Psychiatry*, **3**, 77–83. [196]

GOLDSTEIN, I. B. (1964). Physiological responses in anxious women patients. A study of autonomic activity and muscle tension. *Archives of General Psychiatry*, **10**, 382–8. [105, 106]

GOLDSTEIN, I. B. (1965). The relationship of muscle tension and autonomic activity to psychiatric disorders. *Psychosomatic Medicine*, **27**, 39–52. [130, 134, 135]

GOLDSTEIN, I. B., GRINKER, R. R., HEATH, H. A., OKEN, D., and SHIPMAN, W. G. (1964). Study in psychophysiology of muscle tension. I. Response specificity. *Archives of General Psychiatry*, **11**, 322–30. [135]

GOLDSTEIN, L., MURPHREE, H. B., SUGARMAN, A. A., PFEIFFER, C. C., and JENNEY, E. H. (1963). Quantitative electroencephalographic analysis of naturally occurring (schizophrenic) and drug-induced psychotic states in human males. *Clinical Pharmacology and Therapeutics*, **4**, 10–21. [171]

GOLDSTEIN, L., and SUGARMAN, A. A. (1969). EEG correlates of psychopathology. In Zubin, J., and Shagass, C. (eds), *Neurobiological Aspects of Psychopathology*, Grune & Stratton, New York, pp. 1–19. [169]

GOLDSTEIN, L., SUGARMAN, A. A., STOLBERG, H., MURPHREE, H. B., and PFEIFFER, C. C. (1965). Electro-cerebral activity in schizophrenics and non-psychotic subjects: quantitative EEG amplitude analysis. *Electroencephalography and Clinical Neurophysiology*, **19**, 350–61. [170]

GOLDSTEIN, R., and PRICE, L. L. (1966). Clinical use of EEA with an average response computer: a case report. *Journal of Speech and Hearing Disorders*, **31**, 75–8. [191]

GOLDWATER, B. C. (1972). Psychological significance of pupillary movements. *Psychological Bulletin*, **77**, 340–55. [40]

GOLLA, F. L. (1921). The objective study of neurosis. *Lancet*, **99**:2, 215–21. [97]

BIBLIOGRAPHICAL INDEX

GOODALL, MCC., MCCALLY, M., and GRAVELINE, D. E. (1964). Urinary adrenaline and noradrenaline response to simulated weightless state. *American Journal of Physiology*, **206**, 431–6. [118]

GÖTLIND, E. (1958). *Three Theories of Emotion. Some Views on Philosophical Method*, Gleerup, Lund; Munksgaard, Copenhagen. [207]

GOTTLIEB, G., and PAULSON, G. (1961). Salivation in depressed patients. A longitudinal study. *Archives of General Psychiatry*, **5**, 468–71. [132]

GOTTSCHALK, L. A., CLEGHORN, J. M., GLESER, G. C., and IACONO, J. M. (1965). Studies of relationships of emotions to plasma lipids. *Psychosomatic Medicine*, **27**, 102–11. [123]

GOTTSCHALK, L. A., SEROTA, H. M., and SHAPIRO, L. B. (1950). Psychologic conflict and neuromuscular tension: I. Preliminary report on a method, as applied to rheumatoid arthritis. *Psychosomatic Medicine*, **12**, 315–19. [203]

GRAHAM, D. T. (1971). Psychophysiology and medicine. *Psychophysiology*, **8**, 121–31. [200]

GRAHAM, F. K., and CLIFTON, R. K. (1966). Heart-rate change as a component of the orienting response. *Psychological Bulletin*, **65**, 305–20. [83]

GREENBLATT, M. (1944). Age and electroencephalographic abnormality in neuropsychiatric patients. A study of 1593 cases. *American Journal of Psychiatry*, **101**, 82–90. [137]

GREENFIELD, A. D. M. (1960). Venous occlusion plethysmography. In Bruner, H. D. (ed.), *Methods in Medical Research*, vol. 8, Year Book, Chicago, pp. 293–301. [37]

GREENFIELD, N. S., KATZ, D., ALEXANDER, A. A., and ROESSLER, R. (1963). The relationship between physiological and psychological responsivity: depression and galvanic skin response. *Journal of Nervous and Mental Disease*, **136**, 535–9. [130]

GREENFIELD, N. S., and STERNBACH, R. A. (eds) (1972). *Handbook of Psychophysiology*, Holt, Rinehart & Winston, New York. [3, 81]

GRESHAM, S. C., AGNEW, H. W., and WILLIAMS, R. L. (1965). The sleep of depressed patients. An EEG and eye movement study. *Archives of General Psychiatry*, **13**, 503–7. [141]

GRINKER, R. R. (1961). The physiology of emotions. In Simon, A., Herbert, C. C., and Straus, R. (eds), *The Physiology of Emotions*, Charles C. Thomas, Springfield, Illinois, pp. 3–25. [97]

GRINKER, R. R., MILLER, J., SABSHIN, M., NUNN, R., and NUNNALLY, J. C. (1961). *The Phenomena of Depression*, Hoeber, New York. [129]

GRINKER, R. R., et al. (1957). Use of an anxiety-producing interview and its meaning to the subject. *Archives of Neurology and Psychiatry (Chicago)*, **77**, 406–19. [94]

GROSZ, H. J. (1961). The relation of serum ascorbic acid level to adrenocortical secretion during experimentally induced emotional stress in human subjects. *Journal of Psychosomatic Research*, **5**, 253–61. [112]

GROSZ, H. J., and FARMER, B. B. (1969). Blood lactate in the development of anxiety symptoms. A critical examination of Pitts and McClure's hypothesis and experimental study. *Archives of General Psychiatry*, **21**, 611–19. [126]

GROSZ, H. J., and FARMER, B. B. (1272). Pitts and McClure's lactate-anxiety study revisited. *British Journal of Psychiatry*, **120**, 415–18. [126]

GRUZELIER, J. H. (1973). Bilateral asymmetry of skin conductance orienting activity and levels in schizophrenics. *Biological Psychology*, **1**, 21–41. [163]

GRUZELIER, J. H., LYKKEN, D. T., and VENABLES, P. H. (1972). Schizophrenia and arousal revisited. *Archives of General Psychiatry*, **26**, 427–32. [161]

GRUZELIER, J. H., and VENABLES, P. H. (1972). Skin conductance orienting activity in a heterogeneous sample of schizophrenics. *Journal of Nervous and Mental Disease*, **155**, 277–87. [162]

GRUZELIER, J. H., and VENABLES, P. H. (1973). Skin conductance responses to tones with and without attentional significance in schizophrenic and non-schizophrenic psychiatric patients. *Neuropsychologia*, in press. [162]

GULEVICH, G. D., DEMENT, W. C., and ZARCONE, V. P. (1967). All night sleep recordings of chronic schizophrenics in remission. *Comprehensive Psychiatry*, **8**, 141–9. [176]

GUNNE, L. M., and GEMZELL, C. A. (1956). Adrenocortical and thyroid function in periodic catatonia. *Acta Psychiatrica et Neurologica Scandinavica*, **31**, 367–78. [180]

GURNEY, C., ROTH, M., GARSIDE, R. F., KERR, T. A., and SCHAPIRA, K. (1972). Studies in the classification of affective disorders. The relationship between anxiety states and depressive illness. II. *British Journal of Psychiatry*, **121**, 162–6. [129]

HAKAREM, G. (1967). Pupillography. In Venables, P. H., and Martin, I. (eds), *Manual of Psycho-physiological Methods*, North-Holland, Amsterdam, pp. 335–49. [40]

HALE, H. B., DUFFY, J. C., ELLIS, J. P., and WILLIAMS, E. W. (1964). Flying stress in relation to flying proficiency. *US Air Force School of Aerospace Medicine*, 1–8. [111]

HALE, H. B., ELLIS, J. P., and KRATOCHVIL, C. H. (1959). Effects of piloting supersonic aircraft on plasma corticosteroids and bicarbonate. *Journal of Applied Physiology*, **14**, 629–31. [111]

HALL, S. B. (1927). The blood pressure in psychoneurosis. An investigation of 71 cases. *Lancet*, **2**, 540–3. [103]

HALLIDAY, A. M. (1968). Computing techniques in neurological diagnosis. *British Medical Bulletin*, **24**, 253–9. [191]

HALLIDAY, A. M., and MASON, A. A. (1964). The effect of hypnotic anaesthesia on cortical responses. *Journal of Neurology, Neurosurgery and Psychiatry*, **27**, 300–12. [192]

HAMILTON, M. (1960). Quantitative assessment of the mecholyl test. *Acta Neurologica Psychiatrica Scandinavica*, **35**, 156–62. [136]

HANDLON, J. H. (1962). Hormonal activity and individual responses to stresses and easements in everyday living. In Roessler, R., and Greenfield, N. S. (eds), *Physiological Correlates of Psychological Disorders*, University of Wisconsin Press, Madison, pp. 157–70. [114]

HANDLON, J. H., WADESON, R. W., FISHMAN, J. R., SACHAR, E. J., HAMBURG, D. A., and MASON, J. W. (1962). Psychological factors lowering plasma 17-hydroxycorticosteroid concentration. *Psychosomatic Medicine*, **24**, 535–41. [113]

HARE, R. D. (1965a). Acquisition and generalisation of a conditioned fear response in psychopathic and non-psychopathic criminals. *Journal of Psychology*, **59**, 367–70. [195]

HARE, R. D. (1965b). Temporal gradient of fear arousal in psychopaths. *Journal of Abnormal Psychology*, **70**, 442–5. [195]

HARE, R. D. (1968). Psychopathy, autonomic functioning and the orienting response. *Journal of Abnormal Psychology, Monograph supplement* **73**, No. 3, 1–24. [195]

HARE, R. D. (1970). *Psychopathy: Theory and Research*, Wiley, New York. [194]

HARE, R. D. (1972). Psychopathy and physiological responses to adrenalin. *Journal of Abnormal Psychology*, **79**, 138–47. [196]

HARE, R. D., and QUINN, M. J. (1971). Psychopathy and autonomic conditioning. *Journal of Abnormal Psychology*, **77**, 223–35. [195]

HARPER, M., GURNEY, C., SAVAGE, R. D., and ROTH, M. (1965). Forearm blood flow in normal subjects and patients with phobic anxiety states. *British Journal of Psychiatry*, **III**, 723–31. [104]

HARRIS, J. D. (1943). Habituatory response decrement in the intact organism. *Psychological Bulletin*, **40**, 385–422. [86]

HARRISON, J., MACKINNON, P. C. B., and MONK-JONES, M. E. (1962). Behaviour of the palmar sweat glands before and after operation. *Clinical Science*, **23**, 371–7. [95]

HAWKINS, D. R., and MENDELS, J. (1966). Sleep disturbance in depressive syndromes. *American Journal of Psychiatry*, **123**, 682–90. [140]

HAWKINS, D. R., MONROE, J. D., SANDIFER, M. G., and VERNON, C. R. (1960). Psychological and physiological responses to continuous epinephrine infusion. *Psychiatric Research Reports of the American Psychiatric Association*, **12**, 40–52. [127]

HEATH, H. A., OKEN, D., and SHIPMAN, W. G. (1967). Muscle tension and personality, a serious second look. *Archives of General Psychiatry*, **16**, 720–7. [135]

HEIN, P. L., GREEN, R. L., and WILSON, W. P. (1962). Latency and duration of photically elicited arousal responses in the electroencephalograms of patients with chronic regressive schizophrenia. *Journal of Nervous and Mental Diseases*, **135**, 361–4. [172]

HEMSI, L. K., WHITEHEAD, A., and POST, F. (1968). Cognitive functioning and cerebral arousal in elderly depressives and dements. *Journal of Psychosomatic Research*, **12**, 145–56. [132]

HENINGER, G., and SPECK, L. B. (1966). Visual evoked responses and mental status of schizophrenics during and after phenothiazine therapy. *Archives of General Psychiatry*, **15**, 419–26. [174]

HERNÁNDEZ-PEÓN, R., CHÁVEZ-IBARRA, G., and AGUILAR-FIGUEROA, E. (1963). Somatic evoked potentials in one case of hysterical anaesthesia. *Electroencephalography and Clinical Neurophysiology*, **15**, 889–92. [190]

HERNÁNDEZ-PEÓN, R., and DONOSO, M. (1959). Influence of attention and suggestion upon subcortical evoked electric activity in the human brain. *Electroencephalography and Clinical Neurophysiology*, Suppl. **7**, 385–96. [192]

HERR, V. V., and KOBLER, F. J. (1953). A psychogalvanometric test for neuroticism. *Journal of Abnormal and Social Psychology*, **48**, 410–16. [97]

HERR, V. V., and KOBLER, F. J. (1957). Further study of psychogalvanometric test for neuroticism. *Journal of Clinical Psychology*, **13**, 387–90. [97]

HETZEL, B. S., SCHOTTSTAEDT, W. W., GRACE, W. J., and WOLFF, H. G. (1956). Changes in urinary nitrogen and electrolyte excretion during stressful life experiences, and their relation to thyroid function. *Journal of Psychosomatic Research*, **1**, 177–85. [123]

HIATT, H. H., ROTHWELL, W. S., and HORWITT, M. K. (1952). Eosinopenia produced by ACTH in patients with schizophrenia. *Proceedings of the Society of Experimental Biology and Medicine*, **79**, 707–8. [179]

HICKAM, J. B., CARGILL, W. H., and GOLDEN, A. (1948). Cardiovascular reactions to emotional stimuli. Effect on the cardiac output, arteriovenous oxygen difference, arterial pressure, and peripheral resistance. *Journal of Clinical Investigation*, **27**, 290–8. [95]

HILL, D. (1952). EEG in episodic psychotic and psychopathic behaviour. *Electroencephalography and Clinical Neurophysiology*, **4**, 419–40. [171]

HILL, D. (1957). Electroencephalogram in schizophrenia. In Richter, D. (ed.), *Schizophrenia. Somatic Aspects*, Pergamon, London, pp. 33–51. [167]

HILL, D. (1963). The EEG in psychiatry. In Hill, D., and Parr, G. (eds), *Electroencephalography: a Symposium on its Various Aspects*, 2nd ed., Macdonald, London, pp. 368–428. [108, 137, 196]

HILLMAN, J. (1960). *Emotion*, Routledge & Kegan Paul, London. [207]

HINTON, J. M. (1963). Patterns of insomnia in depressive states. *Journal of Neurology, Neurosurgery and Psychiatry*, **26**, 184–9. [139]

HOAGLAND, H., CAMERON, D. E., and RUBIN, M. A. (1937). The electroencephalogram of schizophrenics during insulin treatments. *American Journal of Psychiatry*, **94**, 183–208. [167]

HOAGLAND, H., ELMADJIAN, F., and PINCUS, G. (1946). Stressful psychomotor performance and adrenal cortical function as indicated by the lymphocyte response. *Journal of Clinical Endocrinology*, **6**, 301–11. [70]

HOAGLAND, H., PINCUS, G., ELMADJIAN, F., ROMANOFF, L., FREEMAN, H., HOPE, J., BALLAN, J., BERKELEY, A., and CARLO, J. (1953). Study of adrenocortical physiology in normal and schizophrenic men. *Archives of Neurology and Psychiatry*, **69**, 470–85. [179]

HOCH, P., KUBIS, J. F., and ROUKE, F. L. (1944). Psychogalvanometric investigations in psychoses and other abnormal mental states. *Psychosomatic Medicine*, **6**, 237–43. [158]

HODGES, J. R., JONES, M. T., and STOCKHAM, M. A. (1962). Effect of emotion on blood corticotrophin and cortisol concentrations in man. *Nature*, **193**, 1187–8. [110]

HOLLOWAY, F. A., and PARSONS, O. A. (1969). Unilateral brain damage and bilateral skin conductance levels in humans. *Psychophysiology*, **6**, 138–48. [197]

HOLLOWAY, F. A., and PARSONS, O. A. (1971). Habituation of the orienting reflex in brain damaged patients. *Psychophysiology*, **8**, 623–34. [197]

HOLMGREN, A., and STRÖM, G. (1959). Blood lactate concentration in relation to absolute and relative work load in normal men, and in mitral stenosis, atrial septal defect and vasoregulatory asthenia. *Acta Medica Scandinavica*, **163**, 185–93. [125]

BIBLIOGRAPHICAL INDEX

HOWE, E. S. (1958). GSR conditioning in anxiety states, normals, and chronic functional schizophrenic subjects. *Journal of Abnormal and Social Psychology*, **56**, 183–9. [101, 158]

HULLIN, R. P., BAILEY, A. D., MCDONALD, R., DRANSFIELD, G. A., and MILNE, H. B. (1967). Variations in 11-hydroxycorticosteroids in depression and manic-depressive psychosis. *British Journal of Psychiatry*, **113**, 593–600. [150]

HUMPHREY, G. (1933). *The Nature of Learning*, Kegan Paul, London. [86]

HURST, L. A., MUNDY-CASTLE, A. C., and BEERSTACHER, D. M. (1954). The electroencephalogram in manic-depressive psychosis. *Journal of Mental Science*, **100**, 220–40. [138]

IGERT, C., and LAIRY, G. C. (1962). Intérêt pronostique de l'EEG au cours de l'évolution des schizophrènes. *Electroencephalography and Clinical Neurophysiology*, **14**, 183–90. [169]

INDERBITZIN, L. B., BUCHSBAUM, M., and SILVERMAN, J. (1970). EEG-averaged evoked response and perceptual variability in schizophrenics. *Archives of General Psychiatry*, **23**, 438–44. [174]

INNES, G., MILLAR, W. M., and VALENTINE, M. (1959). Emotion and blood-pressure. *Journal of Mental Science*, **105**, 840–51. [103]

INOUYE, T., and SHIMIZU, A. (1972). Visual evoked response and reaction time during verbal hallucination. *Journal of Nervous and Mental Disease*, **155**, 419–26. [178]

IRA, G. H., WHALEN, R. E., and BOGDONOFF, M. D. (1963). Heart rate changes in physicians during daily 'stressful' tasks. *Journal of Psychosomatic Research*, **7**, 147–50. [96]

ITIL, M. T. (1964). *Elektroencephalographische Studien bei Endogenen Psychosen und ihren Behandlung mit Psychotropen Medikamenten unter Besonderer Berücksichtigung des Pentothal-Elektroencephalogramms*, Matbassi, Istanbul. [137]

ITIL, T. M., HSU, W., KLINGENBERG, H., SALETU, B., and GANNON, P. (1972). Digital-computer-analyzed all-night sleep EEG patterns (sleep prints) in schizophrenics. *Biological Psychiatry*, **4**, 3–16. [177]

ITIL, T. M., SALETU, B., and DAVIS, S. (1972). EEG findings in chronic schizophrenics based on digital computer period analysis and analog power spectra. *Biological Psychiatry*, **5**, 1–13. [170]

JAKOBSON, T., STENBÄCK, A., STRANDSTRÖM, L., and RIMÓN, R. (1966). The excretion of urinary 11-deoxy- and 11-oxy-17-hydroxycorticosteroids in depressive patients during basal conditions and during the administration of methopyrazone. *Journal of Psychosomatic Research*, **9**, 363–74. [152]

JAMES, W. (1884). What is emotion? *Mind*, **19**, 188–205. [207]

JASPER, H. H. (1958). The ten–twenty electrode system of the international federation. *EEG Clinical Neurophysiology*, **10**, 371–5. [49]

JENKINS, J. S. (1968). *An Introduction to Biochemical Aspects of the Adrenal Cortex*, Edward Arnold, London. [64, 70]

JENNER, F., GJESSING, L., COX, J., DAVIES-JONES, A., HULLIN, R. P., and HANNA, S. (1967). A manic-depressive psychotic with a persistent forty-eight hour cycle. *British Journal of Psychiatry*, **113**, 898–910. [153]

JONES, M., and MELLERSH, V. (1946). A comparison of the exercise response in anxiety states and normal controls. *Psychosomatic Medicine*, **8**, 180–7. [125]

JONES, R. T., BLACKER, K. H., and CALLAWAY, E. (1966). Perceptual dysfunction in schizophrenia: clinical and auditory evoked response findings. *American Journal of Psychiatry*, **123**, 639–45. [173]

JONES, R. T., BLACKER, K. H., CALLAWAY, E., and LAYNE, R. S. (1965). The auditory evoked response as a diagnostic and prognostic measure in schizophrenia. *American Journal of Psychiatry*, **122**, 33–41. [173]

JURKO, M. F., FOSHEE, D. P., and SMITH, J. C. (1964). Hyperactivity and peripheral nerve conductivity. *Archives of General Psychiatry*, **10**, 431–4. [197]

JURKO, M., JOST, H., and HILL, T. S. (1952). Pathology of the energy system: an experimental-clinical study of physiological adaptive capacities in a non-patient, a psycho-neurotic and an early paranoid schizophrenic group. *Journal of Psychology*, **33**, 183–98. [103, 105, 158, 165, 166]

KAISER, E., PETERSÉN, I., SELLDÉN, U., and KAGAWA, N. (1964). EEG data representation in broad-band frequency analysis. *Electroencephalography and Clinical Neurophysiology*, **17**, 76–80. [52]

KALES, A., and BERGER, R. J. (1970). Psychopathology of sleep. In Costello, C. G. (ed.), *Symptoms of Psychopathology*, Wiley, New York, pp. 418–47. [90]

KATKIN, E. S. (1966). The relationship between a measure of transitory anxiety and spontaneous autonomic activity. *Journal of Abnormal Psychology*, **71**, 142–6. [95]

KATKIN, E. S., and MCCUBBIN, R. J. (1969). Habituation of the orienting response as a function of individual differences in anxiety and autonomic lability. *Journal of Abnormal Psychology*, **74**, 54–60. [96]

KELLY, D. H. W. (1966). Measurement of anxiety by forearm blood flow. *British Journal of Psychiatry*, **112**, 789–98. [103, 104]

KELLY, D. H. W. (1967). The technique of forearm plethysmography for assessing anxiety. *Journal of Psychosomatic Research*, **10**, 373–82. [37]

KELLY, D. H. W., MITCHELL-HEGGS, N., and SHERMAN, J. (1971). Anxiety and sodium lactate assessed clinically and physiologically. *British Journal of Psychiatry*, **119**, 129–41. [127]

KELLY, D. H. W., and WALTER, C. J. S. (1969). The relationship between clinical diagnosis and anxiety, assessed by forearm blood flow and other measurements. *British Journal of Psychiatry*, **114**, 611–26. [104, 133, 134, 165, 166]

KELLY, D. H. W., WALTER, C. J. S., and SARGANT, W. (1966). Modified leucotomy assessed by forearm blood flow and other measurements. *British Journal of Psychiatry*, **112**, 871–82. [134]

KELSEY, F. O., GULLOCK, A. H., and KELSEY, F. E. (1957). Thyroid activity in hospitalized psychiatric patients—relation of dietary iodine to I$^{131}$ uptake. *Archives of Neurology and Psychiatry*, **77**, 543–8. [182]

KENDALL, J. W. (1971). Feedback control of adrenocorticotropic hormone secretion. In Martini, L., and Ganong, W. F. (eds), *Frontiers in Neuroendocrinology 1971*, Oxford University Press, New York, pp. 177–207. [69]

KENDELL, R. E. (1968). *The Classification of Depressive Illnesses*, Oxford University Press, London. [155]

KENNARD, M. A., RABINOVITCH, M. S., and FISTER, W. P. (1955). The use of frequency analysis in the interpretation of the EEGs of patients with psychological disorders. *Electroencephalography and Clinical Neurophysiology*, **7**, 29–38. [108]

KENNARD, M. A., and SCHWARTZMAN, A. E. (1957). A longitudinal study of electroencephalographic frequency patterns in mental hospital patients and normal controls. *Electroencephalography and Clinical Neurophysiology*, **9**, 263–74. [170]

KERR, T. A., ROTH, M., SCHAPIRA, K., and GURNEY, C. (1972). The assessment and prediction of outcome in affective disorders. *British Journal of Psychiatry*, **121**, 167–74. [129]

KIELHOLZ, P., and BECK, D. (1962). Diagnosis, autonomic tests, treatment and prognosis of exhaustion depression. *Comprehensive Psychiatry*, **3**, 8–14. [134]

KILOH, L. G., and GARSIDE, R. F. (1963). The independence of neurotic depression and endogenous depression. *British Journal of Psychiatry*, **109**, 451–63. [155]

KISSEL, S., and LITTIG, L. W. (1962). Test anxiety and skin conductance. *Journal of Abnormal and Social Psychology*, **65**, 276–8. [96]

KLYNE, W. (1963). *The Chemistry of the Steroids*, Methuen, London. [65]

KOEPKE, J. E., and PRIBRAM, K. H. (1967). Habituation of the vasoconstriction response as a function of stimulus duration and anxiety. *Journal of Comparative and Physiological Psychology*, **64**, 502–4. [96]

KOLTUV, M., HAYES, R., FUCHS, A., and WELCH, L. (1959). A comparison of the GSRs of psychiatric patients and normals in an avoidance situation. *Journal of Psychology*, **48**, 115–19. [157]

KORESKO, R. L., SNYDER, F., and FEINBERG, I. (1963). 'Dream time' in hallucinating and non-hallucinating schizophrenic patients. *Nature*, **199**, 1118–19. [178]

KORNETSKY, C. (1967). Attention dysfunction and drugs in schizophrenia. In Brill, H., Cole, J. O., Deniker, P., Hippius, H., and Bradley, P. B. (eds), *Neuro-psychopharmacology*, Excerpta Medica, Amsterdam, pp. 948–54. [183]

KORTCHINSKAÏA, E. I. (1965). Étude électroencéphalographique comparée de malades atteints de 'schizophrénie greffée' et de malades atteints de schizophrénie non compliquée à évolution maligne. *Zhurnal Nevropatologii Psikhiatrii*, **65**, 263–7. [168]

KRAUSE, M. S. (1961). The measurement of transitory anxiety. *Psychological Review*, **68**, 178–89. [93]

KRAUSE, M. S., GALINSKY, M. D., and WEINER, I. B. (1961). A bibliography through 1957 of physiological indicators for transitory anxiety. *Journal of Psychological Studies*, **12**, 13–18. [94]

KURLAND, H. D. (1964). Steroid excretion in depressive disorders. *Archives of General Psychiatry*, **10**, 554–60. [148]

LACEY, J. I. (1950). Individual differences in somatic response patterns. *Journal of Comparative and Physiological Psychology*, **43**, 338–50. [85]

LACEY, J. I. (1959). Psychophysiological approaches to the evaluation of psychotherapeutic process and outcome. In Rubinstein, E. A., and

Parloff, M. B. (eds), *Research in Psychotherapy*, American Psychological Association, Washington, pp. 160–208. [85]

LACEY, J. I., BATEMAN, D. E., and VAN LEHN, R. (1953). Autonomic response specificity—an experimental study. *Psychosomatic Medicine*, **15**, 8–21. [85]

LACEY, J. I., and LACEY, B. C. (1958). Verification and extension of the principle of autonomic response-stereotypy. *American Journal of Psychology*, **71**, 50–73. [85]

LACEY, J. I., and VAN LEHN, R. (1952). Differential emphasis in somatic response to stress. An experimental study. *Psychosomatic Medicine*, **14**, 71–81. [85]

LADER, M. H. (1967). Palmar skin conductance measures in anxiety and phobic states. *Journal of Psychosomatic Research*, **11**, 271–81. [99]

LADER, M. H. (1969). The effect of anxiety on response to treatment. *Australian and New Zealand Journal of Psychiatry*, **3**, 288–92. [189]

LADER, M. H. (1970). The unit of quantification of the G.S.R. *Journal of Psychosomatic Research*, **14**, 109–10. [22]

LADER, M. H. (1971). The responses of normal subjects and psychiatric patients to repetitive stimulation. In Levi, L. (ed.), *Society, Stress and Disease*, vol. 1, Oxford University Press, London, pp. 417–32. [86]

LADER, M. H. (1972). The nature of anxiety. *British Journal of Psychiatry*, **121**, 481–91. [94]

LADER, M. H., GELDER, M. G., and MARKS, I. M. (1967). Palmar skin conductance measures as predictors of response to desensitization. *Journal of Psychosomatic Research*, **11**, 283–90. [100]

LADER, M. H., and MONTAGU, J. D. (1962). The psycho-galvanic reflex: a pharmacological study of the peripheral mechanism. *Journal of Neurology, Neurosurgery and Psychiatry*, **25**, 126–33. [21]

LADER, M. H., and NOBLE, P. J. (1974). The affective disorders. In Venables, P. H., and Christie, M. (eds), *Research in Psychophysiology*, in press. [155]

LADER, M. H., and SARTORIUS, N. (1968). Anxiety in patients with hysterical conversion symptoms. *Journal of Neurology, Neurosurgery and Psychiatry*, **31**, 490–7. [188]

LADER, M. H., and TYRER, P. (1975). Vegetative system and emotion. In Levi, L. (ed.), *Parameters of Emotion*, Oxford University Press, London, in press. [208]

LADER, M. H., and VENABLES, P. H. (1973). Biological psychology. *Biological Psychology*, **1**, 1–3. [2]

LADER, M. H., and WING, L. (1964). Habituation of the psycho-galvanic reflex in patients with anxiety states and in normal subjects. *Journal of Neurology, Neurosurgery and Psychiatry*, **27**, 210–18. [98]

LADER, M. H., and WING, L. (1966). *Physiological Measures, Sedative Drugs, and Morbid Anxiety*, Oxford University Press, London. [98, 103, 205]

LADER, M. H., and WING, L. (1969). Physiological measures in agitated and retarded depressed patients. *Journal of Psychiatric Research*, **7**, 89–100. [130, 131, 133, 135, 155]

LANDIS, C., and HUNT, W. A. (1939). *The Startle Pattern*, Farrar & Rinehart, New York. [84]

LANG, P. J., and BUSS, A. H. (1965). Psychological deficit in schizophrenia: II. Interference and activation. *Journal of Abnormal Psychology*, **70**, 77–106. [159, 183]

LASHLEY, K. S. (1916). Reflex secretion of the human parotid gland. *Journal of Experimental Psychology*, **1**, 461–93. [29]

LAZARUS, R. S. (1966). *Psychological Stress and the Coping Process*, McGraw-Hill, New York. [208]

LAZARUS, R. S., SPEISMAN, J. C., MORDKOFF, A. M., and DAVISON, L. A. (1962). A laboratory study of psychological stress produced by a motion picture film. *Psychology Monograph*, **76**, No. 34, Whole No. 553. [94]

LEMERE, F. (1941). Cortical energy production in the psychoses. *Psychosomatic Medicine*, **3**, 152–6. [137]

LESTER, B. K., and EDWARDS, R. J. (1966). EEG fast activity in schizophrenic and control subjects. *International Journal of Neuropsychiatry*, **2**, 143–56. [168]

LEVI, L. (1963). The urinary output of adrenalin and noradrenalin during experimentally induced emotional stress in clinically different groups. *Acta Psychotherapia (Basel)*, **11**, 218–27. [119]

LEVI, L. (1964). The stress of everyday work as reflected in productiveness, subjective feelings, and urinary output of adrenaline and noradrenaline under salaried and piecework conditions. *Journal of Psychosomatic Research*, **8**, 199–202. [119]

LEVI, L. (1965). The urinary output of adrenalin and noradrenalin during pleasant and unpleasant emotional states. *Psychosomatic Medicine*, **27**, 80–5. [118]

LEVI, L. (ed.) (1967). Emotional stress. *Försvarsmedicin*, **3**, Suppl. 2. [84, 117, 124]

LEVI, L. (1969). Neuro-endocrinology of anxiety. In Lader, M. H. (ed.), *Studies of Anxiety*, Royal Medico-Psychological Association, London, pp. 40–52. [122]

LEVI, L. (1972). Psychological and physiological reactions to and psychomotor performance during prolonged and complex stressor exposure. *Acta Medica Scandinavica*, Suppl. **528**, 119–42. [74, 117, 118, 119, 124]

LEVIT, R. A., SUTTON, S., and ZUBIN, J. (1973). Evoked potential correlates of information processing in psychiatric patients. *Psychological Medicine*, **3**, 487–94. [143, 175]

LEVITT, E. E., PERSKY, H., BRADY, J. P., and FITZGERALD, J. A. (1963). The effect of hydrocortisone infusion on hypnotically induced anxiety. *Psychosomatic Medicine*, **25**, 158–61. [113]

LEVY, R., and BEHRMAN, J. (1970). Cortical evoked responses in hysterical hemianaesthesia. *Electroencephalography and Clinical Neurophysiology*, **29**, 400–2. [191]

LEVY, R., ISAACS, A., and BEHRMAN, J. (1971). Neurophysiological correlates of senile dementia. II. The somatosensory evoked response. *Psychological Medicine*, **1**, 159–65. [197]

LEVY, R., ISAACS, A., and HAWKS, G. (1970). Neurophysiological correlates of senile dementia. I. Motor and sensory nerve conduction velocity. *Psychological Medicine*, **1**, 40–7. [197]

LEVY, R., and MUSHIN, J. (1973). Somatosensory evoked responses in patients with hysterical anaesthesia. *Journal of Psychosomatic Research*, **17**, 81–4. [191]

LEWIS, A. J. (1954). Aspetti di medicina psicosomatica. *Recenti Progressi di Medicina*, **16**, 434–53. [200]

LIBERSON, W. T. (1944). Functional electroencephalography in mental disorders. *Diseases of the Nervous System*, **5**, 357–64. [138]

LIFSHITZ, K. (1963a). Rheoencephalography: I. Review of the technique. *Journal of Nervous and Mental Disease*, **136**, 388–98. [12]

LIFSHITZ, K. (1963b). Rheoencephalography: II. Survey of clinical applications. *Journal of Nervous and Mental Disease*, **137**, 285–96. [12]

LIFSHITZ, K., and GRADIJAN, J. (1972). Relationships between measures of the coefficient of variation of the mean absolute EEG voltage and spectral intensities in schizophrenic and control subjects. *Biological Psychiatry*, **5**, 149–63. [171]

LINDSLEY, D. B. (1950). Emotions and the electroencephalogram. In Reymert, M. L. (ed.), *Feelings and Emotions*, McGraw-Hill, New York, pp. 238–46. [108]

LINDSLEY, D. B. (1951). Emotion. In Stevens, S. S. (ed.), *Handbook of Experimental Psychology*, Wiley, New York, pp. 473–516. [89]

LINGJAERDE, P. S. (1964). Plasma hydrocortisone in mental disease. *British Journal of Psychiatry*, **110**, 423–32. [115, 149]

LINGJAERDE, P. S., SKAUG, O. E., and LINGJAERDE, O. (1960). The determination of thyroid function with radioiodine (I-131) in mental patients. *Acta Psychiatrica Neurologica Scandinavica*, **35**, 498–508. [182]

LIPOWSKI, Z. J. (1968). Review of consultation psychiatry and psychosomatic medicine. III. Theoretical issues. *Psychosomatic Medicine*, **30**, 395–422. [198]

LIPPERT, W. W., and SENTER, R. J. (1966). Electrodermal responses in the sociopath. *Psychonomic Science*, **4**, 25–6. [195]

LIPPOLD, O. C. J. (1952). The relation between integrated action potentials in a human muscle and its isometric tension. *Journal of Physiology*, **117**, 492–9. [43]

LIPPOLD, O. C. J. (1967). Electromyography. In Venables, P. H., and Martin, I. (eds), *Manual of Psycho-physiological Methods*, North-Holland, Amsterdam, pp. 245–97. [43]

LOEW, D. (1965). Syndrom, Diagnose und Speichelsekretion bei depressiven Patienten. *Psychopharmacologia*, **7**, 339–48. [132]

LORE, R. K. (1966). Palmar sweating and transitory anxiety in children. *Child Development*, **37**, 115–24. [95]

LOTSOF, E. J., and DOWNING, W. L. (1956). Two measures of anxiety. *Journal of Consulting Psychology*, **20**, 170. [96]

LOVAAS, O. I. (1960). The relationship of induced muscular tension, tension level, and manifest anxiety in learning. *Journal of Experimental Psychology*, **59**, 145–52. [96]

LOVEGROVE, T. D., METCALFE, E. V., HOBBS, G. E., and STEVENSON, J. A. (1965). The urinary excretion of adrenaline, noradrenaline, and 17-hydroxycorticosteroids in mental illness. *Canadian Psychiatric Association Journal*, **10**, 170–9. [153, 180, 181]

LOWENSTEIN, O., and LOWENFELD, I. E. (1958). Electronic pupillography. *Archives of Ophthalmology*, **59**, 352–63. [40]

LOWY, F. H., CLEGHORN, J. M., and MCCLURE, D. J. (1971). Sleep patterns in depression. *Journal of Nervous and Mental Disease*, **153**, 10–26. [140]

LUBY, E. D., and CALDWELL, D. F. (1967). Sleep deprivation and EEG slow wave activity in chronic schizophrenia. *Archives of General Psychiatry*, **17**, 361–4. [177]

LYKETSOS, G., BELINSON, L., and GIBBS, F. A. (1953). Electroencephalograms of nonepileptic psychotic patients awake and asleep. *Archives of Neurology and Psychiatry*, **69**, 707–12. [168]

LYKKEN, D. T. (1957). A study of anxiety in the sociopathic personality. *Journal of Abnormal and Social Psychology*, **55**, 6–10. [194]

LYKKEN, D. T. (1959). Properties of electrodes used in electrodermal measurement. *Journal of Comparative and Physiological Psychology*, **52**, 629–34. [26, 27]

LYKKEN, D. T., and MALEY, M. (1968). Autonomic versus cortical arousal in schizophrenics and non-psychotics. *Journal of Psychiatric Research*, **6**, 21–32. [161]

LYKKEN, D. T., and VENABLES, P. H. (1971). Direct measurement of skin conductance: a proposal for standardization. *Psychophysiology*, **8**, 656–72. [24]

LYNCH, J. J., and PASKEWITZ, D. A. (1971). On the mechanisms of the feedback control of human brain wave activity. *Journal of Nervous and Mental Disease*, **153**, 205–17. [88]

LYNN, R. (1963). Russian theory and research on schizophrenia. *Psychological Bulletin*, **60**, 486–98. [184]

MCCALLUM, W. C., and WALTER, W. G. (1968). The effects of attention and distraction on the contingent negative variation in normal and neurotic subjects. *Electroencephalography and Clinical Neurophysiology*, **25**, 319–29. [109]

MCCAWLEY, A., STROEBEL, C. F., and GLUECK, B. C. (1966). Pupillary reactivity, psychologic disorder, and age. *Archives of General Psychiatry*, **14**, 415–18. [166]

MCCLURE, D. J. (1966a). The diurnal variation of plasma cortisol levels in depression. *Journal of Psychosomatic Research*, **10**, 189–95. [150]

MCCLURE, D. J. (1966b). The effects of antidepressant medication on the diurnal plasma cortisol levels in depressed patients. *Journal of Psychosomatic Research*, **10**, 197–202. [150]

MCCONAGHY, N., JOFFE, A. D., and MURPHY, B. (1967). The independence of neurotic and endogenous depression. *British Journal of Psychiatry*, **113**, 479–84. [155]

MCFARLAND, R. A., and HUDDLESON, J. H. (1936). Neurocirculatory reactions in psychoneuroses studied by the Schneider method. *American Journal of Psychiatry*, **93**, 567–99. [125]

MCGHIE, A., and CHAPMAN, J. (1961). Disorders of attention and perception in early schizophrenia. *British Journal of Medical Psychology*, **34**, 103–16. [183]

MCGHIE, A., CHAPMAN, J., and LAWSON, J. S. (1965a). The effect of distraction on schizophrenic performance. I. Perception and immediate memory. *British Journal of Psychiatry*, **111**, 383–90. [183]

MCGHIE, A., CHAPMAN, J., and LAWSON, J. S. (1965b). The effect of distraction on schizophrenic performance. II. Psychomotor ability. *British Journal of Psychiatry*, 111, 391–8. [183]

MCGUIGAN, F. J. (1966). Covert oral behavior and auditory hallucinations. *Psychophysiology*, 3, 73–80. [167]

MACMAHON, J. F., and WALTER, W. G. (1938). The electro-encephalogram in schizophrenia. *Journal of Mental Science*, 84, 781–7. [167]

MAGGS, R., and TURTON, E. C. (1956). Some EEG findings in old age and their relationship to affective disorder. *Journal of Mental Science*, 102, 812–18. [138]

MALMO, R. B., and SHAGASS, C. (1949). Physiologic study of symptom mechanisms in psychiatric patients under stress. *Psychosomatic Medicine*, 11, 25–9. [201]

MALMO, R. B., and SHAGASS, C. (1952). Studies of blood pressure in psychiatric patients under stress. *Psychosomatic Medicine*, 14, 82–93. [103]

MALMO, R. B., SHAGASS, C., BÉLANGER, D., and SMITH, A. A. (1951). Motor control in psychiatric patients under experimental stress. *Journal of Abnormal and Social Psychology*, 46, 539–47. [106, 167]

MALMO, R. B., SHAGASS, C., and DAVIS, F. H. (1950). Symptom specificity and bodily reactions during psychiatric interview. *Psychosomatic Medicine*, 12, 362–76. [201]

MALMO, R. B., SHAGASS, C., DAVIS, J. F., CLEGHORN, R. A., GRAHAM, B. F., and GOODMAN, A. J. (1948). Standardized pain stimulation as controlled stress in physiological studies of psychoneurosis. *Science*, 108, 509–11. [94]

MALMO, R. B., SHAGASS, C., and HESLAM, R. M. (1951). Blood pressure response to repeated brief stress in psychoneurosis: a study of adaptation. *Canadian Journal of Psychology*, 5, 167–79. [103]

MALMO, R. B., and SMITH, A. A. (1955). Forehead tension and motor irregularities in psychoneurotic patients under stress. *Journal of Personality*, 23, 391–406. [106]

MALMO, R. B., WALLERSTEIN, H., and SHAGASS, C. (1953). Headache proneness and mechanisms of motor conflict in psychiatric patients. *Journal of Personality*, 22, 163–87. [107]

MANDLER, G., and KREMEN, I. (1958). Autonomic feedback: a correlational study. *Journal of Personality*, 26, 388–99. [209]

MANDLER, G., MANDLER, J. M., and UVILLER, E. T. (1958). Autonomic feedback: the perception of autonomic activity. *Journal of Abnormal and Social Psychology*, 56, 367–73. [209]

MARCHBANKS, V. H. (1960). Flying stress and urinary 17-hydroxycorticosteroid levels during 20 hour missions. *Aerospace Medicine*, 31, 639–43. [111]

MARJERRISON, G., KRAUSE, A. E., and KEOGH, R. P. (1968). Variability of the EEG in schizophrenia: quantitative analysis with a modulus voltage integrator. *Electroencephalography and Clinical Neurophysiology*, 24, 35–41. [171]

MARKS, I. M., and HUSON, J. (1973). Physiological aspects of neutral and phobic imagery: further observations. *British Journal of Psychiatry*, 122, 567–72. [102]

MARKS, I., MARSET, P., BOULOUGOURIS, J., and HUSON, J. (1971). Physiological accompaniments of neutral and phobic imagery. *Psychological
Medicine*, **1**, 299–307. [102]

MARTIN, I. (1956). Levels of muscle activity in psychiatric patients. *Acta
Psychologica (Amsterdam)*, **12**, 326–41. [106, 128, 166]

MARTIN, I. (1958). Blink rate and muscle tension. *Journal of Mental
Science*, **104**, 123–32. [47]

MARTIN, I., and DAVIES, B. M. (1962). Sleep threshold in depression.
*Journal of Mental Science*, **108**, 466–73. [136]

MARTIN, I., and DAVIES, B. M. (1965). The effect of sodium amytal on
autonomic and muscle activity of patients with depressive illness. *British
Journal of Psychiatry*, **111**, 168–74. [135]

MARTIN, I., MARKS, I. M., and GELDER, M. G. (1969). Conditioned eyelid
responses in phobic patients. *Behaviour Research and Therapy*, **7**, 115–24.
[107]

MARTIN, I., and VENABLES, P. H. (1966). Mechanisms of palmar skin
resistance and skin potential. *Psychological Bulletin*, **65**, 347–57. [21]

MASON, J. W. (1959). Psychological influences on the pituitary-adrenal
cortical system. *Recent Progress in Hormone Research*, **15**, 345–78. [116]

MASON, J. W. (1968a). A review of psychoendocrine research on the
pituitary-adrenal cortical system. *Psychosomatic Medicine*, **30**, 576–607.
[144, 178]

MASON, J. W. (1968b). A review of psychoendocrine research on the
sympathetic-adrenal medullary system. *Psychosomatic Medicine*, **30**, 631–
53. [153]

MASON, J. W. (1968c). A review of psychoendocrine research on the
pituitary-thyroid system. *Psychosomatic Medicine*, **30**, 666–81. [154]

MASON, J. W. (1972). Organization of psychoendocrine mechanisms. A
review and reconsideration of research. In Greenfield, N. S., and Sternbach, R. A. (eds), *Handbook of Psychophysiology*, Holt, Rinehart &
Winston, New York, pp. 3–91. [84]

MASON, J. W., SACHAR, E. J., FISHMAN, J. R., HAMBURG, D. A., and HANDLON,
J. H. (1965). Corticosteroid responses to hospital admission. *Archives of
General Psychiatry (Chicago)*, **13**, 1–8. [114]

MASTERS, W., and JOHNSON, V. (1966). *Human Sexual Response*, Little,
Brown and Co., Boston. [90]

MATSUMOTO, K., BERLET, H. H., BULL, C., and HIMWICH, H. E. (1966).
Excretion of 17-hydroxycorticosteroids and 17-ketosteroids in relation to
schizophrenic symptoms. *Journal of Psychiatric Research*, **4**, 1–12. [180]

MATTINGLY, D. (1962). A simple fluorimetric method for the estimation of
free 11-hydroxycorticoids in human plasma. *Journal of Clinical Pathology*,
**15**, 374–9. [68]

MEARES, R. (1971). Features which distinguish groups of spasmodic
torticollis. *Journal of Psychosomatic Research*, **15**, 1–11. [199]

MEARES, R., and HORVATH, T. (1972). 'Acute' and 'chronic' hysteria.
*British Journal of Psychiatry*, **121**, 653–7. [189]

MEARES, R., and LADER, M. H. (1971). Electromyographic studies in patients
with spasmodic torticollis. *Journal of Psychosomatic Research*, **15**, 13–18.
[199]

243

MEDICAL RESEARCH COUNCIL COMMITTEE ON CLINICAL ENDOCRINOLOGY (1963). A standard method of estimating 17-oxosteroids and total 17-oxogenic steroids. *Lancet*, **1**, 1415–19. [67]

MEDICAL RESEARCH COUNCIL REPORT (1965). Clinical trial of the treatment of depressive illness. *British Medical Journal*, **1**, 881–6. [5]

MEDNICK, S. A. (1958). A learning theory approach to research in schizophrenia. *Psychological Bulletin*, **55**, 316–27. [157, 185]

MEDNICK, S. A. (1966). A longitudinal study of children with a high risk for schizophrenia. *Mental Hygiene*, **50**, 522–35. [164]

MEDNICK, S. A., and SCHULSINGER, F. (1968). Some premorbid characteristics related to breakdown in children with schizophrenic mothers. In Rosenthal, D., and Kety, S. S. (eds), *The Transmission of Schizophrenia*, Pergamon Press, New York, pp. 267–91. [164]

MEDNICK, S. A., and SCHULSINGER, F. (1974). Nature-nurture aspects of schizophrenia. In Lader, M. H. (ed.), *Studies of Schizophrenia*, Royal College of Psychiatrists, London, pp. 36–41. [164]

MELICK, R. (1960). Changes in urinary steroid excretion during examinations. *Australasian Annals of Medicine*, **9**, 200–3. [110]

MENDELS, J., and COCHRANE, C. (1968). The nosology of depression: the endogenous-reactive concept. *American Journal of Psychiatry*, **124**, Suppl., 1–11. [155]

MENDELS, J., and HAWKINS, D. R. (1967a). Sleep and depression. A controlled EEG study. *Archives of General Psychiatry*, **16**, 344–54. [140]

MENDELS, J., and HAWKINS, D. R. (1967b). Sleep and depression. A follow-up study. *Archives of General Psychiatry*, **16**, 536–42. [140]

MENDELS, J., and HAWKINS, D. R. (1971). Sleep and depression. IV. Longitudinal studies. *Journal of Nervous and Mental Disease*, **153**, 251–72. [140]

MENDELS, J., WEINSTEIN, N., and COCHRANE, C. (1972). The relationship between depression and anxiety. *Archives of General Psychiatry*, **27**, 649–53. [129]

MICHAEL, R. P., and GIBBONS, J. L. (1963). Interrelationships between the endocrine system and neuropsychiatry. *International Review of Neurobiology*, **5**, 243–302. [144, 145, 154]

MILLER, L. H., and SHMAVONIAN, B. M. (1965). Replicability of two GSR indices as a function of stress and cognitive activity. *Journal of Personality and Social Psychology*, **2**, 753–6. [95]

MILLER, R. G., RUBIN, R. T., CLARK, B. R., CRAWFORD, W. R., and ARTHUR, R. J. (1970). The stress of aircraft carrier landings. I. Corticosteroid responses in naval aviators. *Psychosomatic Medicine*, **32**, 581–8. [111]

MILSTEIN, V., and STEVENS, J. (1967). Habituation of the alpha blocking response. *Electroencephalography and Clinical Neurophysiology*, **23**, 95–6. [52]

MILSTEIN, V., STEVENS, J., and SACHDEV, K. (1969). Habituation of the alpha attenuation response in children and adults with psychiatric disorders. *Electroencephalography and Clinical Neurophysiology*, **26**, 12–18. [12]

MITTELMAN, A., ROMANOFF, L. P., PINCUS, G., and HOAGLAND, H. (1952). Neutral steroid excretion by normal and schizophrenic men. *Journal of Clinical Endocrinology*, **12**, 831–40. [179]

MONTAGU, J. D. (1958). The psycho-galvanic reflex—a comparison of AC skin resistance and skin potential changes. *Journal of Neurology, Neurosurgery and Psychiatry*, **21**, 119–28. [28]

MONTAGU, J. D., and COLES, E. M. (1966). Mechanism and measurement of the galvanic skin response. *Psychological Bulletin*, **65**, 261–79. [19, 24]

MOOS, R. H., and ENGEL, B. T. (1962). Psychophysiological reactions in hypertensive and arthritic patients. *Journal of Psychosomatic Research*, **6**, 227–41. [203]

MURPHY, C. W., GOFTON, J. P., and CLEGHORN, R. A. (1954). Effect of long-range flights on eosinophil level and corticosteroid excretion. *Journal of Aviation Medicine*, **25**, 242–8. [111]

MURPHY, D., GOODWIN, F., and BUNNEY, W. (1969). Aldosterone and sodium response to lithium administration in man. *Lancet*, **2**, 458–61. [152]

NELSON, G. N., MASUDA, M., and HOLMES, T. H. (1966). Correlation of behavior and catecholamine metabolite excretion. *Psychosomatic Medicine*, **28**, 216–26. [122]

NOBLE, P. J., and LADER, M. H. (1971a). The symptomatic correlates of the skin conductance changes in depression. *Journal of Psychiatric Research*, **9**, 61–9. [131]

NOBLE, P. J., and LADER, M. H. (1971b). Salivary secretion and depressive illness: a physiological and psychometric study. *Psychological Medicine*, **1**, 372–6. [133]

NOBLE, P. J., and LADER, M. H. (1971c). Depressive illness, pulse rate and forearm blood flow. *British Journal of Psychiatry*, **119**, 261–6. [134]

NOBLE, P. J., and LADER, M. H. (1971d). An electromyographic study of depressed patients. *Journal of Psychosomatic Research*, **15**, 233–9. [135]

NOBLE, R., and LADER, M. H. (1972). A physiological comparison of 'endogenous' and 'reactive' depression. *British Journal of Psychiatry*, **120**, 541–2. [155]

NORMAN, A. (1969). Response contingency and human gastric acidity. *Psychophysiology*, **5**, 673–82. [40]

NORYMBERSKI, J. K. (1961). Methods of group corticosteroid estimation in urine—II. In McGowan, G. K., and Sandler, M. (eds), *The Adrenal Cortex*, Pitman, London, pp. 88–109. [68]

NYMGAARD, K. (1959). Studies on the sedation threshold. *Archives of General Psychiatry*, **1**, 530–6. [136]

ÖDEGAARD, Ö. (1932). The psychogalvanic reactivity in affective disorders. *British Journal of Medical Psychology*, **12**, 132–50. [97]

OKEN, D., and HEATH, H. A. (1963). The law of initial values: some further considerations. *Psychosomatic Medicine*, **25**, 3–12. [85]

ONHEIBER, P., WHITE, P. T., DEMYER, M. K., and OTTINGER, D. R. (1965). Sleep and dream patterns of child schizophrenics. *Archives of General Psychiatry*, **12**, 568–71. [198]

ORNITZ, E. M., RITVO, E. R., BROWN, M. B., LA FRANCHI, S., PARMELEE, T., and WALTER, R. D. (1969). The EEG and rapid eye movements during REM sleep in normal and autistic children. *Electroencephalography and Clinical Neurophysiology*, **26**, 167–75. [198]

OSWALD, I., BERGER, R. J., JARAMILLO, R. A., KEDDIE, K. M. G., OLLEY, P. C., and PLUNKETT, G. B. (1962). Melancholia and barbiturates: a controlled

EEG, body and eye movement study of sleep. *British Journal of Psychiatry*, **109**, 66–78. [140]

PALMAI, G., and BLACKWELL, B. (1965). The diurnal pattern of salivary flow in normal and depressed patients. *British Journal of Psychiatry*, **111**, 334–8. [132, 165]

PALMAI, G., BLACKWELL, B., MAXWELL, A. E., and MORGENSTERN, F. (1967). Patterns of salivary flow in depressive illness and during treatment. *British Journal of Psychiatry*, **113**, 1297–308. [132]

PARSONS, O. A., and CHANDLER, P. J. (1969). Electrodermal indicants of arousal in brain damage: cross-validated findings. *Psychophysiology*, **5**, 644–59. [197]

PASSOUANT, P., DUC, N., and MINVIELLE, J. (1961). Etude E.E.G. du sommeil chez un groupe de schizophrènes. *Revue Neurologique*, **104**, 246–9. [172]

PAUL, G. L. (1969). Physiological effects of relaxation training and hypnotic suggestion. *Journal of Abnormal Psychology*, **74**, 425–37. [101]

PAULSON, G. W., and GOTTLIEB, G. (1961). A longitudinal study of the electroencephalographic arousal response in depressed patients. *Journal of Nervous and Mental Disease*, **133**, 524–8. [141]

PAVLOV, I. P. (1927). *Conditioned reflexes. An Investigation of the Physiological Activity of the Cerebral Cortex*, Clarendon Press, Oxford. [83, 87]

PAVLOV, I. P. (1941). *Conditioned Reflexes and Psychiatry*, Oxford University Press, London. [184]

PECK, R. E. (1959). The SHP test—an aid in the detection and measurement of depression. *Archives of General Psychiatry*, **1**, 35–40. [131, 165]

PECK, R. E. (1966). Observations on salivation and palmar sweating in anxiety and other psychiatric conditions. *Psychosomatics*, **7**, 343–8. [133]

PEREZ-REYES, M. (1968). Differences in sedative susceptibility between types of depression, clinical and neurophysiological. *Archives of General Psychiatry*, **19**, 64–71. [136]

PEREZ-REYES, M., and COCHRANE, C. (1967). Differences in sodium thiopental susceptibility of depressed patients as evidenced by the galvanic skin reflex inhibition threshold. *Journal of Psychiatric Research*, **5**, 335–47. [136]

PEREZ-REYES, M., SHANDS, H. C., and JOHNSON, G. (1962). Galvanic skin reflex inhibition threshold: a new psychophysiologic technique. *Psychosomatic Medicine*, **24**, 274–7. [77]

PERKOFF, G. T., EIK-NES, K., NUGENT, C. A., FRED, H. L., NIMER, R. A., RUSH, L., SAMUELS, L. T., and TYLER, F. H. (1959). Studies of the diurnal variation of plasma 17-hydroxycorticosteroids in man. *Journal of Clinical Endocrinology*, **19**, 432–43. [68]

PERRIS, C. (1973). A new approach to the classification of affective disorders. In Lader, M. H., and Garcia, R. (eds), *Aspects of Depression*, World Psychiatric Association, Barcelona, pp. 95–107. [155]

PERRIS, C., and BRATTEMO, C. E. (1963). The sedation threshold as a method of evaluating antidepressive treatments. *Acta Psychiatrica Scandinavica*, **39**, Suppl. 169, 111–19. [136]

PERSKY, H. (1953). Response to a life stress: evaluation of some biochemical indices. *Journal of Applied Physiology*, **6**, 369–74. [111]

PERSKY, H. (1957a). Adrenal cortical function in anxious human subjects. Effect of corticotrophin (ACTH) on plasma hydrocortisone level and urinary hydroxycorticoid excretion. *Archives of Neurology and Psychiatry*, **78**, 95–100. [115]

PERSKY, H. (1957b). Adrenocortical function in anxious human subjects: the disappearance of hydrocortisone from plasma and its metabolic fate. *Journal of Clinical Endocrinology and Metabolism*, **17**, 760–5. [115]

PERSKY, H. (1962a). Introduction and removal of hydrocortisone from plasma. Rates in normal subjects and anxious patients. *Archives of General Psychiatry*, **7**, 93–7. [115]

PERSKY, H. (1962b). Adrenocortical function in anxiety. In Roessler, R., and Greenfield, N. S. (eds), *Physiological Correlates of Psychological Disorders*, University of Wisconsin Press, Madison, pp. 171–91. [114]

PERSKY, H., GROSZ, H. J., NORTON, J. A., and MCMURTRY, M. (1959). Effect of hypnotically-induced anxiety on the plasma hydrocortisone level of normal subjects. *Journal of Clinical Endocrinology and Metabolism*, **19**, 700–10. [112]

PERSKY, H., MAROC, J., CONRAD, E., and DEN BREEIJEN, A. (1959). Blood corticotrophin and adrenal weight-maintenance factor levels of anxious patients and normal subjects. *Psychosomatic Medicine*, **21**, 379–86. [115]

PERSKY, H., SMITH, K. D., and BASU, G. K. (1971). Relation of psychologic measures of aggression and hostility to testosterone production in man. *Psychosomatic Medicine*, **33**, 265–77. [114]

PERSKY, H., et al. (1956). Adrenal cortical function in anxious human subjects. Plasma level and urinary excretion of hydrocortisone. *Archives of Neurology and Psychiatry*, **76**, 549–58. [115]

PERSKY, H., et al. (1958). Relation of emotional responses and changes in plasma hydrocortisone level after stressful interview. *Archives of Neurology and Psychiatry*, **79**, 434–47. [115]

PERSKY, H., et al. (1959). Effect of two psychological stresses on adreno-cortical function. Studies on anxious and normal subjects. *Archives of Neurology and Psychiatry*, **81**, 219–32. [115]

PETERS, J. F. (1971). Eye movement recording: a brief review. *Psychophysiology*, **8**, 414–16. [46]

PIERCY, M., ELITHORN, A., PRATT, R. T. C., and CROSSKEY, M. (1955). Anxiety and an autonomic reaction to pain. *Journal of Neurology, Neurosurgery and Psychiatry*, **18**, 155–62. [97]

PINCUS, G., and ELMADJIAN, F. (1946). The lymphocyte response to heat stress in normal and psychotic subjects. *Journal of Clinical Endocrinology*, **6**, 295–300. [179]

PINCUS, G., HOAGLAND, H., FREEMAN, H., ELMADJIAN, F., and ROMANOFF, L. P. (1949). A study of pituitary-adrenocortical function in normal and psychotic men. *Psychosomatic Medicine*, **11**, 74–101. [179]

PINCUS, G., SCHENKER, V., ELMADJIAN, F., and HOAGLAND, H. (1949). Responsivity of schizophrenic men to pituitary adrenocorticotrophin. *Psychosomatic Medicine*, **11**, 146–50. [179]

PITTS, F. N., and MCCLURE, J. N. (1967). Lactate metabolism in anxiety neurosis. *New England Journal of Medicine*, **277**, 1329–36. [125]

*

PLATMAN, S. R., and FIEVE, R. R. (1968). Lithium carbonate and plasma cortisol response in the affective disorders. *Archives of General Psychiatry*, **18**, 591–4. [151]

PLUTCHIK, R. (1956). The psychophysiology of skin temperature: a critical review. *Journal of General Psychology*, **55**, 249–68. [38]

POE, R. O., ROSE, R. M., and MASON, J. W. (1970). Multiple determinants of 17-hydroxycorticosteroid excretion in recruits during basic training. *Psychosomatic Medicine*, **32**, 369–78. [69]

POLLIN, W. (1962). Control and artifact in psychophysiological research. In Roessler, R., and Greenfield, N. S. (eds), *Physiological Correlates of Psychological Disorders*, University of Wisconsin Press, Madison, pp. 171–91. [79]

PRANGE, A. J., WILSON, I. C., RABON, A. M., and LIPTON, M. A. (1969). Enhancement of imipramine antidepressant activity by thyroid hormone. *American Journal of Psychiatry*, **126**, 457–69. [155]

PRICE, D. B., THALER, M., and MASON, J. W. (1957). Preoperative emotional states and adrenal cortical activity. Studies on cardiac and pulmonary surgery patients. *Archives of Neurology and Psychiatry (Chicago)*, **77**, 646–56. [112]

PRIDEAUX, E. (1920). The psychogalvanic reflex: a review. *Brain*, **43**, 50–73. [97]

PRYCE, I. G. (1964). The relationship between 17-hydroxycorticosteroid excretion and glucose utilization in depression. *British Journal of Psychiatry*, **110**, 90–4. [152]

PSCHEIDT, G. R., BERLET, H. H., BULL, C., SPAIDE, J., and HIMWICH, H. E. (1964). Excretion of catecholamines and exacerbation of symptoms in schizophrenic patients. *Journal of Psychiatric Research*, **2**, 163–8. [181]

QUARTON, G. C., CLARK, L. D., COBB, S., and BAUER, W. (1955). Mental disturbances associated with ACTH and cortisone: a review of explanatory hypotheses. *Medicine*, **34**, 13–50. [145]

QUAY, H. C. (1965). Psychopathic personality as pathological stimulation seeking. *American Journal of Psychiatry*, **122**, 180–3. [194]

RADVAN-ZIEMNOWICZ, S. (1967). Rheoencephalography. In Brown, C. C. (ed.), *Methods in Psychophysiology*, Williams & Wilkins, Baltimore, pp. 129–57. [38]

RECHTSCHAFFEN, A., SCHULSINGER, F., and MEDNICK, S. A. (1964). Schizophrenia and physiological indices of dreaming. *Archives of General Psychiatry*, **10**, 89–93. [178]

REDFEARN, J. W. T. (1957). Normal and neurotic tremors. *Journal of Neurology, Neurosurgery and Psychiatry*, **20**, 302–13. [107]

REGAN, P. F., and REILLY, J. (1958). Circulating epinephrine and norepinephrine in changing emotional states. *Journal of Nervous and Mental Disease*, **127**, 12–16. [122]

REICHLIN, S. (1959). Peripheral thyroxine metabolism in patients with psychiatric and neurological diseases. *Archives of General Psychiatry*, **1**, 434–40. [182]

REISS, M., HEMPHILL, R. E., MAGGS, R., SMITH, S., HAIGH, C. P., and REISS, J. M. (1951). Thyroid activity in mental patients: evaluation by radioactive tracer methods. *British Medical Journal*, **1**, 1181–3. [125]

REY, J. H., WILLCOX, D. R., GIBBONS, J. L., TAIT, H., and LEWIS, D. J. (1961). Serial biochemical and endocrine investigations in recurrent mental illness. *Journal of Psychosomatic Research*, **5**, 155–69. [148]

RICHTER, C. R. (1928). The electrical skin resistance. Diurnal and daily variation in normal and psychopathic persons. *Archives of Neurology and Psychiatry*, **19**, 488–508. [130]

RIDJANOVIĆ, S. (1964). Problèmes biologiques et psychopathologiques du sommeil des vieillards. *Evolution Psychiatrique*, **2**, 279–336. [176]

RIMÓN, R., STENBÄCK, A., and HUHMAR, E. (1966). Electromyographic findings in depressive patients. *Journal of Psychosomatic Research*, **10**, 159–70. [135]

RIZZO, N. D., FOX, H. M., LAIDLAW, J. C., and THORN, G. W. (1954). Concurrent observations of behavior change and adrenocortical variations in a cyclothymic patient during a period of twelve months. *Annals of Internal Medicine*, **41**, 798–815. [149]

ROBERTS, L. N., SMILEY, J. R., and MANNING, G. W. (1953). A comparison of direct and indirect blood pressure determinations. *Circulation*, **8**, 232–42. [34]

RODIN, E., GRISELL, J., and GOTTLIEB, J. (1968). Some electrographic differences between chronic schizophrenic patients and normal subjects. In Wortis, J. (ed.), *Recent Advances in Biological Psychiatry*, vol. X, 194–204. [170]

ROSE, J. T. (1962). Autonomic function in depression: a modified methacholine test. *Journal of Mental Science*, **108**, 624–41. [136]

ROSE, R. M., POE, R. O., and MASON, J. W. (1968). Psychological state and body size as determinants of 17-OHCS excretion. *Archives of Internal Medicine*, **121**, 406–13. [69]

ROSSI, A. M. (1959). The evaluation of the manifest anxiety scale by the use of electromyography. *Journal of Experimental Psychology*, **58**, 64–9. [96]

ROTH, M. (1960a). Depressive states and their borderlands: classification, diagnosis and treatment. *Comprehensive Psychiatry*, **1**, 135–55. [129]

ROTH, M. (1960b). The phobic anxiety-depersonalization syndrome and some general aetiological problems in psychiatry. *Journal of Neuropsychiatry*, **1**, 293–306. [192]

ROTH, M., et al. (1972). Studies in the classification of affective disorders. The relationship between anxiety states and depressive illness—1. *British Journal of Psychiatry*, **121**, 147–61. [129]

ROTH, W. T., and CANNON, E. H. (1972). Some features of the auditory evoked response in schizophrenics. *Archives of General Psychiatry*, **27**, 466–71. [174]

RUBIN, J., NAGLER, R., SPIRO, H. M., and PILOT, M. L. (1962). Measuring the effect of emotions on esophageal motility. *Psychosomatic Medicine*, **24**, 170–6. [41]

RUBIN, L. S. (1964). Autonomic dysfunction as a concomitant of neurotic behavior. *Journal of Nervous and Mental Disease*, **138**, 558–74. [105]

RUBIN, L. S., and BARRY, T. J. (1972). The effect of the cold pressor test on pupillary reactivity of schizophrenics in remission. *Biological Psychiatry*, **5**, 181–97. [166]

RUBIN, R. T. (1967). Adrenal cortical activity changes in manic-depressive illness. Influence on intermediary metabolism of tryptophan. *Archives of General Psychiatry*, **17**, 671–9. [148]

RUBIN, R. T., and MANDELL, A. J. (1966). Adrenal cortical activity in pathological emotional states: a review. *American Journal of Psychiatry*, **123**, 387–400. [144]

RUBIN, R. T., MILLER, R. O., CLARK, B. R., POLAND, R. E., and ARTHUR, R. V. (1970). The stress of aircraft carrier landings. II. 3-Methoxy-4-hydroxy-phenylglycol excretion in naval aviators. *Psychosomatic Medicine*, **32**, 589–97. [111]

RUBIN, R. T., YOUNG, W. M., and CLARK, B. R. (1968). 17-Hydroxycorti-costeroid and vanillylmandelic acid excretion in a rapidly cycling manic-depressive. *Psychosomatic Medicine*, **30**, 162–71. [149, 154]

RUSSELL, R. W., and STERN, R. M. (1967). Gastric motility: the electro-gastrogram. In Venables, P. H., and Martin, I. (eds), *Manual of Psycho-physiological Methods*, North-Holland, Amsterdam, pp. 219–43. [41]

SABSHIN, M., HAMBURG, D. A., GRINKER, R. R., PERSKY, H., BASOWITZ, H., KORCHIN, S. J., and CHEVALIER, J. A. (1957). Significance of pre-experi-mental studies in the psychosomatic laboratory. *Archives of Neurology and Psychiatry*, **78**, 207–19. [77]

SACHAR, E. J. (1967a). Corticosteroids in depressive illness. I. A re-evaluation of control issues and the literature. *Archives of General Psychiatry*, **17**, 544–53. [70, 114]

SACHAR, E. J. (1967b). Corticosteroids in depressive illness. II. A longi-tudinal psychoendocrine study. *Archives of General Psychiatry*, **17**, 554–67. [147]

SACHAR, E. J., FISHMAN, J. R., and MASON, J. W. (1965). Influence of hyp-notic trance on plasma 17-hydroxycorticosteroid concentration. *Psycho-somatic Medicine*, **27**, 330–41. [113]

SACHAR, E. J., HELLMAN, L., FUKUSHIMA, D. K., and GALLAGHER, T. F. (1972). Cortisol production in mania. *Archives of General Psychiatry*, **26**, 137–9. [151]

SACHAR, E. J., KANTER, S. S., BUIE, D., ENGLE, R., and MEHLMAN, R. (1971). Psychoendocrinology of ego disintegration. In Cancro, R. (ed.), *The Schizophrenic Syndrome, An Annual Review, 1971*, Butterworths, London, pp. 445–65. [180]

SACHAR, E. J., MACKENZIE, J. M., BINSTOCK, W. A., and MACK, J. E. (1967). Corticosteroid responses to psychotherapy of depressions. I. Evaluations during confrontation of loss. *Archives of General Psychiatry*, **16**, 461–70. [147]

SACHAR, E. J., MASON, J. W., FISHMAN, J. R., HAMBURG, D. A., and HANDLON, J. H. (1965). Corticosteroid excretion in normal young adults living under 'basal' conditions. *Psychosomatic Medicine*, **27**, 435–45. [114]

SACHAR, E. J., MASON, J. W., KOLMER, H. S., and ARTISS, K. L. (1963). Psycho-endocrine aspects of acute schizophrenic reactions. *Psychosomatic Medi-cine*, **25**, 510–37. [180, 181]

SACHAR, E. J., *et al.* (1973). Disrupted 24-hour patterns of cortisol secre-tion in psychotic depression. *Archives of General Psychiatry*, **28**, 19–24. [151]

SAINSBURY, P. (1964). Muscle responses: muscle tension and expressive movement. *Journal of Psychosomatic Research*, **8**, 179–85. [46]

SAINSBURY, P., and COSTAIN, W. R. (1971). The measurement of psychomotor activity: some clinical applications. *Journal of Psychosomatic Research*, **15**, 487–94. [46]

SAINSBURY, P., and GIBSON, J. G. (1954). Symptoms of anxiety and tension and the accompanying physiological changes in the muscular system. *Journal of Neurology, Neurosurgery and Psychiatry*, **17**, 216–24. [107, 201]

SAKALIS, G., CURRY, S. H., MOULD, G. P., and LADER, M. H. (1972). Physiological and clinical effects of chlorpromazine and their relationship to plasma level. *Clinical Pharmacology and Therapeutics*, **13**, 931–46. [143, 205]

SALAMON, I., and POST, J. (1965). Alpha blocking and schizophrenia. I. Methodology and initial studies. *Archives of General Psychiatry*, **13**, 367–74. [169]

SALETU, B., ITIL, T. M., and SALETU, M. (1971). Auditory evoked responses, EEG, and thought process in schizophrenics. *American Journal of Psychiatry*, **128**, 336–43. [174]

SATTERFIELD, J. H. (1964). Discussion. *Annals of the New York Academy of Sciences*, **112**, 508–9. [192]

SATTERFIELD, J. H., and DAWSON, M. E. (1971). Electrodermal correlates of hyperactivity in children. *Psychophysiology*, **8**, 191–7. [198]

SAYER, K. E., and TORRES, A. A. (1966). Effect of anxiety on alpha responsiveness to light stimulation. *Psychological Reports*, **19**, 1143–6. [109]

SCHACHTER, J. (1957). Pain, fear, and anger in hypertensives and normotensives. A psychophysiological study. *Psychosomatic Medicine*, **19**, 17–29. [202]

SCHACHTER, S. (1966). The interaction of cognitive and physiological determinants of emotional state. In Spielberger, C. D. (ed.), *Anxiety and Behavior*, Academic Press, New York, pp. 193–224. [121, 206, 208]

SCHACHTER, S., and LATANÉ, B. (1964). Crime, cognition and the autonomic nervous system. In Jones, M. R. (ed.), *Nebraska Symposium on Motivation*, University of Nebraska Press, Lincoln, pp. 221–75. [196]

SCHACHTER, S., and WHEELER, L. (1962). Epinephrine, chlorpromazine, and amusement. *Journal of Abnormal and Social Psychology*, **65**, 121–8. [121]

SCHALLING, D., and LEVANDER, S. E. (1967). Spontaneous fluctuations in skin conductance during anticipation of pain in two delinquent groups, differing in anxiety-proneness. *Reports from the Psychological Laboratories*, University of Stockholm, No. 238. [196]

SCHALLING, D., LIDBERG, L., LEVANDER, S. E., and DAHLIN, Y. (1973). Spontaneous autonomic activity as related to psychopathy. *Biological Psychology*, **1**, 83–97. [196]

SCHAPIRA, K., ROTH, M., KERR, T. A., and GURNEY, C. (1972). The prognosis of affective disorders: the differentiation of anxiety states from depressive illnesses. *British Journal of Psychiatry*, **121**, 175–81. [129]

SCHLOSBERG, H. (1954). Three dimensions of emotion. *Psychological Review*, **61**, 81–8. [89]

SCHNEYER, L. H., and LEVIN, L. K. (1955). Rate of secretion by individual salivary gland pairs of man under conditions of reduced exogenous stimulation. *Journal of Applied Physiology*, **7**, 508–12. [29]

SCHNORE, M. M. (1959). Individual patterns of physiological activity as a function of task differences and degree of arousal. *Journal of Experimental Psychology*, **58**, 117–28. [86]

SCHWARTZ, M., MANDELL, A. J., GREEN, R., and FERMAN, R. (1966). Mood, motility, and 17-hydroxycorticoid excretion; a polyvariable case study. *British Journal of Psychiatry*, **112**, 149–56. [148]

SCHWARTZ, T. B., and SHIELDS, D. R. (1956). Urinary excretion of formal-dehydogenic steroids and creatinine. A reflection of emotional tension. *Psychosomatic Medicine*, **18**, 159–72. [110]

SEGRAVES, R. T. (1970). Personality, body build and adrenocortical activity. *British Journal of Psychiatry*, **117**, 405–11. [113]

SELYE, H. (1936). A syndrome produced by diverse nocuous agents. *Nature*, **138**, 32–3. [84]

SELYE, H. (1950). *Stress*, Acta Inc., Montreal. [84]

SHACKEL, B. (1967). Eye movement recording by electro-oculography. In Venables, P. H., and Martin, I. (eds), *Manual of Psycho-physiological Methods*, North-Holland, Amsterdam, pp. 299–334. [46]

SHAGASS, C. (1954). The sedation threshold. A method for estimating tension in psychiatric patients. *Electroencephalography and Clinical Neurophysiology*, **6**, 221–33. [77]

SHAGASS, C. (1955). Differentiation between anxiety and depression by the photically activated electroencephalogram. *American Journal of Psychiatry*, **112**, 41–6. [108]

SHAGASS, C. (1966). Electrophysiology of depression. In Cole, J. O., and Wittenborn, J. R. (eds), *Pharmacotherapy of Depression*, Charles C. Thomas, Springfield, Illinois, pp. 91–111. [137]

SHAGASS, C. (1968). Averaged somatosensory evoked responses in various psychiatric disorders. In Wortis, J. (ed.), *Recent Advances in Biological Psychiatry*, vol. x, Plenum, New York, pp. 205–19. [142, 144, 174]

SHAGASS, C. (1972). *Evoked Brain Potentials in Psychiatry*, Plenum, New York. [54, 141, 142]

SHAGASS, C., and JONES, A. L. (1958). A neurophysiological test for psychiatric diagnosis: results in 750 patients. *American Journal of Psychiatry*, **114**, 1002–9. [136]

SHAGASS, C., and MALMO, R. B. (1954). Psychodynamic themes and localized muscular tension during psychotherapy. *Psychosomatic Medicine*, **16**, 295–314. [107]

SHAGASS, C., and NAIMAN, J. (1955). The sedation threshold, manifest anxiety, and some aspects of ego function. *Archives of Neurology and Psychiatry*, **74**, 397–406. [136]

SHAGASS, C., and NAIMAN, J. (1956). The sedation threshold as an objective index of manifest anxiety in psychoneurosis. *Journal of Psychosomatic Research*, **1**, 49–57. [136]

SHAGASS, C., NAIMAN, J., and MIHALIK, J. (1956). An objective test which differentiates between neurotic and psychotic depression. *Archives of Neurology and Psychiatry*, **75**, 461–71. [136]

SHAGASS, C., and SCHWARTZ, M. (1961). Reactivity cycle of somatosensory cortex in humans with and without psychiatric disorder. *Science*, **134**, 1757–9. [143]

SHAGASS, C., and SCHWARTZ, M. (1962). Cerebral cortical reactivity in psychotic depressions. *Archives of General Psychiatry*, **6**, 235–42. [143]

SHAGASS, C., and SCHWARTZ, M. (1963a). Cerebral responsiveness in psychiatric patients. Intensity-response gradients and recovery cycles of somatosensory evoked potentials. *Archives of General Psychiatry*, **8**, 177–89. [142]

SHAGASS, C., and SCHWARTZ, M. (1963b). Psychiatric disorder and deviant cerebral responsiveness to sensory stimulation. In Wortis, J. (ed.), *Recent Advances in Biological Psychiatry*, vol. v, Plenum, New York, pp. 321–30. [142]

SHAGASS, C., and SCHWARTZ, M. (1963c). Psychiatric correlates of evoked cerebral cortical potentials. *American Journal of Psychiatry*, **119**, 1055–61. [143]

SHAGASS, C., and SCHWARTZ, M. (1964). Evoked potential studies in psychiatric patients. *Annals of the New York Academy of Science*, **112**, 526–42. [142]

SHAGASS, C., and SCHWARTZ, M. (1966). Somatosensory cerebral evoked responses in psychotic depression. *British Journal of Psychiatry*, **112**, 799–807. [144]

SHAKOW, D. (1963). Psychological deficit in schizophrenia. *Behavioural Science*, **8**, 275–305. [183, 184]

SHAKOW, D. (1971). Some observations on the psychology (and some fewer, on the biology) of schizophrenia. *Journal of Nervous and Mental Disease*, **153**, 300–16. [183]

SHANNON, I. L., PRIGMORE, J. R., HESTER, W. R., MCCALL, C. M., and ISBELL, G. M. (1961). Stress patterns in dental patients. I. Serum free 17-hydroxy-corticosteroid, sodium and potassium in subjects undergoing local anaesthesia and simple exodontic procedures. *Journal of Oral Surgery*, **19**, 486–91. [112]

SHAPIRO, A., and COHEN, H. D. (1965). The use of mercury capillary length gauges for the measurement of the volume of thoracic and diaphragmatic components of human respiration: a theoretical analysis and a practical method. *Transactions of the New York Academy of Science*, **27**, 634–49. [42]

SHARPLESS, S., and JASPER, H. (1956). Habituation of the arousal reaction. *Brain*, **79**, 655–80. [87]

SHATTOCK, F. M. (1950). The somatic manifestations of schizophrenia: a clinical study of their significance. *Journal of Mental Science*, **96**, 32–142. [157]

SHAW, J. C. (1967). Quantification of biological signals using integration techniques. In Venables, P. H., and Martin, I. (eds), *Manual of Psychophysiological Methods*, North-Holland, Amsterdam, pp. 403–65. [44]

SHINFUKU, N., OMURA, M., and KAYANO, M. (1961). Catecholamine excretion in manic depressive psychosis. *Yonago Acta Medica*, **5**, 109–14. [153]

SHORVON, H. J. (1946). The depersonalization syndrome. *Proceedings of the Royal Society of Medicine*, **39**, 779–92. [192]

SILVERMAN, A. J., COHEN, S. I., SHMAVONIAN, B. M., and KIRSCHNER, N.

(1961). Catecholamines in psychophysiologic studies. *Recent Advances in Biological Psychiatry*, **3**, 104–17. [202]

SILVERMAN, J. (1964). The problem of attention in research and theory in schizophrenia. *Psychological Review*, **71**, 352–79. [183]

SILVERMAN, J. (1967). Variations in cognitive control and psychophysiological defense in the schizophrenias. *Psychosomatic Medicine*, **29**, 225–45. [186]

SILVERMAN, J. J., and POWELL, V. E. (1944a). Studies on palmar sweating. *American Journal of Medical Science*, **208**, 297–305. [97]

SILVERMAN, J. J., and POWELL, V. E. (1944b). Studies on palmar sweating. III. Palmar sweating in an army general hospital. *Psychosomatic Medicine*, **6**, 243–9. [97]

SIMPSON, G. M., CRANSWICK, E. H., and BLAIR, J. H. (1963). Thyroid indices in chronic schizophrenia. *Journal of Nervous and Mental Disease*, **137**, 582–90. [182]

SIMPSON, G. M., CRANSWICK, E. H., and BLAIR, J. H. (1964). Thyroid indices in chronic schizophrenia. II. *Journal of Nervous and Mental Disease*, **138**, 581–5. [182]

SLATER, E. (1965). Diagnosis of 'hysteria'. *British Medical Journal*, **1**, 1395–9. [188]

SLOANE, R. B., and LEWIS, D. J. (1956). Prognostic value of adrenaline and mecholyl responses in electroconvulsive therapy. *Journal of Psychosomatic Research*, **1**, 273–86. [136]

SLOANE, R. B., SAFFRAN, M., and CLEGHORN, R. A. (1958). Autonomic and adrenal responsivity in psychiatric patients: effect of methacholine and corticotropin. *Archives of Neurology and Psychiatry*, **79**, 549–53. [115]

SMALL, J. G., and SMALL, I. F. (1971). Contingent negative variation (CNV). Correlations with psychiatric diagnosis. *Archives of General Psychiatry*, **25**, 550–4. [144, 175]

SMALL, J. G., SMALL, I. F., and PEREZ, H. C. (1971). EEG, evoked potential, and contingent negative variations with lithium in manic depressive disease. *Biological Psychiatry*, **3**, 47–58. [144]

SMALL, J. G., and STERN, J. A. (1965). EEG indicators of prognosis in acute schizophrenia. *Electroencephalography and Clinical Neurophysiology*, **18**, 526–7. [169]

SNYDER, F., and SCOTT, J. (1972). The psychophysiology of sleep. In Greenfield, N. S., and Sternbach, R. A. (eds), *Handbook of Psychophysiology*, Holt, Rinehart & Winston, New York, pp. 645–708. [90]

SOKOLOV, Y. N. (1963). Higher nervous functions: the orienting reflex. *Annual Review of Physiology*, **25**, 545–80. [83]

SOLOMON, A. P., and FENTRESS, T. L. (1934). Galvanic skin reflex and blood pressure reactions in the psychoneuroses. *Journal of Nervous and Mental Disease*, **80**, 163–82. [97]

SPECK, L. B., DIM, B., and MERCER, M. (1966). Visual evoked responses of psychiatric patients. *Archives of General Psychiatry*, **15**, 59–63. [144]

SPIELBERGER, C. D., LUSHENE, R. E., and MCADOO, W. G. (1971). Theory and measurement of anxiety states. In Cattell, R. B. (ed.), *Handbook of Modern Personality Theory*, Aldine, Chicago, chap. 10. [208]

SPOHN, H. I., THETFORD, P. E., and CANCRO, R. (1970). Attention, psychophysiology, and scanning in the schizophrenic syndrome. In Cancro, R. (ed.), *The Schizophrenic Reactions: A Critique of the Concept, Hospital Treatment, and Current Research*, Brunner, Mazel, New York, pp. 259–69. [163]

STACHENKO, J., and GIROUD, C. J. P. (1962). Some aspects of steroidogenesis in the zona glomerulosa. In Currie, A. R., Symington, T., and Grant, J. K. (eds), *The Human Adrenal Cortex*, Livingstone, Edinburgh, pp. 30–43. [65]

STANAWAY, R. G., and HULLIN, R. P. (1973). The relationship of exercise response to personality. *Psychological Medicine*, 3, 343–9. [127]

STAVNEY, L. S., HAMILTON, T., SIRCUS, W., and SMITH, A. N. (1966). Evaluation of the pH-sensitive telemetering capsule in the estimation of gastric secretory capacity. *American Journal of Digestive Diseases*, 11, 753–60. [40]

STEINSCHNEIDER, A., and LIPTON, E. L. (1965). Individual differences in autonomic responsivity. Problems of measurement. *Psychosomatic Medicine*, 27, 446–56. [85]

STENBÄCK, A., JAKOBSON, T., and RIMÓN, R. (1966). Depression and anxiety ratings in relation to the excretion of urinary total 17-hydroxycorticosteroid in depressive subjects. *Journal of Psychosomatic Research*, 9, 355–62. [147]

STERN, J. A., SURPHLIS, W., and KOFF, E. (1965). Electrodermal responsiveness as related to psychiatric diagnosis and prognosis. *Psychophysiology*, 2, 51–61. [164]

STERNBACH, R. A. (1966). *Principles of Psychophysiology*, Academic Press, New York. [1]

STEWART, M. A., et al. (1959). Adaptation and conditioning of the galvanic skin response in psychiatric patients. *Journal of Mental Science*, 105, 1102–11. [100]

STRAUSS, H. (1945). Clinical and electroencephalographic studies: the electroencephalogram in psychoneurotics. *Journal of Nervous and Mental Disease*, 101, 19–27. [108]

STROEBEL, C. F. (1972). Psychophysiological pharmacology. In Greenfield, N. S., and Sternbach, R. A. (eds), *Handbook of Psychophysiology*, Holt, Rinehart & Winston, New York, pp. 787–838. [204]

STRÖM-OLSEN, R., and WEIL-MALHERBE, H. (1958). Humoral changes in manic-depressive psychosis with particular reference to the excretion of catecholamines in urine. *Journal of Mental Science*, 104, 696–704. [153]

STRONGIN, E. I., and HINSIE, L. E. (1938a). Parotid secretory rate in schizophrenic patients. *Journal of Nervous and Mental Disease*, 87, 715–24. [164]

STRONGIN, E. I., and HINSIE, L. E. (1938b). Parotid gland secretions in manic-depressive patients. *American Journal of Psychiatry*, 94, 1459–62. [131]

STRONGIN, E. I., and HINSIE, L. E. (1939). A method for differentiating manic-depressive depressions from other depressions by means of parotid secretions. *Psychiatric Quarterly*, 13, 697–704. [131]

STRUVE, F. A., and BECKA, D. R. (1968). The relative incidence of the B-mitten EEG pattern in process and reactive schizophrenia. *Electroencephalography and Clinical Neurophysiology*, 24, 80–2. [168]

255

STRUVE, F. A., BECKA, D. R., and KLEIN, D. F. (1972). B-mitten EEG pattern in process and reactive schizophrenia. *Archives of General Psychiatry*, **26**, 189–92. [168]

SUGARMAN, A. A., GOLDSTEIN, L., MURPHREE, H. B., PFEIFFER, C. C., and JENNEY, E. H. (1964). EEG and behavioral changes in schizophrenia. *Archives of General Psychiatry*, **10**, 340–4. [171]

SUWA, N., and YAMASHITA, I. (1972). *Psychophysiological Studies of Emotion and Mental Disorders*, Hokkaido University School of Medicine, Sapporo, Japan. [180]

SUWA, N., YAMASHITA, I., OWADA, H., SHINOHARA, S., and NAKAZAWA, A. (1962). Psychic state and adrenocortical function: a psychophysiologic study of emotion. *Journal of Nervous and Mental Disease*, **134**, 268–76. [115]

SYMINGTON, T. (1962). The morphology and zoning of the human adrenal cortex. In Currie, A. R., Symington, T., and Grant, J. K. (eds), *The Human Adrenal Cortex*, Livingstone, Edinburgh, pp. 3–20. [65]

TAIT, J. F., TAIT, S. A. S., LITTLE, B., and LAUMAS, K. (1962). The metabolism of aldosterone in man. In Currie, A. R., Symington, T., and Grant, J. K. (eds), *The Human Adrenal Cortex*, Livingstone, Edinburgh. [66]

TAN, B. K. (1964). Physiological correlates of anxiety. A preliminary investigation of the orienting reflex. *Canadian Psychiatric Association Journal*, **9**, 63–71. [101]

TANNER, J. M., HEALY, M. J. R., WHITEHOUSE, R. H., and EDGSON, A. C. (1959). The relation of body-build to the excretion of 17-ketosteroids and 17-ketogenic steroids in healthy young men. *Journal of Endocrinology*, **19**, 87–101. [69]

TARCHANOFF, J. (1890). Über die galvanischen Erscheinungen an der Haut des Menschen bei Reizung der Sinnesorgane und bei verschiedenen Formen der psychischen Tätigkeit. *Pflügers Archiven der Gesammten Physiologie*, **46**, 46–55. [19]

TECCE, J. J. (1971). Contingent negative variation and individual differences. *Archives of General Psychiatry*, **24**, 1–16. [57]

TECCE, J. J. (1972). Contingent negative variation (CNV) and psychological processes in man. *Psychological Bulletin*, **77**, 73–108. [57, 109, 110]

TECCE, J. J., FRIEDMAN, S. B., and MASON, J. W. (1965). Anxiety, defensiveness and 17-hydroxycorticosteroid excretion. *Journal of Nervous and Mental Disease*, **141**, 549–54. [112]

THAYER, J., and SILBER, D. E. (1971). Relationship between levels of arousal and responsiveness among schizophrenic and normal subjects. *Journal of Abnormal Psychology*, **77**, 162–73. [159]

THOMAS, P. E., and KORR, I. M. (1957). Relationship between sweat gland activity and electrical resistance of the skin. *Journal of Applied Physiology*, **10**, 505–10. [22]

THOMASSON, B. (1959). Studies on the content of 17-hydroxycorticosteroids and its diurnal rhythm in the plasma of surgical patients. *Scandinavian Journal of Clinical and Laboratory Investigation*, **11**, Suppl. 42. [112]

THOMPSON, R. F., and SPENCER, W. A. (1966). Habituation: a model phenomenon for the study of neuronal substrates of behavior. *Psychological Review*, **73**, 16–43. [87]

THORPE, J. G., and BARKER, J. C. (1957). Objectivity of the sedation threshold. *Archives of Neurology and Psychiatry*, **78**, 194–6. [77]

TIMSIT, M., KONINCKX, N., DARGENT, J., FONTAINE, O., and DONGIER, M. (1970). Variations contingentes négatives en psychiatrie. *Electroencephalography and Clinical Neurophysiology*, **28**, 41–7. [175]

TINGLEY, J. O., MORRIS, A. W., and HILL, S. R. (1958). Studies on the diurnal variation and response to emotional stress of the thyroid gland. *Clinical Research*, **6**, 134. [123]

TOLSON, W. W., MASON, J. W., SACHAR, E. J., HAMBURG, D. A., HANDLON, J. H., and FISHMAN, J. R. (1965). Urinary catecholamine responses associated with hospital admission in normal human subjects. *Journal of Psychosomatic Research*, **8**, 365–72. [114, 120]

TONG, J. E. (1959). Stress reactivity in relation to delinquent and psychopathic behaviour. *Journal of Mental Science*, **105**, 935–56. [194]

TONG, J. E., and MURPHY, I. C. (1960). A review of stress reactivity research in relation to psychopathology and psychopathic behaviour disorders. *Journal of Mental Science*, **106**, 1273–95. [194]

TUCKER, G. J., DETRE, T., HARROW, M., and GLASER, G. H. (1965). Behavior and symptoms of psychiatric patients and the electroencephalogram. *Archives of General Psychiatry*, **12**, 278–86. [169]

ULETT, G. A., GLESER, G., WINOKUR, G., and LAWLER, A. (1953). The EEG and reaction to photic stimulation as an index of anxiety-proneness. *Electroencephalography and Clinical Neurophysiology*, **5**, 23–32. [108]

UNO, T., and GRINGS, W. W. (1965). Autonomic components of orienting behavior. *Psychophysiology*, **1**, 311–21. [83]

VANDERHOOF, E., and CLANCY, J. (1964). Physiological correlate of therapeutic change. *Archives of General Psychiatry*, **11**, 145–50. [104]

VANDERHOOF, E., CLANCY, J., and ENGELHART, R. S. (1966). Relationship of a physiological variable to psychiatric diagnoses and personality characteristics. *Diseases of the Nervous System*, **27**, 171–7. [166]

VAN DER MERWE, A. B. (1948). The diagnostic value of peripheral vasomotor reactions in the psychoneuroses. *Journal of Psychosomatic Medicine*, **10**, 347–54. [104]

VAN EGEREN, L. F., FEATHER, B. W., and HEIN, P. L. (1971). Desensitization of phobias: some psychophysiological propositions. *Psychophysiology*, **8**, 213–28. [102]

VASCONETTO, C., FLORIS, V., and MOROCUTTI, C. (1971). Visual evoked responses in normal and psychiatric subjects. *Electroencephalography and Clinical Neurophysiology*, **31**, 77–83. [144, 174]

VENABLES, P. H. (1960). The effect of auditory and visual stimulation on the skin potential response of schizophrenics. *Brain*, **83**, 77–92. [160]

VENABLES, P. H. (1963a). Selectivity of attention, withdrawal and cortical activation. *Archives of General Psychiatry*, **9**, 74–8. [160]

VENABLES, P. H. (1963b). The relationship between level of skin potential and fusion of paired light flashes in schizophrenic and normal subjects. *Journal of Psychiatric Research*, **1**, 279–87. [160]

VENABLES, P. H. (1963c). Changes due to noise in the threshold of fusion of paired light flashes in schizophrenics and normals. *British Journal of Social and Clinical Psychology*, **2**, 94–9. [183]

VENABLES, P. H. (1964). Input dysfunction in schizophrenia. In Maher, B. (ed.), *Progress in Experimental Personality Research*, Academic Press, New York, vol. 1, pp. 1–47. [159, 183]

VENABLES, P. H. (1966a). A comparison of two-flash and two-click thresholds in schizophrenic and normal subjects. *Quarterly Journal of Experimental Psychology*, **18**, 371–3. [160]

VENABLES, P. H. (1966b). Psychophysiological aspects of schizophrenia. *British Journal of Medical Psychology*, **39**, 289–97. [161]

VENABLES, P. H. (1967). The relation of two-flash and two-click thresholds to withdrawal in paranoid and nonparanoid schizophrenics. *British Journal of Social and Clinical Psychology*, **6**, 60–2. [161]

VENABLES, P. H., and CHRISTIE, M. (eds) (1975). *Research in Psychophysiology*, Wiley, New York. [3, 81]

VENABLES, P. H., and MARTIN, I. (eds) (1967). *Manual of Psycho-physiological Methods*, North-Holland, Amsterdam. [6, 9, 19, 21, 24]

VENABLES, P. H., and WING, J. K. (1962). Level of arousal and the sub-classification of schizophrenia. *Archives of General Psychiatry*, **7**, 114–19. [160]

VENNING, E. H., DYRENFURTH, I., and BECK, J. C. (1957). Effect of anxiety upon aldosterone excretion in man. *Journal of Clinical Endocrinology*, **17**, 1005–7. [114]

VOGEL, G. W. (1968). REM deprivation. III. Dreaming and psychosis. *Archives of General Psychiatry*, **18**, 312–29. [177]

VOGEL, G. W., and TRAUB, A. C. (1968). REM deprivation. I. The effect on schizophrenic patients. *Archives of General Psychiatry*, **18**, 287–300. [177]

VOGEL, G. W., TRAUB, A. C., BEN-HORIN, P., and MEYERS, G. M. (1968). REM deprivation. II. The effects on depressed patients. *Archives of General Psychiatry*, **18**, 301–11. [141]

VOLAVKA, J., GROF, P., and MRKLAS, L. (1967). EEG frequency analysis in periodic endogenous depressions. *Psychiatria Neurologia, Basel*, **153**, 384–90. [138]

VOLAVKA, J., MATOUŠEK, M., and ROUBÍČEK, J. (1966). EEG frequency analysis in schizophrenia. An attempt to reconsider the role of age. *Acta Psychiatrica Scandinavica*, **42**, 237–45. [170]

VOLPÉ, R., VALE, J., and JOHNSTON, MACA. W. (1960). The effects of certain physical and emotional tensions and strains on fluctuations in the level of serum protein-bound iodine. *Journal of Clinical Endocrinology and Metabolism*, **20**, 415–28. [123]

WALTER, W. G. (1964). Slow potential waves in the human brain associated with expectancy, attention and decision. *Archiv für Psychiatrie und Nervenkrankheiten*, **206**, 309–22. [109]

WALTER, W. G. (1966). Electrophysiologic contributions to psychiatric therapy. *Current Psychiatric Therapies*, **6**, 13–25. [109, 196]

WASMAN, M., MOREHEAD, S. D., LEE, H.-Y., and ROWLAND, V. (1970). Interaction of electro-ocular potentials with the contingent negative variation. *Psychophysiology*, **7**, 103–11. [57]

WATSON, J. P., GAIND, R., and MARKS, I. M. (1972). Physiological habituation to continuous phobic stimulation. *Behaviour Research and Therapy*, **10**, 269–78. [102]

WEARN, J. T., and STURGIS, C. C. (1919). Studies on epinephrin. I. Effects of the injection of epinephrin in soldiers with 'irritable heart'. *Archives of Internal Medicine*, **24**, 247–68. [122]

WEIL-MALHERBE, H. (1955). The concentration of adrenaline in human plasma and its relation to mental activity. *Journal of Mental Science*, **101**, 733–55. [181]

WEINER, S., *et al.* (1963). Effect of anxiety of increasing the plasma hydrocortisone level. *Psychosomatic Medicine*, **25**, 69–77. [113]

WEINMAN, J. (1967). Photoplethysmography. In Venables, P. H., and Martin, I. (eds), *Manual of Psycho-physiological Methods*, North-Holland, Amsterdam, pp. 185–217. [38]

WEITZMAN, E. D., *et al.* (1971). Twenty-four hour pattern of the episodic secretion of cortisol in normal subjects. *Journal of Clinical Endocrinology*, **33**, 14–22. [69]

WELLS, C. E., and WOLFF, H. G. (1960). Electrographic evidence of impaired brain function in chronically anxious patients. *Science*, **131**, 1671–2. [108]

WENGER, M. A. (1941). The measurement of individual differences in autonomic balance. *Psychosomatic Medicine*, **3**, 427–34. [82]

WENGER, M. A. (1947). Preliminary study of the significance of measures of autonomic balance. *Psychosomatic Medicine*, **9**, 301–9. [82]

WENGER, M. A. (1962). Some problems in psychophysiological research. In Roessler, R., and Greenfield, N. S. (eds), *Physiological Correlates of Psychological Disorder*, University of Wisconsin Press, Madison, pp. 97–114. [79]

WENGER, M. A. (1966). Studies of autonomic balance: a summary. *Psychophysiology*, **2**, 173–86. [82]

WENGER, M. A., CLEMENS, T. L., COLEMAN, D. R., CULLEN, T. D., and ENGEL, B. T. (1961). Autonomic response specificity. *Psychosomatic Medicine*, **23**, 185–93. [86]

WENGER, M. A., and CULLEN, T. D. (1972). Studies of autonomic balance in children and adults. In Greenfield, N. S., and Sternbach, R. A. (eds), *Handbook of Psychophysiology*, Holt, Rinehart & Winston, New York, pp. 535–69. [82]

WENGER, M. A., HENDERSON, E. B., and DINNING, J. S. (1957). Magnetometer method for recording gastric motility. *Science*, **125**, 910. [40]

WEYBREW, B. B. (1959). Patterns of reaction to stress as revealed by a factor analysis of autonomic-change measures and behavioral observations. *Journal of General Psychology*, **60**, 253–64. [94]

WHATMORE, G. B. (1966). Some neurophysiologic differences between schizophrenia and depression. *American Journal of Psychiatry*, **123**, 712–6. [167]

WHATMORE, G. B., and ELLIS, R. M. (1958). Some motor aspects of schizophrenia. *American Journal of Psychiatry*, **114**, 882–9. [166]

WHATMORE, G. B., and ELLIS, R. M. (1959). Some neurophysiologic aspects of depressed states. An electromyographic study. *Archives of General Psychiatry*, **1**, 70–80. [135]

WHATMORE, G. B., and ELLIS, R. M. (1962). Further neurophysiologic aspects of depressed states: an electromyographic study. *Archives of General Psychiatry*, **6**, 243–53. [135]

WHEATLEY, D. (1972). Potentiation of amitriptyline by thyroid hormone. *Archives of General Psychiatry*, **26**, 229–33. [155]

WHITE, B. V., and GILDEA, E. F. (1937). 'Cold pressor test' in tension and anxiety. A cardiochronographic study. *Archives of Neurology and Psychiatry*, **38**, 964–84. [102]

WHITEHORN, J. C., and RICHTER, H. (1937). Unsteadiness of the heart rate in psychotic and neurotic states. *Archives of Neurology and Psychiatry*, **38**, 62–70. [102]

WILDER, J. (1957). The law of initial value in neurology and psychiatry. Facts and problems. *Journal of Nervous and Mental Disease*, **125**, 73–86. [85]

WILKINS, R. W., and EICHNA, L. W. (1941). Blood flow to the forearm and calf. I. Vasomotor reactions: role of the sympathetic nervous system. *Bulletin, Johns Hopkins Hospital*, **68**, 425–49. [35]

WILLIAMS, H. L. (1971). The new biology of sleep. *Journal of Psychiatric Research*, **8**, 445–78. [92]

WILLIAMS, M. (1953). Psychophysiological responsiveness to psychological stress in early chronic schizophrenic reactions. *Psychosomatic Medicine*, **15**, 456–62. [158, 165, 166]

WILSON, W. P., and PARKER, J. B. (1957). Humoral arousal responses in mental disease. *Diseases of the Nervous System*, **18**, 272–4. [172]

WILSON, W. P., and WILSON, N. J. (1961). Observations on the duration of photically elicited arousal responses in depressive psychoses. *Journal of Nervous and Mental Disease*, **133**, 438–40. [141]

WING, L. (1964). Physiological effects of performing a difficult task in patients with anxiety states. *Journal of Psychosomatic Research*, **7**, 283–94. [80, 98]

WOHLBERG, G. W., KNAPP, P. H., and VACHON, L. (1970). A longitudinal investigation of adrenocortical function in acute schizophrenia. *Journal of Nervous and Mental Disease*, **151**, 245–65. [180]

WOLFF, C. T., FRIEDMAN, S. B., HOFER, M. A., and MASON, J. W. (1964). Relationship between psychological defenses and mean urinary 17-hydroxycorticosteroid excretion rates. I. A predictive study of parents of fatally ill children. *Psychosomatic Medicine*, **26**, 576–91. [112]

WOLFF, H. H. (1970). Practice and teaching of psychosomatic medicine in general hospitals. In Hill, O. W. (ed.), *Modern Trends in Psychosomatic Medicine—2*, Butterworth, London, pp. 298–311. [199]

WOODS, E. F., RICHARDSON, J. A., RICHARDSON, A. K., and BOZEMAN, R. F. (1956). Plasma concentrations of epinephrine and arterenol following the actions of various agents on the adrenals. *Journal of Pharmacology and Experimental Therapeutics*, **116**, 351–5. [127]

WYATT, R. J., PORTNOY, B., KUPFER, D. J., SNYDER, F., and ENGELMAN, K. (1971). Resting plasma catecholamine concentrations in patients with depression and anxiety. *Archives of General Psychiatry*, **24**, 65–70. [122]

WYATT, R. J., STERN, M., FRAM, D. H., TURSKY, B., and GRINSPOON, L. (1970). Abnormalities in skin potential fluctuations during the sleep of acute schizophrenic patients. *Psychosomatic Medicine*, **32**, 301–8. [177]

WYATT, R. J., TERMINI, B. A., and DAVIS, J. (1971). Sleep studies. *Schizophrenia Bulletin*, No. **4**, 45–66. [178]

ZAHN, T. P., ROSENTHAL, D., and LAWLOR, W. G. (1968). Electrodermal and heart rate orienting reactions in chronic schizophrenia. *Journal of Psychiatric Research*, **6**, 117–34. [158]

ZARCONE, V., GULEVICH, G., and DEMENT, W. (1967). Sleep and electro-convulsive therapy. *Archives of General Psychiatry*, **16**, 567–73. [141]

ZARCONE, V., GULEVICH, G., PIVIK, T., and DEMENT, W. (1968). Partial REM phase deprivation and schizophrenia. *Archives of General Psychiatry*, **18**, 194–202. [176]

ZUBEK, J. P., and SCHUTTE, W. (1966). Urinary excretion of adrenaline and noradrenaline during prolonged perceptual deprivation. *Journal of Abnormal Psychology*, **71**, 328–34. [118]

ZUCKERMAN, M. (1971). Physiological measures of sexual arousal in the human. *Psychological Bulletin*, **75**, 297–329. [90]

ZUCKERMAN, M., PERSKY, H., and CURTIS, G. C. (1968). Relationships among anxiety, depression, hostility and autonomic variables. *Journal of Nervous and Mental Disease*, **146**, 481–7. [98]

ZUCKERMAN, M., PERSKY, H., HOPKINS, T. R., MURTAUGH, T., BASU, G. K., and SCHILLING, M. (1966). Comparison of stress effects of perceptual and social isolation. *Archives of General Psychiatry*, **14**, 356–65. [124]

ZUNG, W. W. K., WILSON, W. P., and DODSON, W. E. (1964). Effect of depressive disorders on sleep EEG responses. *Archives of General Psychiatry*, **10**, 439–45. [142]

# Subject index